The Human Tradition in
the Black Atlantic, 1500–2000

The Human Tradition around the World
Series Editors: William H. Beezley and Colin M. MacLachlan

The Human Tradition in the Black Atlantic, 1500–2000

Edited by
Beatriz G. Mamigonian and Karen Racine

ROWMAN & LITTLEFIELD PUBLISHERS, INC.
Lanham • Boulder • New York • Toronto • Plymouth, UK

Published by Rowman & Littlefield Publishers, Inc.
A wholly owned subsidiary of The Rowman & Littlefield Publishing Group, Inc.
4501 Forbes Boulevard, Suite 200, Lanham, Maryland 20706
http://www.rowmanlittlefield.com

Estover Road, Plymouth PL6 7PY, United Kingdom

British Library Cataloguing in Publication Information Available

Library of Congress Cataloging-in-Publication Data

The human tradition in the black Atlantic, 1500–2000 / edited by Beatriz G.
Mamigonian and Karen Racine.
        p. cm. — (The human tradition around the world)
    Includes bibliographical references and index.
    ISBN 978-0-7425-6729-0 (cloth : alk. paper) — ISBN 978-0-7425-6730-6 (pbk. : alk.
paper) — ISBN 978-0-7425-6731-3 (electronic)
    1. Blacks—Atlantic Ocean Region—Biography. 2. Blacks—Atlantic Ocean
Region—History. 3. Blacks—Atlantic Ocean Region—Social conditions. 4. Blacks—
Civil rights—Atlantic Ocean Region—History. 5. Slave trade—Atlantic Ocean
Region—History. 6. Slavery—Atlantic Ocean Region—History. 7. Atlantic Ocean
Region—Biography. 8. Atlantic Ocean Region—Race relations. 9. Atlantic Ocean
Region—Social conditions. I. Mamigonian, Beatriz G. (Beatriz Gallotti) 1969– II.
Racine, Karen, 1967–
    CT105.H786 2010
    920.0092960163—dc22
                                    2009031113

⊗ ™ The paper used in this publication meets the minimum requirements of
American National Standard for Information Sciences—Permanence of Paper for
Printed Library Materials, ANSI/NISO Z39.48-1992.

Printed in the United States of America

~

Contents

~

Introduction

People in the Making of the Black Atlantic

Beatriz G. Mamigonian and Karen Racine

Imagine the scene: A streetcar crosses residential neighborhoods of Salvador da Bahia, Brazil, picking up men dressed in white sheets and wearing white turbans made of towels. Many of them hang out from the car; others try to squeeze in. A latecomer brings a small drum. One of the men holds the banner of the group, while another greets the photographer, cheering with opened arms. It is Carnival, and the men will gather to parade the streets of Salvador as the Sons of Gandhi. It is 1959.[1]

The photographer who immortalized this scene was Pierre Verger, a Frenchman from a rich family who had left Europe to become a photo-journalist and who had, by that time, traveled extensively in northern and western Africa, Latin America, the Caribbean, and the United States before settling in Brazil. He had seen orisha cults, voodoo ceremonies, street festivals, work routines, and architecture in West Africa and in different parts of the Americas, sometimes strikingly similar, coming from peoples both joined and set apart by the Atlantic. For Verger, his snapshots captured more than a festive scene showing a group of black workers going to the Carnival parade; instead, these vivid images of the Sons of Gandhi connected those men to other men and women of African descent whose daily activities and celebrations of life and death he had witnessed and captured through his lenses, in Africa and elsewhere in the Atlantic.

This book is a collection of biographies that, like the photograph of the Sons of Gandhi, connects men and women of African descent to the larger human tradition of the Black Atlantic. The "Black Atlantic" is a concept rather than a physical region. It rests on hard historical facts: The migration of Africans across the Atlantic was the largest forced migration in history, and Africans represented three of every four immigrants to the Americas before 1820.[2] Without the coerced labor supplied mostly by Africans and their descendants, the development of the Americas would have been impossible. Moreover, the successive generations of enslaved Africans and their Creole offspring left indelible marks in the cultural landscape, despite their subordinated status.

Like the idea of "Atlantic World," that of the "Black Atlantic" considers the shared history and the links established among peoples of western Europe, Africa, and the Americas since the beginning of the age of exploration. In doing so, both concepts represent attempts to move beyond the boundaries of imperial and national histories and consider the wider Atlantic framework for the study of the economic, cultural, and biological exchanges that shaped the modern world.[3] The concept of the Black Atlantic departs from the more general Atlantic World perspective in significant ways. First, it rejects the Eurocentrism embedded in the analysis of the emergence of the modern world as a European achievement. In that, it follows the recent contributions from Africanist historians like John Thornton, who has established the central role played by Africans and the importance of Africa in the making of the early modern Atlantic World.[4] Second, while both concepts acknowledge that the slave system was central to the making of an integrated economic, social, and cultural space joining the various shores of the Atlantic, under the Black Atlantic framework the slave trade is more than the commercial supply of a labor force for the burgeoning plantation system in the Americas. The slave trade is also significant because of its human consequences, as a massive forced migration that displaced people within Africa and dispersed millions of them across the Atlantic, the Mediterranean, and the Indian Oceans, fueling chattel slavery and leaving a legacy of race discrimination. Third, the Black Atlantic framework has been used most recently as an alternative reading of modern history, a counternarrative that addresses the cultural transformations, resistance, and struggles that peoples of African descent waged against enslavement, exploitation, racism, and other forms of oppression.[5]

Through the biographies that make up this collection, readers will follow the major themes in the history of the Black Atlantic from the forced migration of people of African descent to the Atlantic islands and to Europe beginning in the fifteenth century to the struggles against colonialism and racial discrimination in the second half of the twentieth century. The Atlantic slave trade, the major migration of modern times, which forcefully displaced and transplanted around twelve million Africans to Europe and the Americas from about 1450 to 1861, holds a central role in this history. It resulted from complex trading relations involving merchants from Europe and the Americas, rulers of African kingdoms and smaller groups, and numerous other collaborators who benefited from the systematic sale and forced transportation of enslaved human beings across the Atlantic. Displaced from their original land, family, and kin, and subjected to domination and exploitation on different levels, Africans and their descendants in the New World had to adapt to new conditions, to fight and overcome domination in diverse settings. From the traumatic middle passage to the small tobacco holdings of Virginia, the gold mines of Minas Gerais, the sugar plantations of Cuba, or urban slavery in New Orleans, the various forms of adaptation account for a wide range of experiences. Recent scholarship has demonstrated that the recourse to family and community ties to face adversities and confront difficulties, the quest for autonomy and self-sufficiency through the cultivation of land or commerce, and the spectacular range of forms of resistance were strategies that transcended local histories and could be said to connect separate groups to the larger Black Atlantic tradition.

Besides the traumatic and transformative experience of enslavement, the reaction to racism constitutes another common experience in the Black Atlantic tradition. The end of slavery in the Americas and the rise of colonialism in Africa in the nineteenth century saw the emergence of scientific racism, and the multiplication of social, political, and economic mechanisms to prevent African descendants from the enjoyment of full citizenship and economic independence. "Race" came to be used as the basis for discrimination, and in many places it justified spatial segregation of people according to their skin color and ancestry. It is important to note that "racial" categories varied from one region to the other and changed over time, and that racism took different forms, yet there was an overall trend in the early twentieth century to discriminate against people of African descent in the public sphere. The reaction of African descendants combined different strategies and varied according to the circumstances. In many places they refused to be classified by racial categories and fought for universal rights regardless of color, aiming at integration. In other places or moments they rallied behind the racial category of "black" by reinforcing their religious, labor, and community organizations, and by fighting for rights equal to those of "whites" while maintaining separate lives.[6] The problem of racial discrimination was brought to the public debate through collective mobilization, publications, literature, and other forms of art throughout the century. Ultimately, it became evident that the cause transcended regional and national boundaries.

In the twentieth century, the fight against the racial discrimination toward African descendants in the Americas came to be associated with a wider struggle against colonial domination and economic exploitation. When students and intellectuals from Caribbean and African colonies met in capitals like London and Paris, they made common cause. Pan-Africanism for the English-speaking and *Négritude* for the French-speaking became rallying ideals to fight against oppression and foster a common identity among Africans and African descendants throughout the world. In many places of the Iberian world, activists had to dispute first the pervasive assumption that their regimes were benevolent and inclusive, not racist. The political engagement of this generation led to the independence movements in Africa, fed the struggle for civil rights in the United States and against apartheid in South Africa, and inspired the present-day struggle of rural "Maroon" communities for land titles in Colombia and Brazil.

While race has been a strong element in the discrimination toward peoples of African ancestry dispersed throughout the world, a "black" identity among them should not be assumed. Identities are socially and historically constructed. Historians and anthropologists have been dealing with this "conundrum" for quite some time. Studies of slave societies have shown that not all enslaved men and women would join together to fight their masters and that freedpersons would not necessarily join slaves in their resistance either. Neither legal condition nor African origin favored instant association.

Moreover, those born in the Americas (generally called "Creoles") and those transplanted from Africa rarely found common cause in their attempts to negotiate their daily lives. Identity stems from relationships and therefore depends on local conditions, and varies over time. The individuals forcefully transplanted to the Americas belonged to a multitude of cultural groups and political units and did not identify themselves as "Africans" in the first place. Historian Robert Slenes has argued that an identity that linked individuals from various groups of West Central Africa was probably constituted between the time they were gathered to be shipped and their passage across the Atlantic, facilitated by their mutually understandable languages (at least partially) and common cultural traits.[7]

Once in the Americas, the proportion of Africans in the population of a given place, their origins, and their ability to retain certain practices and traditions greatly influenced the transformation of African cultures in the New World. The influx of successive waves of "saltwater" slaves, newcomers from

Africa bearing the experiences of enslavement and displacement and the burden of adaptation, shaped each region differently according to the flows of the Atlantic slave trade. New ethnic identities and new "nation" names, or ethnonyms, emerged from this process. People of different West Central African groups ended up identified more generally as Congo, Angola, or Benguella in South America, while Yoruba-speaking individuals identified themselves as Lucumís in Cuba, as Nagôs in Bahia, or as Minas elsewhere in Brazil, for example. Rarely did West Africans and West Central Africans join for religious activities or plotting against their masters. But over time, as the proportion of slaves and freedpersons born in the Americas in the overall population grew, African "nations" slowly disappeared and gave way to different identities. After the end of the Atlantic slave trade, that transition was inevitable.[8]

Slave emancipation represented a watershed everywhere. People of African descent tirelessly claimed rights of full citizenship, and social divisions were redefined, often along racialized lines. In the next century, the black-white divide became pervasive, as racism was entrenched in public policy as well as in social behavior. As early as 1903, American activist and intellectual W. E. B. DuBois anticipated the struggles ahead by declaring, "The problem of the twentieth century is the problem of the color line."[9] By then, a regular flow of people and ideas across the Atlantic in all directions favored the formulation of a common African-diasporic identity and a strong sense of a shared history linking the experience of African descendants in North America, Latin America, and the Caribbean, and eventually pulling them to consider their ties to Africa, land of the forebears. While a single "black" identity did not encompass all people of African descent, the history of the twentieth century shows that in a variety of ways they banded together, sometimes with other "minority" groups, to fight racism and domination and present alternatives to a version of modernity that excluded and alienated.[10]

One of the most important challenges when addressing the human tradition in the Black Atlantic is that of finding sources on individuals, particularly prior to the twentieth century. Illiteracy and numerous other constraints prevented slaves and freedpersons from leaving personal accounts. The rare exceptions are the treasured slave narratives from the late eighteenth and nineteenth centuries and the interviews with ex-slaves and descendants collected in the 1930s.[11] Most of the time, it is from transcripts of judicial cases, police investigations, and notarial and ecclesiastical records that historians draw the information necessary to reconstitute individual lives that might otherwise fall into oblivion. The nature of the sources—official, indirect, often prejudiced—augments the challenge of uncovering those individuals' own perspectives of their experiences. But social historians, like archaeologists of everyday life in the past, are used to interpreting fragments, reading between the lines, and listening to muted voices. The chapters collected in this volume testify to the painstaking research conducted in scattered archives and libraries and to the hidden treasures that they hold.

Not even many volumes would cover the full human experience in the Black Atlantic. This collection takes readers to a unique choice of places, periods, and themes. The chapters span the sixteenth through the twentieth centuries, covering and weaving together the colonial Americas, precolonial and colonial Africa, and the more contemporary experience. The persons whose life histories are depicted in this collection were, with two exceptions, voluntary or involuntary migrants across the Atlantic themselves, thus experiencing the cultural encounters and the challenge of identity that placed them within this collective experience. Their lives were marked by change and fluidity. Among them we find Roman Catholics, Muslims, and Anglicans who were always in contact with people who professed faiths other than their own. Their labor experience was quite diverse: from the watched routine of a rural slave to the mobility of being a cook in a slave vessel, from the waged industrial position in the Soviet Union to the precariousness of an illegal migrant's work as a domestic servant. Some of them gained prominence among their peers: Among them we find Alonso de Illescas, a Maroon leader in sixteenth-century Ecuador; Philip Quaque, a missionary in West Africa; a number of intellectuals and activists; and Romare Bearden, a renowned artist. Music, an essential element in the lives of Africans and their descendants, can be heard in the background throughout the book: Catholic prayers surely brought consolation to Gregoria Lopez; Harry Washington overheard the plantation slaves singing work songs; drumming and dancing animated the *cabildo* celebrations Buenaventura Lucumí attended; jazz inspired Bearden's work; drums and berimbau gave rhythm to the capoeira movements of Mestre Pastinha. As editors of this volume we have sought to convey the extraordinary complexity and diversity of this field, which was shaped in the last decades by the examination of human agency. The assumption that human beings make choices and, within the limits of possibility, impose those choices on their world has challenged researchers to understand history "in the making" instead of predetermined by abstract processes that left little room for historical actors. The biographies presented here give a sense of how individuals at different places and times took part in the cultural transformations and the struggles to overcome adversity that shaped the Black Atlantic.

Each one of the biographical chapters will pose questions and challenge readers to read beyond them, to connect those individuals to larger historical processes, and to make up a complex image of the Black Atlantic, transcending local histories. Going back to the streetcar scene in Salvador in 1959, one could ask: Why would that particular group of Bahian men choose to pay tribute to Gandhi? Why do so during Carnival? Why was that not a group of Sons and Daughters of Gandhi, but an all-male group? And all-black, too? Pierre Verger knew all too well that the cultural expressions of African descendants in the New World had become a theme of academic research and public interest. Newsmagazines in Europe and the Americas commissioned such photographic essays to respond to the curiosity among their readership. In the 1950s, the Brazilian racial scene had even become a laboratory for public policy: UNESCO commissioned researchers to decipher the "recipe" for seemingly good racial integration and the apparent lack of racial prejudice. Carnival and other profane and religious festivities, celebrated by blacks and whites alike, demonstrated, at first glance, that a racial paradise existed, and that the formula could perhaps be exported to places where racial tensions ran high, like the United States. And yet Pierre Verger's intention was not to praise the mythical Brazilian racial paradise, but to illuminate the vibrant cultural expressions of Africans and peoples of African descent as demonstrations of alternative worldviews. He knew the men who founded the Sons of Gandhi belonged to the stevedores' trade union of the Salvador harbor and had a long tradition of labor resistance and ethnic cooperation, which may eventually be traced back to the 1857 strike by slave "earners" who stopped the transportation of goods in the city for about a week.[12] Verger was also used to the fact that the Carnival parade was the occasion to voice social criticism and comment on current affairs, sometimes in a sarcastic tone. According to the official history of the group, prior to 1949, the stevedores paraded in lavish costumes to demonstrate their status, but state intervention on the trade unions left them short of means, and it was for this reason that some of them formed the group, chose costumes that represented the simplicity of Indian clothes, and decided to pay tribute to Gandhi, the pacifist leader of Indian independence.[13]

Yet historians stress the social and racial tensions of those years, reminding us that the group feared repression by the police for their display of Afro-Brazilian religious symbols.[14] As a Babalaô, or father of secrets in the West African cult of Ifa himself, Pierre Verger understood the meaning attributed by the participants of the group to the bead necklaces that they wore as part of the costume, and the importance of their religious affiliation, which they tried to disguise. White and blue bead necklaces connected those men to

Oxalá and Ogum, Candomblé deities associated with peace and strength. The beads are used as amulets among Candomblé followers, and to this day the bead necklaces of the Sons of Gandhi symbolize good fortune for those who use them. From the beginning, women could only help in making the costumes and providing food and drinks during the parade, and this tradition persists, justified by the fact that there were no women among the stevedores. How about the racial exclusivity? Agnaldo Silva, a member of the group, in a recent interview declared that the Sons of Gandhi never discriminated against whites, only reflected the composition of the labor category. Minimizing past and present racial tensions in Bahia, he insisted that the group's message "was one of peace, regardless of color."[15]

From a parade of forty men who feared repression in 1949 to about five thousand participants in recent years, the Sons of Gandhi have become one of the symbols of Carnival in Bahia. This fact alone testifies to the importance and institutional recognition of the cultural expressions of African descendants have achieved in the early twenty-first century. Yet the entangled and contradictory racial, social, and cultural meanings attributed to the group by its own members and outside observers clearly demonstrate the complexities of the human tradition in the Black Atlantic that we have tried to convey in this collection of biographies, like snapshots from centuries past.

CHAPTER ONE

~

Alonso de Illescas (1530s–1590s)

African, Ladino, and
Maroon Leader in Colonial Ecuador

Charles Beatty Medina

In the fifteenth and sixteenth centuries, the presence of Africans in the Atlantic World was quite different from what it would become later, with the development of plantation slavery. Alonso de Illescas was what historian Ira Berlin called a typical "Atlantic Creole": born and raised in Cape Verde, off the coast of Africa, he came of age in Seville, a city connected to the Atlantic through its burgeoning commerce with Spain's newly contacted territories in the Americas. There, Alonso learned how to play by the emerging Spanish Atlantic society's rules, which incorporated Africans and their descendants according to color and status. First a slave of one of Seville's powerful merchants, he later became the leader of a runaway African slave community on the coast of Ecuador. Historian Charles Beatty Medina shows an unusual story of collaboration between Africans, Native Indians, and renegade Iberians in resisting Spanish colonization in sixteenth-century Ecuador, one in which the leadership and the Atlantic experience of an "Atlantic Creole" such as Illescas were instrumental in guaranteeing to his group not only freedom, but autonomy.

For Africans like Alonso de Illescas, the sixteenth-century Atlantic World was one of harsh realities, momentous change, and rare opportunity. The few pieces of biographical information that we have on his early life state that he was born on the Cape Verde Islands. At the age of eight or ten he was taken to live in Seville, where he became a servant to one of the city's

wealthiest merchant families: the Illescas. In Spain he learned Hispanic traditions, culture, language, and religion, enough to be considered *muy ladino*,
or very Hispanic in his ways. As a young man, his owners, deeply invested
in the commerce of the Indies, sent him first to the Caribbean, then to
Panama, and finally to Peru, the silver-producing capital of the early Spanish
Empire. In the 1550s on a voyage from Panama to Lima, a shipwreck off the
coast of colonial Ecuador provided Alonso the opportunity to escape from
captivity. His life, and those of twenty-two fellow Africans, took on even
greater drama. Within just a few years, Illescas became the leader of their
fledgling community, or *Maroon society*, made up of Africans, Amerindians,
and even a few Europeans. In his later years, he was considered the greatest
of the "Lords of *Esmeraldas*," the coastal province that became a permanent
homeland to their people.

Illescas' life is inextricably bound up with the history of Iberian expansion.
Born in the 1530s on the Cape Verde Islands off the coast of Africa, he was
a child of the emerging Atlantic age. Portuguese exploration in the fifteenth
century led to the discovery and settlement of Cape Verde. Its proximity to
the West African coast made it ideal as a slave-trading post, and later as a
key hub of transatlantic navigation it became a provisioning port for ships
bound to and from the Americas.

As a child, Illescas was given the name Enrique. However, he was confirmed with the name he commonly used, which was also the name of his
owner, who was the patriarch of one of Seville's trading dynasties, the Illescas. Even for an African slave in the sixteenth century, one's name was
important. It not only provided a statement of family background, but also
alluded to quality, status, honor, and origins—Christian forebears. And
though Alonso could not share in the benefits of association with the Illescas
as a true family member, that association with one of the best-connected and
wealthiest of the great merchant families of the early Atlantic age must have
brought some level of prestige. The Illescas traded in many of the luxury and
staple goods sent overseas in the first century of the Spanish conquest, and
they even held many of the contracts for the delivery of African slaves to
the Indies from the time of the earliest discoveries until well into the seventeenth century. As the conquest progressed and expanded, so did the Illescas
trade network. From the rich centers of the "Spanish Indies," they relayed
their orders for goods and African slaves to Seville and beyond.

Unlike the majority of Africans forcibly brought to the Americas, Alonso
probably never saw a day of work on a sugar plantation or in a rice field.
Every bit of evidence indicates that he was a trusted personal servant, expected to perform many duties for his owners. Further evidence of his close

relationship to the Illescas family is gained from his personal history. Once purchased, he was taken from Cape Verde to Seville, where he lived for seventeen years before his journey to the Indies. These were his formative years, when he acquired the traits that observers would later describe as *muy ladino*. Sources indicate that he learned the Spanish style of formal address, could play the *vihuela*, or Spanish guitar, and was versed in Catholic prayers and understood the sacraments. He acquired much of this cultural knowledge in Seville, the busy nucleus of Spain's commerce with her American empire: a great city with a social and economic world quite different from that of Cape Verde. While Seville and Cape Verde had important roles in the early Atlantic trade network, sixteenth-century Seville was a large cosmopolitan metropolis. More than just a trading center, it had been a great administrative city under Muslim rule and could boast of classic Roman origins. With the discovery of the Indies, Seville's fortunes increased further. It became a city swirling on the wealth of travel and commerce with the Indies. It was home to the *Casa de contratación*, the royal customs storehouse that handled nearly all of Spain's commercial exchange with the Americas. As trade increased, Seville's population expanded rapidly along with its massive wealth, much of it in the form of silver that poured in from the colonies. The city was a magnet for foreign traders, embarking colonizers, artists, and ex-conquistadors, as well as beggars and vagrants. A population of 50,000 in 1530 had risen to over 120,000 by 1580.

As the city's fortune rose, so did Seville's African slave population. Growing up in and around the Illescas household, Enrique would have seen this society at its extremes. At one end, slaves were increasingly visible as household servants and personal lackeys. But they were considered social inferiors, recent converts to Christianity, and thus were also seen as having impure blood. At the other end stood the cadre of well-to-do merchants, church prelates, returning conquistadors, and local nobility, who exhibited the newfound wealth of the Indies. For them, personal servants and slaves were among the more visible symbols of their affluence. Female slaves could be found in the city's kitchens, markets, and patios. And the men, especially young men like Illescas, who belonged to a merchant family, "could be found in all the focal points of the city—along the wharves and in the public squares and markets."[1] Demand for African labor increased through the first half of the sixteenth century, and the price for able-bodied males rose from about twenty ducats to between eighty and ninety ducats in just a few decades.

As the African population grew, observers noted that the city's population appeared like a chessboard—with "equal numbers of black and white pieces,"[2] milling around in their daily activities. In fact, Africans probably made up no more than 8–12 percent of the population at the time. However, their roles in the heart of the city's commercial center made them more apparent. Outside the commercial zones, Africans were known to inhabit specific neighborhoods, or *barrios*, namely San Bernardino and San Roque, working-class districts beyond the city walls. It was in these quarters that some of the Atlantic World's earliest African diasporic communities were born.

In these enclaves, Africans of different *naciones*, or ethnic groups, mingled with one another. Removed from the many local communities that sustained them in Africa, they became *negros*—blacks. Indeed the term, once used to describe African Americans, is a literal translation from Spanish. Nonetheless, the continuance of their identity through culture and language was an important facet of life for Africans in Seville. Already by the end of the fourteenth century they were allowed to gather among themselves on feast days to perform songs and dances. They had their own *mayoral*, a steward who aided in protecting them from owner abuses and assisted when they had to appear before judicial courts. Through African mutual aid they established a hospital, Our Lady of the Angels. A black religious brotherhood or confraternity shouldered its maintenance and upkeep. These institutions also received aid from Seville's elite. Thus African diasporic life in southern Spain was marked by a notable segregation of physical space for social, cultural, medical, and residential purposes. Africans and Spaniards surely intermingled a great deal, but Africans also took refuge within their network of friends, neighbors, and religious brotherhoods. They developed new identities that Spanish observers came to call *African* or *black ladino* and are today sometimes described more broadly as *Atlantic Creole*.

In contrast to the plebeian standards of life in the city's African quarters, the elite areas demonstrated an ever-increasing wealth. The commercial nouveau riche eschewed the old architectural styles, inherited from the Muslims, which emphasized the interior decoration of the house. Private as well as public buildings, like the Casa Lonja, or trade warehouse, demonstrate that sixteenth-century Seville was refashioning itself. Tenement-type buildings sprang up in the working-class barrios, while the townhouses of the merchant and elite class declared a new opulence.[3]

Alonso was quite familiar with life in each of these urban settings. His owners, the Illescas, were among the richest and most prominent of Seville's merchant families. It was their charge to train him in Spanish ways and to develop his faith in Christianity. It was during his teenage years that Enrique received the sacrament of confirmation and took on his second name, Alonso. The name belonged to the patriarch of the Illescas family, a *converso*, who was also director of Seville's merchant guild, called the *consulado de mercaderes*. Enrique may even have been the elder Illescas' personal servant during his youth.

Like many Africans in Seville, Enrique was taken to the Indies to assist his owners. Records show that Alvaro and Alonso de Illescas were active in Peru by 1551.[4] Previous to that they established their enterprise on the island of Santo Domingo. In addition to providing many shipments of the merchandise that the Spanish clamored for in the Indies such as clothing, cured meats, swords, horses, olive oil, and wine, the Illescas were among the first to market Africans in the New World. In 1530 they received a concession directly from Emperor Charles V to transport one hundred slaves to the colonies.

The trade that began on the Caribbean islands expanded within decades to include Mexico and then shifted once more with the conquest of the mainland of South America. Merchant families like the Illescas sent their factors to conduct the necessary commerce at the same time that conquistadors founded cities upon the ashes of defeated indigenous empires. The discovery of silver mines in Peru prompted the rapid arrival of thousands of Spaniards and furthered the growth of cities like Lima, the capital of the Peruvian viceroyalty and a key center of the Illescas family business. Alvaro de Illescas acted as family agent and remained in Peru for decades. His African, Alonso, like other ladino slaves, would have assisted in all areas of labor and trade, and perhaps even the protection and safety of his owner.

Peru, however, was not Spain. With a large indigenous population and the beginnings of mass importation of African laborers, Lima's social makeup and the role acquired by some Africans brought their Hispanic learning into high relief.[5] As Atlantic Creoles, Africans were often among the auxiliary forces of conquest; they acted as the hands and feet of their owners, playing key roles in the many battles and skirmishes that took place during Peru's subjugation and afterward. They could also be given managerial duties. They might have power over indigenous workers and entire communities. African ladinos were a constant sight in the company of conquistadors and the colonial elite.

From the indigenous perspective, they were often seen quite negatively. Writing in the early seventeenth century, a native observer named Guaman Poma de Ayala noted that black *criollos* were often mistreated by their owners. However, unlike the newly arrived Africans, or *bozales*, they were given to vices, cheating, abusing the indigenous people, and running away. Hispanicized Africans, therefore, were seen as a threat to the social order, perhaps because they understood it so well.

Notwithstanding the different views held of Creoles and *bozales*, both classes began to run off in acts of *marronage*, resisting enslavement from early on. They also formed renegade Maroon communities throughout Spanish America. In Panama, Mexico, and colonial Colombia, Maroons succeeded in founding permanent settlements. In sixteenth-century Esmeraldas, however, escape was not preplanned but rather the result of unforeseen events.

Alonso and the twenty-three "Guinea slaves" who departed the port of Panama on the southbound journey to Lima in 1553 could not have guessed the fate soon to befall them.[6] It was a typical journey in that the ship's pilot had to contend with the north and westerly Pacific Ocean currents that hampered vessels sailing south. The periodic ocean-atmospheric phenomena now called El Niño and La Niña may have further complicated his task. When the winds were not favorable, as in 1553, the journey could lengthen by weeks, and ships often put in at harbors along the coast to hunt up provisions. The captain of Illescas' ship did just that when he brought the ship carrying Alonso and the other African slaves into San Mateo Bay on the Esmeraldas coast. Tired and low on food, the crew and passengers looked forward to acquiring fresh water and perhaps some provisions from the local indigenous population. It was not a decision they would have taken lightly. The indigenous inhabitants had shown aggression toward the Spanish since their first landing in the 1520s, and even after numerous expeditions, there was no Spanish settlement in the region.

Disaster struck when the ship ran aground inside the bay and stranded the crew, passengers, and slaves onshore. It was a terrible turn for the worse; the only way out for them was to march south along ragged shorelines broken by rivers and estuaries to reach the nearest settlement, called Puerto Viejo. Alonso and the Africans took to the forest instead, seizing the moment to claim their freedom. Perhaps they also surmised that their chances of survival were better than the Europeans', because none of the crew or passengers ever reached Puerto Viejo.[7]

Becoming Maroons, however, did not mean that life would be much easier for the Africans. There were many reasons that they, too, might have perished on the Esmeraldas coast, and perhaps few imagined that they would succeed in planting firm roots there. First, they were alone, facing an environment quite unlike their African homeland and inhabited by Amerindians indifferent to their arrival. In addition, they could not raid or attack nearby Spanish settlements and plantations as Maroons often did in other parts of the Indies. During their first years, they struggled to survive in difficult circumstances, making alliances with and attacks upon indigenous communities. We cannot tell what model of warfare they used—Spanish, African, Amerindian, or some combination thereof. We do know that Alonso was not their first leader. An African named Antón led the escaped slaves at first but was said to have died in battle. It is also possible that he was ostracized from the community, and he may be the same person who was taken and executed as a sorcerer by Spanish soldiers in the 1580s. In either case Alonso did not rise to a position of leadership immediately but by way of alliances that he struck with local Nigua indigenous communities. These societies were remnants of the preconquest era. In some cases, they had retreated from highland homes with the arrival of Spanish dominance in the Andes. In either case, their social and political forms evolved out of communities inhabiting the region for centuries.

The Esmeraldas coast was home to a series of highly developed cultures centuries before the Spanish arrival. Archeological evidence demonstrates the existence of complex ritual structures and organized chieftaincies. Located exactly at the northern frontier of the Inca Empire it was a region largely independent of Incaic control before the conquest. The Spanish encountered midsized coastal villages at the Bay of Atacames when they arrived. However, Spanish colonization brought raiding and devastation to the region that resulted in a steep population decline. Linda Newson's demographic study estimates that a preconquest population of over one hundred thousand was reduced by 80 percent to about twenty thousand in only a few decades.[8] By the time the African slaves landed in 1553, the coastal communities were gone, and only small chieftaincies remained hidden throughout the interior lands. This contributed to the Spanish incapacity to settle the region. Although numerous expeditions entered Esmeraldas, the declining population and Amerindians' ability to evade Spanish detection made the province unattractive to settlement.

By the 1560s conquest expeditions were also declining in number. Spaniards were no longer as interested in conquest. They came to the Indies to populate cities, carry on trade, and manage profitable ventures from mining to cloth production and the collection of tribute. Furthermore, the depredations of the conquistadors upon indigenous peoples and the manpower demands that accompanied the establishment of new coastal settlements made the Crown reluctant to permit further conquests. Martín de Carranza, from the coastal city of Guayaquil, undertook the only well-recorded expedition to Esmeraldas during this period. His soldiers entered Esmeraldas in 1569 searching for Amerindians to enslave and hoping to establish a settlement, but as with earlier expeditions, indigenous people used flight as well as effective attacks to keep the colonizers out. Carranza traveled throughout southern Esmeraldas hoping to entice the indigenous chiefs peacefully. Instead, local Campaz Indians twice engaged him in battle. His men were routed, and Carranza himself suffered serious injuries. Around the same time, the Crown established a high court, or *audiencia*, in the city of Quito. Although it was the northern capital of the fallen Incan state, Quito was far removed from the coast. To increase trade and the region's connection to the silver economy, very soon administrators and merchants began to explore the opening of a port settlement closer to the highland city. Among their first choices was the province of Esmeraldas.

It was at this point in the late 1560s and early 1570s that Alonso's role began to take on greater importance. Although the years between 1553 and 1570 saw numerous Spanish failures in settling Esmeraldas, the Maroons under Alonso de Illescas' (as he was now known) leadership had succeeded in allying themselves with the indigenous population, defending their independence from Spanish invaders, achieving a level of strategic dominance in Esmeraldas in relation to surrounding native communities, and earning the gratitude of the people periodically shipwrecked along the coast. These many successes were a testament to Alonso's abilities and required him to be a diplomat, military leader, and interlocutor between the Amerindian peoples and his African followers.

By the 1570s the community that the Maroons created had indeed become a multiethnic society. The Africans intermarried with local native women (with the men typically forming polygamous partnerships). The Spanish called their children *mulattoes*, an Old World term for someone of mixed African race, though by the 1590s they would begin to use the label *zambos*, a new caste category developed in the Americas. These *zambos* were described as culturally and racially mixed *mestizos*. They spoke indigenous languages as their mother tongue and used native dress and physical ornaments. At the same time they inherited knowledge of African and European culture. Two of Illescas' sons, Sebastián and Antonio, would emerge as the next generation of community leaders. There were also some European members of the community, most notably Illescas' chief assistant, a Portuguese soldier named Gonzalo de Avila, who remained among the Maroons after the unsuccessful military campaign of Martín de Carranza.

In addition, Illescas began engaging in trade with Spanish ships that periodically stopped in Esmeraldas, and he had to contend with another group of African Maroons, called the Mangaches, that formed after one more of the many coastal shipwrecks. While a new generation of Maroons was coming of age and would soon lead the Esmeraldeños, Illescas was perceived as the single most powerful person in the region. These attributes convinced the Spanish that Illescas could be a useful tool for advancing the establishing of a port settlement in Esmeraldas.

In 1577, following another rescue of shipwrecked passengers, the Maroons expressed their desire to become subjects of the Crown. Within a few months, with the *audiencia*'s approval and under the guidance of Quito's bishop, a diplomatic mission arrived in Esmeraldas under the command of a clergyman named Miguel Cabello de Balboa.[9] The *audiencia* offered Illescas the title of *gobernador*, which would make him ruler of the province by royal decree. It was an unprecedented honor for an African Maroon. While the Spanish had established treaties with rebel Africans in other regions, they had never before offered them the title of *gobernador*. Neither did this practice conform entirely to those used with the indigenous leaders called *caciques*. According to Cabello Balboa, Illescas' title gave him the leadership of the entire province, not just over the indigenous and African people of his community. The *audiencia* even accorded Illescas the title of *Don*, a form of address denoting noble status. According to Cabello's own report, there is no doubt that Illescas was pleased to receive the honor. He kissed the written decree with the *audiencia*'s orders and then placed it over his head, vowing in the name of God to obey and serve the Crown faithfully.

From their first meeting, however, it was also clear that offering Illescas titles was not all that Cabello had come for, and the new role the *audiencia* imagined for the Maroon leader came with notable risks and consequences. First, the *audiencia* required that Alonso and his people move from their interior homeland, a safe haven—although described as a place filled with mosquitoes and unhealthy "airs" (perhaps referencing the Spanish distaste for hot, humid climates) to the Bay of San Mateo, near the mouth of the Esmeraldas River. In addition, it was to be his job to congregate the communities of numerous *caciques* (native lords) in the same settlement. The Spanish expected San Mateo to serve as the beginnings of the port that would become the feeder line to increased trade in the highlands. It was a difficult undertaking, one that required Illescas to consolidate his control over the surrounding native peoples and, in leaving his hidden forest settlement, expose himself to possible Spanish treachery and attack.

During the weeks that followed, Illescas visited with the Spanish numerous times, praying with them in a small makeshift chapel they erected on the shore, and promising faithfully to return with his people. On one occasion he came with local native chiefs to hold a great feast, during which Cabello conversed with Illescas extensively. In these conversations Cabello came to know that Alonso was *muy ladino* and believed his willingness to submit to the *audiencia*'s requests. However, the constant delays that followed convinced Cabello and his men that the Maroons had decided not to fulfill their promise. Finally, after more than one month spent stranded on those shores, falling short of provisions and fearing for their safety, they decided to leave. But first, Cabello scouted inland to find out what had happened. He returned to report that the Maroons were nowhere to be found. He had visited a landing point on the river where he found rafts and food destroyed, and the Spaniards deduced that there was war in the land, and immediately made plans to depart. Cabello's mission was a failure, and the *audiencia* was soon busied by rebellion in other regions of Quito. It would not take up the matter of Esmeraldas again until early in 1583.

Needless to say, Illescas did not resettle his community, and Esmeraldas remained outside the grip of Spanish power. Six years later, Quito's *audiencia* attempted to remove the Maroons by force once again. They sent an army of one hundred men under the command of Captain Diego López de Zúñiga. The company managed to travel to the coast by way of the local river networks, but then became bogged down in the forests. They found no Maroons or Amerindians. The strategy of evasion that had worked so well for the indigenous people of Esmeraldas was equally effective when employed by the Maroons. Within a few weeks, however, half the soldiers took ill, and over twenty soon died from fevers. The ultimate cause of their deaths was unknown, but before the illness wiped them all out, many abandoned the expedition and trudged their way back to Quito. In the meantime a young friar named Alonso de Espinosa set out to give the soldiers their last rights and tend to the infirm. Instead, he arrived and befriended the Maroons. For the next two years Espinosa became the rebels' advocate, pleading their case before the *audiencia*. Unlike Cabello de Balboa, Espinosa seemed to have true missionary devotion to the Maroons. Although Alonso de Illescas had remained reclusive for years after his interaction with Cabello, he took a quick liking to Espinosa and requested that the young friar remain among them as their minister. Espinosa baptized the Maroon children and soon became the liaison between Quito and Esmeraldas.

The *audiencia* approved the move and hoped that Espinosa could persuade Illescas not only to become a faithful vassal but to aid in a new colonizing project, this one headed by a leading merchant of Quito named Rodrigo de Ribadeneyra.[10] Ribadeneyra's plan was different from all previous attempts. It involved the introduction of settlers brought from Spain with specific license to land in Esmeraldas and establish two towns. However, Ribadeneyra realized early on that success depended on peaceable relations with Alonso de Illescas and the other Maroon bands. In the following months, the renegades were invited to Quito with their indigenous followers and other native lords, where they received gifts from Ribadeneyra. Alonso would not travel to Quito himself but sent allied Maroons, the Mangaches, and some indigenous leaders. Ribadeneyra gave them many gifts of clothing, hats, pins, long shirts, and blankets. He provided them with machetes, knives, and axes, imported iron goods that were highly prized on the coast. Finally he wrote to the Crown suggesting that any requests made by Illescas be honored because he was the "key to the land." In effect, Alonso de Illescas had become the gatekeeper to Spanish colonization projects in the region.

Given Ribadeneyra's nonviolent methods and Illescas' apparent satisfaction with the gifts he received, an agreement seemed close at hand. However, in 1586 Illescas wrote a letter to the Crown and the *audiencia* that reversed all of Ribadeneyra's efforts. In all likelihood, Espinosa was the scribe for Illescas' thoughts because this is the one and only letter that the Maroon leader is known to have written. What is more difficult to gauge is the degree of Espinosa's influence on Illescas' ideas and proposals.

In his missive, Illescas stated his desire to place himself "in the service of our lord, God, and . . . your royal highness." But then he went on to say that after discussions with his people, they believed that sending Spanish settlers and soldiers to the region was unnecessary because Illescas and his people were fully ready to serve the Crown. In addition he gently chided the king for granting Ribadeneyra permission to bring settlers to Esmeraldas, and stated that "what can be conquered with the indoctrination of the holy gospel would only be of disservice to God and to your majesty if conquered by the force of arms and at the cost of many souls." In effect Illescas was saying that he would neither submit to nor aid Ribadeneyra, and that he did not trust any other Spaniards who entered the region. However, he offered to become a subject of the Crown and subdue the most bellicose Amerindians of the region, called the Campazes, himself. Illescas insisted that because Spanish captains had broken their word to him time and again, he would neither trust them nor help them to settle in Esmeraldas.

Without the support of the Maroons, Ribadeneyra was forced to abandon the project. When the colonizers arrived from Spain, they were dropped on the shores of Esmeraldas, but no one was there and no provisions arrived to help them found the new settlement. They stayed for only a few months before reembarking for Guayaquil. To the Spanish the situation must have been perfectly clear—without Maroon assistance they had no chance of successfully settling Esmeraldas. At the same time, they knew they could not dislodge the Maroons by military means. The Africans had become a permanent fixture on the landscape. Where the Spanish failed the Maroons had succeeded.

The *audiencia*, however, took a dim view of Illescas' letter. They arrested Espinosa on trumped-up charges and subsequently banished him from the

Indies. He was viewed as a traitor and treated as such. In a fascinating twist, Fray Espinosa was rumored to have returned to Esmeraldas after escaping his captors, but he was never heard from again, as if the forests of Esmeraldas had swallowed him whole. Unfortunately, this was also one of the last times that Alonso de Illescas was to interact directly with Spanish authorities.

We do not find Alonso de Illescas in the historical record after 1590. At some point between 1587 and 1596, he passed away in the homeland that he had created in Esmeraldas. Yet it was in this coastal province that he came to rule and find the only period of independence in his life. For most enslaved Africans slavery lasted from birth until death. Alonso de Illescas spent more than thirty years of freedom on the Esmeraldas shores. As importantly, however, Illescas passed this freedom on to his children and followers. They paid a heavy price to achieve it, both in blood and in the everyday struggle for survival. Many of their strategies involved aggressions and alliances with native people. These strategies were, in large measure, determined by the political and social realities of the place where their ship had run aground back in 1553. That was the decisive moment when the Africans could have chosen to follow their Spanish masters, but they chose freedom instead.

After 1590 the Esmeraldas Maroons were able to conclude a peace agreement with the *audiencia* of Quito. While Alonso de Illescas did not live to see it, his son Sebastián received the title of *Don* and was recognized as leader over the Illescas Maroons by 1600. Not only did the Crown legitimize the mulattoes, but a missionary was also sent to preach among them, and they were excluded from tribute obligations. Pedro de Arevalo, a Spaniard who colonized in the Esmeraldas region for over thirty years, beginning in about 1570, provided an embellished but noble testament to Alonso's independence. In a report to the Crown written in 1600, years after Alonso's death, he wrote,

> Alonso de Illescas . . . has been such a discerning and astute warrior that although he often harmed Spanish forces at no time going back more than sixty years have the many Spanish governors and captains that entered to conquer and subdue the region of Esmeraldas . . . done any harm to him, nor overtaken him, nor even seen his face.[11]

His son Sebastián de Illescas finally took the journey to Quito that his father had never managed to take. In 1600, by the hand of Quito's bishop he received the sacrament of confirmation and honored the man who helped free him from slavery by taking Alonso as his confirmation name. After Alonso Sebastián's death in the early 1600s, at least two more generations of

Illescas would rule in Esmeraldas, each one demonstrating the transcultural fusion between Africans and Indians that came to mark the mulatto population and the process of ethnogenesis—the creation of new ethnic groups through intermarriage and the mixing of ethnic identities. The descendants of the charter generation of Africans, led by Alonso de Illescas and the band of slaves that escaped Spanish authorities, became neither African nor Indian but a unique New World hybrid that racially and culturally defied the expectations of the Iberian colonizers. In their process of intermingling they demonstrated that the colonization of the New World and the encounters between people were not only between Europeans and "others" but also among and between the "others." In the case of Esmeraldas this unusual intermingling produced an alternative colonial order that assimilated Old World populations into New World communities, a reversal that aided both groups in retaining their independence from European colonial rule.

CHAPTER TWO

~

Gregoria López (1680s)

A Mexican Mulata Defends Her Honor

Aaron P. Althouse

The seventeenth-century Atlantic World saw the foundation of lasting British, French, and Dutch settlements in the New World and an increased demand for African slaves in the Americas, but also the consolidation of colonial societies in Spanish and Portuguese territories that already included people of African descent, slave and free. The important presence of free blacks, often of mixed descent, marked Hispanic American societies from the outset, and required the fearful attention of metropolitan authorities and colonial elites. Aaron Althouse unearthed from the archives the story of Gregoria López, a freeborn mulata *from the mountain region of Mexico who took her father to the courts for sexual assault. Not the typical powerless victim, Gregoria knew her rights and fought to have them recognized, even if it meant challenging the prevailing hierarchy that called for obedience to her father. As for many other women of African descent in the Americas, this disposition to autonomy was seen by contemporaries as a threat to the social order. Historians today take such episodes as entries into otherwise hidden conflicts over social norms.*

One summer evening in the mountains of Mexico, a sixteen-year-old *mulata* (of African and Spanish descent) named Gregoria López readied for sleep, arranging her "bed" in the corner of a small room in the cramped house where she lived with her *mulato* father, Mateo, and her *castiza* (of Spanish and native descent) stepmother, Bernarda de San Joseph. The fact that all three slept in the same room testifies to the humble character of the residence to which Gregoria recently had moved following time spent with her paternal grandmother in a nearby town. Gregoria did not last more than a few weeks in her new home before trouble emerged. As the afternoon in question turned to twilight, Gregoria lay down to sleep. Suspiciously, rather than join his wife in the opposite corner of the dwelling, Mateo piled his bedding near the center of the room, roughly equidistant from both Bernarda and Gregoria. Sometime around midnight, with the room cloaked in darkness, Mateo crept to Gregoria's bed and began fondling and kissing his daughter despite her unequivocal cautions that he was her father and should not commit such offenses. In testimony she would soon present to criminal court authorities, Gregoria commented that these actions led her to "understand that [Mateo] . . . wanted to commit incest with her."[1] During his own statement before these same officials, Mateo insisted that he was merely operating within his acceptable realm of fatherly duty, as he wished to verify that Gregoria was still a virgin. Likely grasping for some means to extricate herself from this horrible predicament, Gregoria suggested to her father that there were "other ways" to garner such information, and that he might inspect her using his fingers rather than depend upon actual intercourse. Mateo replied that, though it was a shame and he would have to commit a "sin," he wished to discover the truth "with his own parts." Mateo then forced himself upon his daughter. After completing this dreadful act, Mateo expressed contrition, at least regarding his concern that his behavior would be discovered by those outside the household. He kissed Gregoria's hands "with much care, asking her forgiveness, that she not tell anyone" and that all of what occurred would remain "en casa." While his language reflected little preoccupation with the moral implications of having committed incest, Mateo clearly hoped to keep the matter private. Beginning with events that unfolded the following day, when Gregoria complained to a Spanish neighbor woman about the rape, and some days later when she proceeded to bring criminal charges against Mateo, Gregoria proved steadfast in both her unwillingness to keep the matter quiet, and her ability to confront the colonial Spanish American system of social values that assumed a woman's complicity in any sort of sexual encounter, even one such as this, marked by violent coercion.

Although this sort of situation might have occurred in many different places and junctures—including the present—it is unfortunately not a fictional account akin to Jim Trueblood's incestuous liaison in Ralph Ellison's novel *Invisible Man*. The events actually took place in the small provincial city of Pátzcuaro, Mexico, in 1685. We know of the circumstances surrounding the incident through what remains of the criminal suit Gregoria filed against her father. While key aspects of the episode are unequivocally abhorrent and at times difficult to consider in detached, analytical fashion, recounting details of the case serves a positive purpose for the modern student of the African diaspora in the Americas, providing a rare, intimate perspective on the life experiences of a free woman of color in colonial Mexico. It also serves to remind us that people of African descent represented important segments of the population in areas beyond the largest cities and coastal plantation regions—specifically, in this case, the secondary urban center of Pátzcuaro, located in the heart of the preconquest Tarascan Empire more than seven thousand feet above sea level in the mountains of west central Mexico.

As a *mulata*, Gregoria pressed her lawsuit in a climate of socialized and institutionalized inequality. In general, elites of European descent viewed Afro-Mexicans with no small degree of disdain, and women were doubly targeted as their supposed racial inferiority became connected with unique sexual powers that influenced characterizations of black women and *mulatas* as inherently sexual, less honorable than elite white women, and in some cases potentially dangerous to social order. Such images assumed that Afro-Mexican women thought little about issues such as sexual selectivity, defense of virginity, or determination to marry rather than maintain consensual unions. Therefore, Gregoria's defense of body and refusal to accept that the rape resulted in any way from her own actions stand in contrast to the modes of behavior ascribed to women of African heritage. Her words and actions, included in the pages of the criminal suit she lodged against her father, suggest that women of African descent in Spanish America did not necessarily choose the path of resistance, but, rather, in certain cases sought to establish and defend measures of personal honor generally associated only with Spaniards and Creoles.

Material like Gregoria's case that preserves the life experiences of Afro-Mexican women during this time period is rare. The majority were illiterate and of few means, and consequently, they are difficult to encounter in extant colonial documents such as notarial transactions or last wills and testaments. When they do appear, it is often as participants in baptismal or marriage ceremonies, and these records divulge very little about their individual beliefs, opinions, or motives. Inquisition cases prove more fruitful, since they contain statements made by women of African descent in the course of investigations into accusations regarding activities such as sorcery or witchcraft. Testimony in these cases, however, must be used carefully, since it was often geared toward beating the charges that were frequently leveled at women of color rather than accurately reflecting individual values. Finally,

Afro-Mexican women do appear in manumission cases, but these too are not particularly numerous and, due to their nature, cast women largely as slaves. Collectively, in recent years the aforementioned sources have augmented historians' understanding of the ties between gender, honor, and witchcraft. Unfortunately, stories about free Afro-Mexican women like Gregoria, who were neither criminal suspects nor (so far as we know) viewed as "dangerous" women, remain extremely rare.

Highland Mexico in the Black Atlantic

Although people of African descent are not commonly associated with highland provincial regions where indigenous peoples survived after the shock of postconquest population decline, Gregoria's experiences illustrate the long reach of the Black Atlantic. This ethnocultural zone represented an extraordinarily large geographic and cultural area, originating in sub-Saharan West Africa, and extending westward to the Americas and northward to western Europe. In the Americas, the forced arrival of Africans began as early as the sixteenth century. At this formative juncture, many were destined for the emerging viceregal centers of Lima and Mexico City. By the later sixteenth century and into the seventeenth century, African slave labor increasingly became associated with plantation-style agriculture, and increasing numbers of black slaves from diverse ethnolinguistic backgrounds populated sprawling estates in coastal regions of South and Mesoamerica, as well as the Caribbean islands. Consequently, blacks came to outnumber both European whites and indigenous peoples in the plantation societies of northeastern Brazil, Cuba, and even sections of eastern Mexico. Such areas became the foci of a burgeoning American culture designed by Europeans but shaped by Africans and their descendants. There, the Black Atlantic of Spanish America was most visible.

However, African-influenced contributions to a developing Latin American society were not limited to the coastal lowlands and Caribbean islands. Rather, in regions like New Spain, which was dominated by the area of present-day Mexico, Africans and people of African descent resided in both urban centers such as Mexico City, Querétaro, and Antequera (modern day Oaxaca), as well as smaller provincial cities, their even smaller satellite towns, and the haciendas and ranches that dotted the central mountain plateaus. While slave imports to Mexico grew in the sixteenth century and continued until roughly 1650, this traffic entered a period of permanent decline by the middle of the seventeenth century. Yet the diminution of new slave arrivals did not mean the end of either slavery or the African presence in Mexico. By the later seventeenth century, the formerly enslaved Afro-Mexican population was becoming increasingly free and defined less frequently as "black." By that point, the growing sector of free people of color was described more often with labels that denoted racially mixed ancestry, such as *mulato* (African-European background), *lobo* (African–indigenous American), or *pardo* (in general, a dark-skinned person). This transition occurred due to an ongoing process of race mixture that started in the earliest moments of sixteenth-century cultural contact and exploded in the 1600s, when the overall native population—particularly what remained in the heartland of the former Aztec Empire—spiraled toward its nadir.

Spanish elites interpreted the growth of the mixed population as a threat to social order, not only in terms of challenging continued white monopolization of economic resources, social preeminence, and dictation of acceptable behavior and values, but also because race mixture facilitated unity among nonelites of various hues. In other words, Spaniards feared that race mixture would foster an interracial front capable of overthrowing the colonial state. Responding to the disorder race mixture represented, European and American-born Spaniards turned to caste hierarchies as a means of bringing order to this perceived chaos. The resulting *sociedad de castas* assigned highest rank to individuals of "pure" European descent—those who were untainted by Moorish, Jewish, African, or Indian heritage. Indian commoners and African slaves resided at the bottom of the social ladder, and numerous admixtures of indigenous, African, and European blood fell somewhere in between, depending upon their alleged degree of "Spanishness." Making use of these racial characterizations, fiscal and sumptuary measures were imposed upon Indians and people of African descent beginning in the 1500s and continuing through the end of the colonial period in the 1800s. Despite these apparently formal rules, however, the caste system was not codified in law until the later 1700s and varied substantially according to local practice.

The rise of caste rankings—with specific privileges and status denied many racially mixed people—served to further limit opportunities for many Mexican *castas*, particularly those of African descent. Thus, the majority of Afro-Mexicans remained poor and illiterate, living quite public lives in the streets and marketplaces of cities and towns, as well as in poorly constructed and maintained housing that afforded them little privacy to keep potentially embarrassing domestic situations quiet. Further ramifications accompanied these conditions, notably the interplay between African descent and the colonial honor complex, in which "honor embodied interrelated concepts of nobility, Catholicism, 'pure blood lines' (*limpieza de sangre*), privilege, precedence, title, office, form of address, dress, and the lifestyle that the conquistadors, first

settlers, and later Castilian emigrants carried to colonial Spanish America."
In this context, "honor required public esteem," and those with the most
honor were, not surprisingly, Spaniards and Creoles.[2]

A preoccupation with racial status and honor typified elites, but was not
limited to only the upper crust of colonial society. In certain situations,
status-conscious Afro-Mexicans tried to and did establish honorable reputations. Furthermore, by the latter stages of the eighteenth century, official
measures that allowed certain individuals to formally wipe away their African heritage through the purchase of whiteness were functioning throughout Spanish America. Such cases, however, were not common, and the
attainment of honor remained out of reach to most Afro–Latin Americans.
Acquiring honor became even more tenuous when gender was a consideration. Clearly, women of African descent interacted with elites, particularly
in terms of consensual unions with elite men or service as domestic slaves
and servants in the residences of wealthy families. As marriage across caste
lines was never prohibited (though it was discouraged by elites), people of
varying degrees of African, European, and native background could cement
intercaste matrimonial ties. For the most part, however, these relationships
remained informal, and only in the minority of cases did they facilitate one's
rise from plebeian to elite circles. In practice, gender signified yet another
set of issues that could be used to cement negative attributes to Afro–Latin
American women, and consequent images of their sexuality drew upon expectations of sorcery and excessive promiscuity, quite the opposite of that
anticipated from elite women.

Gregoria Defends Her Honor

Gregoria's employment of criminal tribunals to press charges against her
father is not shocking in the sense that a woman of African descent understood colonial legal institutions well enough to use them for the pursuit of
individual motives. In general, while Spanish colonial practice accorded
people of native and African descent secondary social and legal status, both
men and women of African descent maintained a different relationship with
colonial tribunals than did native peoples. Africans and their American
descendants were considered part of the Hispanic realm, even though they
were not accorded sumptuary or legal status equal to that of Spaniards and
Creoles. As part of the Hispanic realm, they were—despite Spanish views
of their inherent shortcomings—expected to follow Iberian social mores,
particularly in terms of proper observation of Christian practice. In fact,
beginning as early as the sixteenth century in places like Mexico (as well

as Peru), people of African descent fought to control the unfolding of their lives through use of legal channels, namely criminal, civil, and ecclesiastical tribunals, not infrequently with some measure of success.

Gregoria's case is a bit more surprising, however, because she publicized actions that had occurred in the confines of her father's house, generally considered a private space where men and women might struggle for dominance, yet one that was not regularly contested in public by women regardless of their caste. In light of the paternalistic and racially unequal society that characterized late seventeenth-century Mexico, Gregoria's story seems most remarkable because of the enormous personal courage and resolve she displayed when facing this social climate as the victim of a violent sex crime, as well as her ability to negotiate what could have been a hopeless situation into one that to some degree met her expectations of honor and morality. As noted earlier, Gregoria's problems began in mid-June of 1685, when Mateo, a *mulato* shoemaker from Pátzcuaro, arrived at the house in Sayula where Gregoria lived with her paternal grandmother, Sebastiana de la Cruz. This living arrangement had evidently been in place since the death of Gregoria's Spanish mother. Mateo decided to retrieve his daughter at that particular point only because he had received news that his father had passed away, leaving Gregoria in the sole care of Sebastiana. Early on in this new arrangement with her father, Gregoria sensed trouble. As Gregoria, Mateo, and two of her younger siblings traveled the road to Pátzcuaro, she concluded that her father harbored "incestuous" thoughts toward her. However, no problems arose until they reached Pátzcuaro and Gregoria moved into the house her father shared with his second wife, Bernarda. Some weeks later, Gregoria found her intuitions regarding her father's feelings to be correct.

The abuse did not end with the first assault—described in this chapter's introduction—and matters actually grew worse for Gregoria the next day. After relating the incident to her Spanish neighbor, Doña Francisca de Nava, Gregoria returned home to Mateo and Bernarda. At that point, she remained uncertain as to whether she would approach Pátzcuaro's criminal authorities or let the matter rest, her indecision stemming from suggestions by Mateo, Bernarda, and Doña Francisca that she remain quiet. However, events that afternoon erased her doubt regarding the course she would follow. Once back inside the small house, Mateo locked himself and Gregoria in the bedroom, where he beat her to the point that he left visible marks upon her body. After this, Mateo carried her to her bed, where he again forced her to have sexual intercourse. After more than an hour spent in this manner, Mateo repeated his instructions for Gregoria to keep the incident secret, then left her and emerged from the room to take his midday meal.

At that point, twice the victim of incest, Gregoria wrestled with what must have been a series of agonizing concerns. First, the general horror and shock resulting from nonconsensual sex cannot be overestimated. Second, some sense of humiliation and perhaps even shame could have accompanied such an experience, for even though Gregoria bore no responsibility for Mateo's actions, societal values of the time could judge her as somehow complicit in the act. Third, to punish her father through the criminal system, Gregoria would have to recount the rape in detail in a public setting. Fourth, based on Gregoria's own words, we can assume that she was still a virgin before the assault. If she had remained so until that point, preserving her virginity mattered to her, and losing it to her father would only have compounded her pain, and perhaps made her unable to marry in the future. Finally, Gregoria's status as a female minor of Afro-Mexican background certainly would have played upon how the authorities would view her, since nonwhites were thought to be both more innately sexual and vulnerable to premarital sex not only because of their alleged racial inferiority, but also because they had less physical separation from such temptations in their daily lives.

Despite these obstacles, however, Gregoria aired the allegations. Within days of the crimes, she provided a deposition to Don Francisco de Solis y Alcazar, lieutenant to the province of Michoacán's highest-ranked justice official (*alcalde mayor*). In doing so, she left resolution of the matter in the hands of Pátzcuaro's criminal tribunal. In the Spanish colonial world, cases were routinely generated through the provision of complaints such as Gregoria's, or when news of a crime—often a report of a beaten or deceased victim—reached criminal officials through informal channels (an uninvolved informant) or more formal lines (village justice officials sending news or reporting in person to Pátzcuaro). While local officials could rule on the probable guilt of defendants and whether they should be jailed while case-related investigations occurred, case files were ultimately sent off to the high court (*audiencia*) in Mexico City, where judgments were rendered and returned to their community of origin.

Importantly, in Gregoria's initial sworn statement to criminal tribunal authorities, she placed the blame squarely upon her father and voiced her complaints quite publicly. This refusal to exhibit guilt over her father's actions and refusal to desist from presenting an official complaint allowed her to define—at least to some extent—how the issue could be resolved. This was the case because Gregoria interacted independently and on her own behalf with criminal authorities who represented the colonial state, and so she negotiated her case without the assistance of either male friends and relatives or women who had reached their legal majority. And she did so despite warnings from her father, stepmother, and Spanish neighbor that such a step might provoke scandal. Of particular significance is the way that Gregoria couched her concern in religious terms, mentioning the sinful nature of what transpired in "God's eyes" as well as relating her desire to attend mass on the morning following the initial incident. Thus, by filing charges, Gregoria was not refuting the honor complex, but rather seeking a more personally favorable resolution to the issue that would preserve what individual honor she still possessed. This was despite the fact that Afro-Mexican women were comprehensively stripped of their virtue in images fostered by elites, who saw them as less virginal and more inclined toward sexual witchcraft than their more "European" counterparts. Gregoria simply refused to fulfill the existing societal expectations about her behavior.

Although she exhibited an intention to possess honor as defined by colonial elites, Gregoria did challenge the status quo along two interrelated lines. First, she brought the charges against her father even though the home was largely considered private space that, though subject to female influence, was still under male guidance and dominion. Second, as we shall see below, despite the slight credibility and autonomy conceded her by the criminal system due to her racial and gender status, Gregoria related often highly intimate details of this assault to Pátzcuaro's colonial officials with a confidence that served to reestablish control over her body.

Mateo, Bernarda, and Doña Francisca de Nava, the Spanish neighbor whom Gregoria approached the morning after the rape, expressed concern with the implications about honor of filing a criminal complaint. In fact, despite the racial differences between Mateo and Bernarda, both of African descent, and Nava, a "Spaniard," the language they employed in warning Gregoria against pursuing the charges was similar in the sense that each appealed to the public dimensions associated with spreading news of the crime, particularly because this would transform a private matter into a public spectacle. Beginning with Mateo, each articulated the need to keep the unpleasant tale private. As we saw earlier, after assaulting his daughter, Mateo requested that she not mention the matter. There certainly was a practical side to the request, as Mateo knew he could be punished severely were he judged guilty of incest, and he appeared to reserve special fear for the Inquisition, which had operated in Mexico since the sixteenth century, and which handled "moral" crimes such as incest, blasphemy, sodomy, and even the rarely occurring episode of bestiality. In an attempt to ensure that Gregoria did not repeat what had happened between them, Mateo followed her to Doña Francisca's house, where he pleaded with her not to say anything of the rape, because "it was an inquisition case and he had only [used] his finger."

On the other hand, Mateo clearly expressed worry about how news of his actions might impact his public reputation, and ostensibly his position of domestic command. He went so far as to claim that he beat Gregoria as a matter of honor after her revelations to Doña Francisca, telling the investigating officials that he gave her ten lashes "because she left to dishonor him in the street." Furthermore, Mateo rationalized the initial rape of his daughter in a way that reflected commonly held beliefs that a woman's sexual behavior might stain the honor of an entire family. He alleged that Gregoria had been involved with a young tailor from Valladolid named Joseph—whose last name he conveniently did not know—and that because of this relationship, Mateo feared Gregoria had bowed to temptation and engaged in sexual activity, which led him to find out whether or not she was still a virgin.

Importantly, while Mateo obviously had reason to attempt to quiet Gregoria, Bernarda and Doña Francisca also voiced trepidation over Gregoria's going public, since this would only serve to attract unwanted attention due to the obvious violation of the colonial honor code, as well as the generally scandalous nature of airing household issues outside the home. The morning after the first assault, Gregoria questioned Bernarda as to how she could remain asleep even though Mateo made noise when he moved to the middle of the room, during his "inspection" of Gregoria, and while forcing the sexual intercourse that followed. With a tearful Gregoria posing these questions to her and stating that she planned to approach the local criminal justices, Bernarda's only response was to direct the young woman to "guard" the information lest it provoke scandal. Doña Francisca proved a more willing advocate for Gregoria. Although the case reveals nothing about why Gregoria sought out Francisca, it would have been a sound decision when lodging a criminal complaint against Mateo to enlist the aid of a Spaniard who also carried the honorific title *Doña*. Interestingly, *patzcuarense* society must have been intimate enough that the arrival of a young and unknown *mulata* at her house between six and seven on a Sunday morning was not unusual enough to merit any mention of the uniqueness of the occasion. At any rate, just as Gregoria concluded her account, Mateo discovered her in Doña Francisca's house, where he entered only to fall subject to a verbal barrage from the Spaniard, who yelled at him to "look how he lived" in such scandalous fashion. Once through with her estimation of Mateo's moral shortcomings, Francisca herself voiced doubt over the wisdom of pursuing the case further. She told Mateo that if he had committed the act, he should "fix it," and that he and Gregoria should not "make any scandal nor publicize it" since it was a woman's matter. Interestingly, despite being Mateo's superior in caste and title, Doña Francisca validated his right to manage his family life as he saw fit. In deciding to press charges, Gregoria was choosing to defend her honor and establish that her father had wronged her, thereby illustrating that she had not willfully disgraced herself.

The second strategy Gregoria used to fight for some role in shaping her public reputation lay in her confident recounting of the intimate details of the assault. Offering this testimony no doubt must have been exceedingly difficult given not only the brutal nature of Mateo's crime, but also the fact that Gregoria's psychological wounds were still quite recent. Established notions of gender and race made Gregoria's position even more difficult, because as a woman and a minor she was not given full dominion over her body. Clues from the case suggest that as her father, Mateo could assume some right to physical inspection when the question of virginity was involved. In giving his own testimony and countering Gregoria's accusations along lines he hoped would eliminate his guilt, Mateo forthrightly acknowledged manually inspecting Gregoria's genitals, but denied the intercourse. Such testimony implies that he saw nothing wrong with checking Gregoria for any signs of prior sexual activity, nor did he believe that revealing such information would damage his cause. From this language, one could safely assume that his attitude was not altogether uncommon in late seventeenth-century provincial society.

To pursue legal action, Gregoria had to publicly reconstruct the most excruciating details of the incident. Notwithstanding this and the gender, racial, and age biases that operated against her, Gregoria faced the municipal justices and offered them highly intimate details of the rape. In the process, she conveyed both her utter lack of complicity in the incident and her refusal to accept such future behavior from Mateo. Gregoria reserved her greatest show of resolve for the recitation of the facts surrounding the nature of the sexual contact between her and her father. Since the issue of genital penetration evidently could influence the outcome of her complaint, she had to address exactly what transpired during the assaults. Hence, she related that Mateo first manually checked her, and afterwards moved on to actual intercourse, during which "he penetrated her with violence." Gregoria also faced her audience with remarkable courage when elaborating upon the beating administered by Mateo the following day. She explained how Mateo had locked the two of them inside the bedroom and repeatedly struck her with a strip of leather, ostensibly as "punishment" for her seeking support from Doña Francisca. For court purposes, her accusations did not stand as sufficient proof, and so the presiding justice requested that she show the "signs" of the beating to him, the attending notary, and two more attending witnesses (both men), which was the norm when recording official affidavits during criminal investigations. Here again, Gregoria did not shrink from the request, nor, according to the case proceedings, did she lose her composure. Finally, Gregoria entered the delicate arena of describing sexual response in detail, as she specified becoming "wet" after a brief period of time during the intercourse. This language stands as remarkable for the time period, given that such sentiments were not likely to have been shared freely between women and their familiars in the best of situations. In this case—considering the violent physical and psychological nature of the crime, the fact that she recounted these details to men who were effectively strangers, and her ability to do so without anyone present to lend her moral support or legal sponsorship—Gregoria's unabashed, systematic, and analytical testimony clearly indicates a great deal of self-confidence regarding characterizations of her body.

While Gregoria advanced her cause with a clarity that manifested her sense of individual autonomy, sexual freedom, and still intact honor, she also related her concern over the moral consequences of the rape in ways that might not have been anticipated by the colonial officials. Specifically, she saw the violation of her body as a moral quandary tied to her religious beliefs, for she explained how in the long hours that immediately followed Mateo's first assault, she was "ashamed and in pain" because an "offense against God . . . had been committed." Due to her concern, she could not sleep the remainder of the night, and felt the need to attend mass the next morning. The genuine religiosity highlighted by Gregoria demonstrates an alternative angle on Afro-Mexicans' relationship with the church, for it presents one woman's highly personal reckoning of her connection with her creator. In this light, Gregoria's beliefs contrast a dual-faceted negative perception of Afro-Mexicans associated with their role in popular religious observance. On one hand, certain religious officials decried the behavior of blacks and *mulatos* as a potentially destabilizing force against the religious foundation of society. On the other hand, as previously mentioned, Afro-Mexicans were lumped together with other poor people as key purveyors of sorcery and sexual remedies.

Gregoria's courageous actions in facing familial and broader social pressures differ from those of her stepmother, Bernarda—also of African descent—who wavered regarding whether or not to support Gregoria's apparently truthful claim or Mateo's account of the incident. No doubt the decision to side with a rape victim over her husband was more difficult than a modern vantage point might suggest, since Bernarda's indecision reflects the pressure of daily survival that women of African descent (and most poor women) often faced. Dependency upon men was, though not always necessary, useful because nonelite women had few legal rights not tied to male spouses or relatives and faced difficult financial straits without the additional support that a spouse could provide. In addition, nonwhite racial status served as a broad limitation on individual success. These conditions likely explain why Bernarda validated Gregoria's testimony during the early stages of the case, yet later sought to withdraw her statement by claiming that she had testified falsely against Mateo. She did so in dramatic fashion, as several days after Mateo's incarceration, Bernarda approached the window of the municipal jail to speak with Mateo. In front of him, as well as several other jailed criminal suspects, she told Mateo that "I did not ask anything against you" and that Gregoria had manipulated her into offering her initial incriminating statement. With Mateo locked away, perhaps Bernarda was beginning to feel the pressure that accompanied material insecurity. It is also plausible, however, that the threat of physical violence from her husband drove her to reverse her earlier testimony. Several Spaniards who entered the court record in providing testimony on Gregoria's behalf explain that on the evening after the beating and second assault, Bernarda went to the royal notary's house—making a great deal of racket—to enter a complaint against Mateo. When told that the notary was "occupied in very important business" and she would have to return later, Bernarda told several men who happened to be present that she wanted her husband to be arrested because he had raped his daughter and tried to kill her, Bernarda, with a machete because she had fought with him over his actions.

Much of what transpired in Gregoria's life after this regrettable incident remains unknown, as even the conclusion of the case remains missing. However, Gregoria's name reappears in other documents recorded shortly thereafter. Among the list of marriages conducted in Pátzcuaro's parish church of San Salvador during April 1686, we find mention of Gregoria de Xaso, a free *mulata*. Although she carried the surname Xaso rather than López in the entry, there is no doubt that she is the same Gregoria, as she is listed as the daughter of Mateo López and Bernarda de San Joseph, also free *mulatos*. The man she married was a free black named Nicolas de la Cruz. Though it is impossible to say how Gregoria viewed herself and her marriage in light of what transpired the preceding year, it is satisfying to imagine that her determination to hold a role in defining herself, and her refusal to passively accept the hand life dealt her in a society rife with inequities for women of African descent, may have helped restore a sense of normalcy to her life and brought her some happiness.

Sources

Primary

The source material for this chapter comes from the Archivo Histórico del Ayuntamiento de Pátzcuaro, Caja 16, Expediente 1, Fojas 9-31, "De oficio de la real justicia contra Mateo López, mulato libre y por querella de Gregoria López, así misma su hija, por haberla esturpado," and Genealogical Society of Utah, Pátzcuaro Parish Registers, Film 0644957.

Secondary

Behar, Ruth. "Sexual Witchcraft, Colonialism, and Women's Powers: Views from the Mexican Inquisition." In *Sexuality and Marriage in Colonial Latin America*, edited by Asunción Lavrin, 178–206. Lincoln: University of Nebraska Press, 1989.

Bennett, Herman L. *Africans in Colonial Mexico: Absolutism, Christianity and Afro-Creole Consciousness, 1570–1640*. Bloomington: Indiana University Press, 2003.

Bristol, Joan C. "From Curing to Witchcraft: Afro-Mexicans and the Mediation of Authority." *Journal of Colonialism and Colonial History* 7, no. 1 (Spring 2006).

Chaves, Maria Eugenia. "Literate Culture, Subalternity and Resistance: The Case of Slave Women in the Colonial Courts." *Journal of Colonialism and Colonial History* 7, no. 1 (Spring 2006).

Few, Martha. *Women Who Live Evil Lives: Gender, Religion, and the Politics of Power in Colonial Guatemala*. Austin: University of Texas Press, 2002.

———. "On Her Deathbed, María de Candelaria Accuses Michaela de Molina of Casting Spells (Guatemala, 1696)." In *Colonial Lives: Documents on Latin America History, 1550–1850*, edited by Richard Boyer and Geoffrey Spurling, 166–177. Oxford: Oxford University Press, 2000.

Johnson, Lyman L., and Sonya Lipsett-Rivera, eds. *The Faces of Honor: Sex, Shame, and Violence in Colonial Latin America*. Albuquerque: University of New Mexico Press, 1998.

Lewis, Laura A. "From Sodomy to Superstition: The Active Pathic and Bodily Transgression in New Spain." *Ethnohistory* 54, no. 1 (Winter 2007): 129–157.

McKnight, Kathryn Joy. "Blasphemy as Resistance: An African Slave Woman before the Mexican Inquisition." In *Women in the Inquisition: Spain and the New World*, edited by Mary Giles, 229–253. Baltimore: Johns Hopkins University Press, 1999.

Twinam, Ann. *Public Lives, Private Secrets: Gender, Honor, Sexuality, and Illegitimacy in Colonial Spanish America*. Stanford, CA: Stanford University Press, 1999.

~

CHAPTER THREE

Philip Quaque (1741–1816)

African Anglican Missionary on the Gold Coast

Ty M. Reese

The eighteenth century witnessed the Atlantic slave trade soar, fuelled by the rising demand for slaves on plantations in the Americas and for the commodities they produced in the North Atlantic market. The Gold Coast, in West Africa, was the oldest area where Europeans had set up slaving forts: The Portuguese had built Elmina Castle in the fifteenth century, and the Dutch took it in 1637, and the British had captured Cape Coast Castle from the Swedes in 1664. Cape Coast remained the most important British base on the West African coast, dotted by Portuguese, Dutch, French, Danish, and Swedish forts and factories. Missionary activity in Africa and European concern about the spiritual welfare of native Africans were still very limited in the eighteenth century. The experience of Philip Quaque, a native of the towns surrounding Cape Coast Castle, who was educated in England and under the auspices of the Society for the Propagation of Gospel in Foreign Parts attempted to educate and proselytize West Africans, echoes later (equally failed) experiments. Historian Ty Reese explores the individual and social implications of this experience as well as the fascinating and complex relationships Quaque established with the English and African servants to the Cape Coast Castle and the residents of the surrounding area, exploring the contradictions of his mandate as a Christian preacher and an educator at the time when the slave trade, the reason for being of Cape Coast Castle until then, started to be criticized as sinful, and was finally prohibited.

In 1766, upon returning home to Cape Coast after an extended stay in England, African Anglican missionary Philip Quaque reported to England's Society for the Propagation of the Gospel in Foreign Parts (hereafter SPG) that this "country is very destructive to the health of men of the British constitutions and though myself being a native by birth, am not exempted from undergoing the common fate equally with those who are not." A year later, as his mission stalled and problems with the local Europeans continued, he announced that he had made himself "ready to go to town to mingle my tears amongst my own countrymen." In both of these statements, Quaque accepted his African origins, yet his stay in England added new character traits that provided him with an often confusing and contradictory identity that neither the Africans nor Europeans of Cape Coast accepted. Both of these realistic and conflicting reflections vividly illustrate the transformations that countless Africans faced within the context of the transatlantic slave trade and of their experiences in the eighteenth-century Atlantic World. Quaque was one of a small group of West Africans taken to Europe to be both educated and proselytized in an attempt to introduce Christianity into West Africa. Quaque's life, from 1741 to 1816, saw both the pinnacle and abolition of England's slave trade along with numerous social, economic, and political changes at Cape Coast and the Gold Coast (modern Ghana) in general. His trials and tribulations teach us that Africans participated in the Atlantic World both inside and outside the shackles of slavery and, while he was a creation of Anglican activity in the Atlantic, there was not yet a defined or accepted place for people like him.

On a personal level, Philip Quaque's story involved a boy taken from his native environment and introduced into a new society and culture within which he served the plans of others. Unlike the approximately fifteen million Africans removed from Africa to be utilized as slaves in the Americas, Quaque's removal occurred through the permission of his family and the local elite. There exists no evidence to show if Quaque had any say in this decision, but most likely his experience with Rev. Thomas Thompson prepared him for his journey. Philip Quaque was a harbinger of social, cultural, and religious change for West Africa, and he played a small part in the spread of Western civilization throughout the Atlantic World. His life, like many others, allows us to understand the long-term consequences of the cultural interaction that occurred between Africans and Europeans from the early 1400s to early 1800s. Within the Atlantic World, Quaque's story was unique not for his acceptance of English society or for his conversion to Christianity but for his role in using these changes to introduce Christianity and a Western educational system into the Gold Coast. Quaque was a proselytized and Western-educated African who became an outsider to both the Africans and Europeans of Cape Coast. At this slave trade and administrative center, Quaque was no longer Fetu as he lost his native language and culture during his stay in England, yet he was not English because of his African origins. Quaque's transformation began with his initial contact with Thompson, intensified with his arrival in England, and continued until his death in 1816.

When the Portuguese arrived on the Gold Coast in the late fifteenth century, Quaque's birthplace, Cape Coast, originally Oguaa, was a Fetu fishing village and coastal marketplace. The ensuing redirection of trade into the Atlantic allowed Cape Coast's importance to grow especially when, in the mid-seventeenth century, Sweden, with the permission of the local elite, constructed a trade castle there. The castle at Cape Coast changed hands several times until finally in 1664 the English acquired it. In 1672, England's Royal African Company received a monopoly over England's African trade and from this decided to make its administrative center its castle at Cape Coast. It remained this way until 1750, when the parliamentary-created Company of Merchants Trading to Africa (CMTA) replaced the Royal African Company and took over its African possessions. This company, whose purpose was to maintain coastal structures and relations that English slave traders could utilize to their advantage, remained in existence until 1821. This meant that Quaque was born into a town where a European presence had existed for almost a century, and in that period the local peoples had learned to take advantage of this presence. This experience with Europeans created a situation in which the local peoples continually searched for ways to acquire goods from the company and education meant opportunity within the company's administrative structure.

Quaque's unique journey started in 1750 when Thomas Thompson, after serving as an SPG missionary for five years in British North America, asked for permission to sail to Guiney (Africa) to introduce Christianity to West Africa. After receiving approval, Thompson traveled to New York City, where, in late November 1751, he sailed for the Gold Coast. On 13 May 1752, his ship arrived at Cape Coast Castle and, on the first Sunday after his arrival, he preached to a mixture of Europeans and Africans. Thompson quickly attempted to befriend Cudjoe Caboceer, the de facto leader of Cape Coast, and the local *penyins* (elders) in the belief that if the elite converted, the rest would follow. Cudjoe promptly informed him that the local peoples were more interested in education than religion, but Thompson saw an opportunity for both. By 1755, as his mission and health failed, Thompson returned to England, but not before he developed and initiated a plan that changed Quaque's life forever. Thompson, with the SPG's permission, sent three local boys to England to be proselytized and educated, after which they would be returned to the Gold Coast to spread Christianity to the local peoples.

Negotiations between Thompson, Cudjoe, and the company officers led to the decision that three boys, Thomas Caboro, William Cudjoe, and Philip Quaque, would participate in Thompson's plan. Upon their arrival in England, the SPG placed the three boys under the care of Mr. Hickman of Islington, who was the master of the Islington parish charity school. The death of Thomas Caboro, coupled with the strain caring for the boys placed upon Hickman, caused the SPG to transfer Quaque and Cudjoe to the custody of Rev. John Moore, a lecturer at St. Sepulchre's church, where they stayed for seven years. Rev. Moore was the logical choice as he possessed experience in educating Africans sent to England. In 1754, Moore provided board and schooling for John Aqua and George Sackee, whom the company sent to England to convince their fathers—important Fante officials—to sign a treaty. Moore's experience with Aqua and Sackee proved vital to his role in educating and converting Quaque as he already possessed insight into Quaque's culture. While the aspects of Quaque's stay in England remain unclear, F. L. Bartels argued that evidence existed that Quaque received more than a charity school education. Bartels based his argument on the fact that Quaque knew Latin and that the total cost of caring for all three boys in England was six hundred pounds. In all likelihood, Quaque was better educated than most of the English servants residing in West Africa upon his return, yet he was not the only educated African at Cape Coast or along the Gold Coast. Many coastal Africans received the opportunity to acquire a European education as the various European companies and states situated along the coast worked to appease the coastal elite. The appeal of education was that it allowed an individual to gain company employment that meant company pay. This pay was often in the form of goods that the individual could use to barter for other items, and that increased status on the coast, as the redistribution of these goods allowed the individual to acquire clients. These clients increased power, as a person's position was related to the number of people dependent upon that individual.

In mid-January 1766, the Rev. John Moore reported the progress of the two African youths to Rev. Dr. Daniel Burton, SPG secretary. According to Moore, Philip Quaque worked hard and excelled at his religious and scholarly studies, while William Cudjoe became mentally unstable and was placed in St. Luke's hospital. During Quaque's final two years in England several important events occurred. The first was his marriage to Catherine Blunt. He was ordained a deacon by the bishop of Exeter and then, a little over a month later, a priest by the bishop of London. This new status qualified Quaque to begin his missionary work, and he soon received appointments to positions in West Africa as an SPG missionary and as the company's chaplain at Cape Coast. In late 1765, Quaque sailed from England, with his wife and her female servant, and arrived at Cape Coast in February 1766. His voyage to Cape Coast included numerous storms, a near grounding of the ship, and his daily interaction with an uncaring and atheistic captain. While stopping on the Portuguese island of Madeira, Quaque encountered Catholicism for the first time and then engaged in a lengthy conversation with a Quaker minister. Upon landing at Cape Coast, Quaque's family and friends welcomed him and inquired into his journey and plans. While the local peoples eagerly awaited his instruction, the European garrison of Cape Coast Castle worried Quaque in that the people there differed from those he had interacted with in England. As Quaque and Catherine adjusted to their new life, he sent the SPG a letter that focused mainly upon William Cudjoe. Quaque reported that William's parents inquired about their son and anxiously awaited his return, especially as the health of William's father was deteriorating. At one point, William's family offered to send money to facilitate William's return, but the ship sailed early. They would not be reunited with their son, as he died in England. It is interesting to note that Quaque says little about his own family throughout his entire correspondence to the SPG and others.

Quaque's arrival marked the fulfillment of Thompson's plan, yet very quickly the plan's shortcomings became clear. Thompson's attempt to bring Christianity to Cape Coast in the 1750s failed, and Thompson rationalized this through a racial argument. As he worked to establish his mission, the cultural and language differences caused Thompson to conclude that Africans could not relate to European missionaries, and that African missionaries would succeed because they could better relate to the Africans. Little did Thompson understand that although Quaque left as an African, he returned changed, for during his stay in England he embraced not only Christianity but also the Anglican culture that surrounded him. Quaque arrived with great expectations for himself and his Godly mission in West Africa, yet as he settled into his new life, an awareness of the reality of his situation, position, and challenge quickly replaced his initial optimism. By September 1766, he already believed that his mission was doomed to failure. A major reason for his despair was that his only coastal supporter, Governor John Hippisley, died, leaving Quaque without any friends or allies. At this point it appeared to Quaque that none of the local European servants cared about planting Christianity in West Africa, and he quickly discovered that Cudjoe Caboceer made many empty promises. Quaque realized the problem:

"I being only then as a new comer, not knowing the manners and customs of my native place." This was the problem with Thompson's plan: He could not foresee how much a young child changed when taken from his native environment and placed in a foreign environment. The peoples he preached to and the Europeans he lived with felt that Quaque was not one of them.

As Quaque attempted to establish his mission, he interacted with three groups: the company's European servants, the local Africans, and the local mulattoes; each group created unique problems for him. Of the three, the first group perplexed Quaque the most because he believed that they, as Christians, would facilitate his mission in any way possible. When Governor John Hippisley died, Quaque complained not only that support was lacking but also that there were too few Anglicans in the garrison. In the early stages of his missionary activity, Quaque hoped that the company's European servants would set an example as proper Christians for the local African and mulatto population, but this was to no avail. The Englishmen who lived and worked at Cape Coast were different from those who had educated and cared for him in England. At Cape Coast, the local environment, a new diet, and the fact that they received their pay in alcohol, tobacco, and other goods created within the castle an environment of death, drunkenness, violence, and aggressive self-interest. Few cared about what Quaque could offer, and most did not appreciate his attempt to convert the local population. At one point, he reported that he was sick and could not conduct Easter services, but it did not matter because nobody cared. Quaque declared that "the only plea they offer is that while they are here acting against light and conscience, they dare not come to the Holy Table." Their role in the slave trade provided the servants with a solid and convincing reason not to attend services and a reason not to support his missionary activity. The fear was that if the local people accepted Christianity, then this might undermine the profitable trade in slaves. Throughout Quaque's long reign as Cape Coast missionary, the European servants' refusal to attend services weighed heavily upon him.

An example of the problems Quaque faced with the local Europeans, especially those involved in the slave trade, occurred in January 1767, when he traveled four leagues to the important slave-trading enclave of Anomabu. At Anomabu lived Richard Brew, who resigned his company position to establish himself as a private trader at Anomabu. During his weeklong stay, Quaque gave Sunday service and baptized Brew's two mulatto daughters at his request. In his next correspondence, Quaque's growing frustration with the local Europeans exploded. He referred to the garrison's lack of education and their growing degeneration as they indulged in vice. The cause of this outburst was that after his departure from Anomabu, Richard Brew stated that he "would never come to Cape Coast Castle to be subservient to and to sit under the nose of a black boy to hear him pointing or laying out their faults before them." This growing resistance to Quaque's mission caused him to conclude that "I think myself only but as a sheep in the jaws of so many ravenous wolves."

While Quaque expected the European servants to be good Christians, the group that he was the most concerned with was the Cape Coast people. Like Thompson, Quaque believed that to be successful in proselytizing the local population he needed the support of the local elite. On 26 June 1767, Quaque meet with Cudjoe to inform him of the importance of baptism and the superior attributes of Christianity. Quaque then provided service to Cudjoe and other local elite, and upon its conclusion Cudjoe expressed a desire to build a two-room schoolhouse in Cape Coast. In mid-August, Quaque again preached to Cudjoe, the *penyins*, and a group of forty to fifty Africans and mulattoes. At the completion of his sermon, the group started drinking, and when Quaque intervened they announced that he could not change them. At the following service the Igwa *penyins*, who had promised to attend, failed to show up as they were sacrificing a sheep to their god. To counter the lack of interest, Quaque started providing liquor at his services, but even this did not bring the numbers and interest that he hoped for. One problem for Quaque was that his services were on Sunday, whereas the local day of rest was Tuesday; for almost everyone at Cape Coast, including the company servants, Sunday was another day to work. A final and critical problem for Quaque was that he required a translator, having lost his native language, and at one point his translator, Frederick Adoy, asked him to shorten his services because he could not keep up.

During this early period, Quaque's concerted effort to proselytize the local Africans taught him much about indigenous religious beliefs and practices. Because of this insight, Quaque spent time during his services chastising them for their beliefs. Early on, he informed the *penyins* that they were "so very deluded as to place [their] confidence in dumb stones and bushes." Another time, when preaching to a group of Africans and mulattoes, Quaque challenged their "idolatrous and superstitious customs of adoring fetishes." He then told a *penyin* that "their fetishes and false Gods and Goddesses are nothing but conjuring and witchcraft made by the slight of hand." The failure of both liquor and ridicule to bring more Africans to his services forced Quaque to try something new. He informed the SPG that he introduced the singing of psalms because the Africans liked music, but like his other plans, this did not work. By late 1768, Quaque made the decision that he would achieve little success among the adult Africans of Cape Coast, and while he did not explicitly state it in his letters to the SPG, it is clear that he turned his attention to the large mulatto population and his young African scholars.

This change in focus became clear on 12 December 1768 when "a convocation by consent of parties" occurred at Cudjoe's home. This meeting was "purposely intended for the spiritual benefit of the mulatto ladies and gentlemen belonging to this town." One thing that Quaque noticed was that the mulattoes "glory and boast of their mixture, valuing themselves better than the rest of the native people on account of their coming from the loins of European people and so nominally styling themselves Christians on that account." Quaque expected that as they considered themselves Christians, they would readily embrace his mission and message. At this meeting he demanded that they act like Christians and "constantly attend divine services" while "rid[ding them]selves of ridiculous notions, customs and manners." He asked them to be baptized, to follow his teaching, and to agree to a set of "solutions," and that if they broke one, they must pay four ackies of gold (equal in value to one pound coastal money). In his next letter to the SPG, Quaque described this as the creation of his "congregation," yet he recognized that the "gentlemen of the fort" opposed his activities because it took away their "wenches." Quaque's high hopes for the local mulatto population, and for creating a congregation, just like his hopes for the European servants and Africans, quickly disappeared.

As none of his original plans for success worked, Quaque made another decision in 1770 that involved focusing upon educating local African and mulatto children. This was something that Cudjoe, the *penyins*, and the mulattoes demanded from the beginning, and Quaque hoped that through this endeavor he could proselytize the local peoples. This new focus upon education was a smart move on Quaque's part because the company required educated servants, both European and African, and thus justified an emphasis on education over proselytization. The appeal of Christianity along the Gold Coast was limited. For the company and the English slavers who visited the coast, the introduction of Christianity caused concern as they feared that if Quaque succeeded in converting the local peoples then they might refuse to sell slaves on Christian principles. For the local Africans and mulattoes, company employment was important in that it increased their local status while providing them with access to an array of commodities. Both sides accepted education because it complemented the existing system, and they rejected Christianity because it challenged it.

While 1770 marked the year in which Quaque focused more energy upon education, these activities had started when he returned to the coast. In late 1767, he reported that three of his students read their primers well. In 1768,

Jack, a local healer and company slave, entered Quaque's school and quickly impressed Quaque with his willingness and ability to learn along with his contention that he had been christened. Quaque not only taught Jack but attempted to convince him to stop drinking alcohol and wearing fetishes. The company was so impressed by Jack's progress that they planned to send him to England to study in an apothecary shop, and then he would return to Cape Coast to care for the local peoples with a mixture of European and African medical treatments. Quaque ended his 1768 letter with the announcement of his scholar's development and requested that the SPG send him an assortment of journals and prayer books.

Throughout his life on the Gold Coast, the number of students that Quaque taught at any one time varied, but he always hoped to create a school and mission within the town. In late January 1789, Quaque reported to the SPG that the castle gentlemen created a society that accepted the responsibility of raising twelve African children. The association would feed, clothe, and educate these children, who were either orphans or children of the poor. The society took the name Torridzonians, referring to the local environment and the European belief in how a hot humid climate affected individuals. Quaque was asked to care for the children, and he expected his son, Samuel, to assist him. On 28 September, Quaque baptized ten of the children and initiated regular services that the children attended in their blue uniforms. Included in the school were four children of European officers. In his next letter of 1791, Quaque reported that the Torridzonian children were doing "tolerably" well and knew most of the catechism. By mid-1792, Quaque reluctantly announced to the SPG that his school was declining because of the loss of interest among the children. When they stopped attending, they lost their allowance, and this forced them to find work. While his school declined, Quaque continued to teach, and in June of 1795 he sent to the SPG writing samples from three of his scholars. Of all his ventures, Quaque's attempt to provide a Western education to the local African and mulatto peoples was the most successful.

Quaque had arrived in West Africa with great expectations and the belief that he would be supported, financially and morally, by the SPG and the CMTA. Little did Quaque know how wrong these beliefs were. His letters show that Quaque clearly experienced great despair over the appearance, at least to him, that the SPG had abandoned him. In late 1767, Quaque wrote concerning events that had occurred since his last letter and expressed his hopes of receiving a letter from the SPG. In September 1768, he reminded the SPG that he had yet to receive a letter from them. Quaque desperately needed affirmation for his work and acknowledgment from the SPG of the great obstacles he faced. While he continually reported to the SPG on his progress and the obstacles that he faced, it was not until 1773, seven years after he established his mission at Cape Coast, that the SPG replied to him. He received several other letters after this but never on a regular basis. Quaque perceived this lack of support as a lack of acceptance because of his African background, and the lack of SPG support shows that they viewed him more as a fortuitous experiment than a true Anglican missionary. This became clear in 1788 when the SPG claimed that Quaque had gone native.

One of the many fascinating aspects of Quaque's life involved how, through his being taken at a young age to England to be proselytized and Westernized, he changed as a person. In England, a new cultural identity replaced much of his African cultural identity; hence his return to Africa seemed more like moving to a foreign location rather than returning home. This change can be seen in how Quaque viewed his native land and its inhabitants. In 1767, Quaque referred to the local peoples as "a very stubborn . . . people extremely bigoted to their principles and customs." His next letter referred to Africa as a "barren land," and he contended that the local customs and religions were illogical. While Quaque's letters clearly showed that the local culture within which he grew up was no longer comprehensible to him, paradoxically, they often illustrated an affinity for his home. As he waited for the governor's decision concerning public service, he reported that "I have made myself ready to go to town to mingle my tears amongst my own countrymen." Yet in 1770 his countrymen were "poor illiterate people" who existed within "a crooked nation." This was followed in 1773 by Quaque stating that "this part of Africa is deaf to the voice of reason." By this point, the lack of success weighed heavily upon him.

As Quaque denigrated his homeland, by explaining to the SPG the situation he faced, he served as a cultural observer whose letters provide historians with insight concerning Cape Coast, Fetu, and Fante society in the second half of the eighteenth century. One important area concerned the local religious beliefs and customs of the Cape Coast peoples. In late 1767, he informed the SPG how the Igwa *penyins*, who promised to attend his Sunday service, failed to do so because they intended to make a sacrifice to their "chief God, the Goddess Aminsa." A malady affected their townspeople, and they believed that if they sacrificed a sheep, caught by force, then Aminsa would heal them. He then explained how at Cape Coast a "set day" existed to sacrifice sheep to the local fetish Taberah and his wife, Neyeir. Taberah lived within the high rock that protruded upon the water and on which the English had constructed Cape Coast Castle. They sacrificed animals to Taberah because they believed it helped their fishing. Quaque described

Neyeir as a "spacious thick bush just by the seaside," and around the bush he constantly saw "snakes of all kinds, serpents, alligators, crocodiles, adders, tigers (and) leopards." Quaque's letters, when utilized with a variety of other sources, allow us to develop an understanding of Cape Coast society in the eighteenth century.

A final aspect of Quaque's life concerns his correspondence with several abolitionists in British North America. In March 1767, Quaque reported that he had recently replied to the Rev. Dr. Johnson of Rhode Island, who expressed interest in the success of his mission and the number of converted Africans. That same year, Quaque received a letter from Dr. Johnson of New York, who sent him some grammars for his school. In 1771, an inquiry arrived from Rev. Mr. Bass of Newbury Port, New England, who wanted to know if the slave trade hindered his success. The next letter he received, in 1772, came from Rev. Mr. Samuel Fayerweather of Narragansett, who inquired into the number of converts and mentioned that Rev. Dr. Johnson spoke very highly of him. In 1773, both Rev. Fayerweather and Rev. Bass wrote Quaque to inform him of the Rev. Dr. Samuel Johnson's death. In March 1773, Quaque received a letter from one of the better-known American abolitionists, the Rev. Mr. Samuel Hopkins of Newport, who asked that Quaque provide him with a description of the local culture. He also asked if two men could resume their lives if they were returned to Anomabu or if they would again be sold into slavery. The two men were Christians and former slaves who wished to return home. Quaque responded that Africans will accept Christianity only if they live in an area "that yields the light and knowledge of the hidden gospel." By this he meant Europe, not Africa. He then warned him not to send the men to Anomabu because "those gentlemen could not spring from a race more vicious, villainous, revengeful, malicious and none more brutal and obdurate in their disposition, than the natives of Anomabu." It was in his letters to the abolitionists, rather than the SPG, that Quaque clearly announced his disdain for the slave trade and the insurmountable problems that it caused him.

The SPG summed up its view of Quaque's life and mission in 1788 when the English government asked the SPG if they had ever sent missionaries to West Africa. The SPG replied that they had sent two. The first, Thomas Thompson, was not successful but had developed a plan to utilize African missionaries. The second, Philip Quaque, was "never . . . able to fulfill the objects of his mission." The SPG reported that he failed to convert a single African, and their only explanation was that he had become more enamored with trade than God. Quaque was indeed involved in trade because the salary he received from the CMTA was in the form of commodities, especially textiles, alcohol, and tobacco. Quaque, like all other company servants, had to trade his pay for the necessities of survival. The rumors concerning Quaque's lack of success traveled around the Atlantic, causing Phillis Wheatley to mention Quaque in a letter to Samuel Hopkins. Wheatley hoped that the rumors were untrue and believed that Quaque, just by setting a proper example, could bring "light" to West Africa. The problem for Quaque was that he was clearly abandoned during his missionary activity at Cape Coast, and this lack of support weighed heavily upon him. It did not prevent him from doing his job, for in 1806 the castle governor reported that despite Quaque's age he continued to provide service and "exerts himself wonderfully." Even in 1806, after being abandoned, ignored, and often slandered, Quaque continued to work to fulfill his duties and mission.

The trials and tribulations of Philip Quaque emerged out of a variety of factors circulating throughout the eighteenth-century Atlantic World. The location of his birth was important in that Cape Coast was the administrative center of England's slave trade in West Africa; therefore, he lived in an important hub of cultural interaction and economic integration. His family connections to the local elite made him a logical choice for Thomas Thompson's plan, and his age made him more susceptible to the processes of Westernization and proselytization. As a youth, he was thrust into a foreign environment where he was expected to assimilate and one day further the spread of Christianity. His return to Africa marked the success of his conversion in that he no longer identified with his homeland. Quaque's struggle to change the local African people into what he had become was one full of despair. He attempted to convert the Cape Coast people who, because of the transatlantic slave trade and the English presence there, saw value and opportunity in education but not in conversion, especially as they possessed their own belief system that served them well. Concurrently, the castle garrison, and the numerous slave traders plying the coast, saw Quaque's mission as a challenge to the slave trade. Many probably wondered whether his attempt at conversion was an attempt to end the slave trade. While both his mission and school have been passed over by many historians as a failure and therefore irrelevant, his life is interesting for both what he did and what he became.

Suggested Readings

Primary

Quaque, Philip. *The Letters of Philip Quaque*. East Ardsley, UK: E. P. Microform, 1979.

Thompson, Thomas. *An Account of Two Missionary Voyages*. Westminster, UK: Society for the Propagation of the Gospel in Foreign Parts, 1937.

Secondary

Bartels, F. L. "Philip Quaque, 1741–1816." *Transactions of the Gold Coast and Togo-land Historical Society* 1, no. 5 (1955).

Hastings, Adrian. *The Church in Africa, 1450–1950.* Oxford: Clarendon Press, 1994.

Priestley, Margaret. "Philip Quaque of Cape Coast." In *Africa Remembered: Narratives by West Africans from the Era of the Slave Trade*, edited by Philip D. Curtin. Madison: University of Wisconsin Press, 1967.

Reese, Ty M. "Sheep in the Jaws of So Many Ravenous Wolves: The Slave Trade and Anglican Missionary Activity at Cape Coast Castle, 1752–1816." *Journal of Religion in Africa* 34, no. 3 (2004): 348–372.

Sanneh, Lamin. *Abolitionist Abroad: American Blacks and the Making of Modern West Africa.* Cambridge, MA: Harvard University Press, 2001.

~

CHAPTER FOUR

Harry Washington (1760s–1790s)

A Founding Father's Slave

Cassandra Pybus

The American Revolution inaugurated an era in which colonists throughout the Americas rejected domination by the European mother countries and fought for independence. The limits of "freedom," however, would remain an issue of contention throughout the next two centuries. For George Washington, "freedom" encompassed the right to self-rule, citizens' individual rights, and free trade. For Harry, an African man who worked as a slave first in Washington's Ferry Plantation, then in his household, "freedom" meant not being enslaved, and having a family and a piece of property for financial autonomy. Historian Cassandra Pybus followed Harry in his quest, from British lines during the war and as a black loyalist to Canada and then to West Africa. Neither in Nova Scotia nor in Sierra Leone, recently founded as the "Province of Freedom," were black loyalists recognized as rightful subjects. In fact, the ability and mobilization to claim the rights of the age, seen as natural for whites, would be severely punished when exercised by Africans and African descendants from then on.

As Harry Washington faced a British military tribunal on the west coast of Africa, charged with rebellion against the colonial government of Sierra Leone, he may have seen the irony that fourteen years earlier he had fled his enslavement to the commander in chief of the rebel forces in colonial America to find freedom with the British military and a return to his African homeland. Harry was almost certainly from West Africa and possibly born in the region around the Gambia River around 1740. He was brought to America early in the 1760s on one of the shipments to the Lower Potomac River area in 1760 and 1761. Late in 1763 George Washington purchased Harry from the estate of Daniel Tebbs, a plantation owner on the Lower Potomac River.

Washington had formed a syndicate called the Dismal Swamp Company with the intention of draining forty thousand acres of a huge swamp in the southeast corner of Virginia. The Dismal Plantation was managed by his brother John, and Washington's contribution to the enslaved workforce was four people he bought from Tebbs's estate—Harry and Topsom, plus a woman called Nan and a boy named Toney—and two men from Mount Vernon named Jack and Caesar. They worked in appalling humidity, enveloped in clouds of mosquitoes, to cut a canal three feet deep and ten feet wide that would drain into a lake five miles away. To get ready cash for the project, they also cut shingles of white cedar and cypress out of the vine-entangled woods. Harry and Nan might have been a couple because two years later they were both taken from the Dismal Swamp to Mount Vernon. If indeed they were a couple, they were not permitted to live together. Harry was employed in or around the house, while Nan labored on one of the outlying farms.

Harry was later described as a very valuable hostler, so his job must have included looking after Washington's horses. He continued to work as a house servant until June 1771, when he appeared in a list of the enslaved laborers on Ferry Plantation, most distant of the Mount Vernon farms. For Harry to be moved from skilled work, which was in some measure self-directed, to grueling plantation labor must have dismayed him sufficiently to precipitate his flight on 29 July 1771. Washington paid one pound and sixteen shillings to advertise for the recovery of his property. The investment paid off when Harry was returned within a matter of weeks, and once again put to work back at Ferry Plantation, where he stayed until 1773, when he was redeployed to the house service.

These were turbulent times in Virginia. Late in 1774 Washington had written to a friend that "the crisis is arrived when we must assert our rights, or submit to every imposition that can be heap'd upon us; till custom and use, will make us as tame, and abject slaves, as the blacks we rule over with such arbitrary sway." Sentiments of this nature had been echoed around the dining tables and drawing rooms of Virginian plantations for many months, discreetly absorbed by the footmen and cooks, the valets and maids, the coachmen and hostlers. Doubtless Harry listened with more than idle interest to this talk about the tyranny of the British masters and the inviolable concept of liberty. Despite having been unsuccessful in his escape in 1771, and having made no further attempt to abscond, he had not abandoned the idea of freedom that now so animated his owner. Even if Washington had been canny enough to send his slave-hostler out of earshot, it would not have been possible to quarantine the ideas that Washington discussed with his friends and neighbors. Snatches of talk overheard were almost instantaneously channeled from plantation to plantation through the complex networks of the enslaved community. The message that Harry would have extracted from the ardent talk swirling around him was that his own attachment to liberty would find no place in the revolutionary ferment sweeping Virginia. As the king was now Washington's enemy, it was to His Majesty that Harry should entrust his aspirations for freedom.

In June 1775, as tension between the colonists and the Crown intensified, the embattled royal governor of Virginia, Lord Dunmore, took refuge on a British warship in the James River and began to assemble a squadron to strike back at the rebellious Virginians, welcoming any fugitive slaves who made their way to his fleet. On 14 November 1775 Dunmore declared martial law and published a proclamation that freed any slaves willing to bear arms for the Crown. Here was every white Virginian's nightmare. Along the length of Chesapeake Bay, alarmed plantation owners and managers did their best to staunch slave defections. At Mount Vernon the manager, Lund Washington, promoted benevolent paternalism over the precarious dangers of freedom. He was confident that the enslaved community understood that General Washington's care and protection was the best option for them and had "not the least dread" that the slaves might make a bolt for Dunmore's fleet, although he could not vouch for the white indentured servants. Washington was not so sanguine. In his capacity as the commander in chief of the Continental Army, he warned that Dunmore must be crushed or the momentum of slave defections would increase like a snowball rolling.

Despite savage penalties and increased patrols, a great many runaways still managed to reach Dunmore's fleet in the James River. At the end of November, Dunmore could report, "Two and three hundred already come in and these I form into a Corps as fast as they come." Those who got safely to Dunmore came mostly from plantations close to navigable waterways, traveling on small craft, though some came on foot, propelled by sheer willpower, to swim out to Dunmore's ships. Lord Dunmore's Ethiopian Regiment, as the governor styled his new corps, was provided with weapons and taught how to use them. Rumor had it that they were outfitted in a uniform bearing the provocative inscription "Liberty to Slaves," but in reality Dunmore was hard pressed to find any clothing for them. By January

1776 the crowded and inadequate conditions on board Dunmore's fleet had precipitated disaster in the form of epidemic disease.

When smallpox first appeared in Dunmore's overcrowded flotilla, the British were largely immune and the Virginians highly susceptible. The disease hit the black recruits especially hard. They died by the hundreds. In late May, to isolate the sick and allow the surgeons to inoculate his recruits, Dunmore moved his base to Gwynn Island, near the mouth of the Rappahanock River, where hundreds of sick men and women endured the awful progress of the disease. Dunmore reported that "there was not a ship in the fleet that did not throw one, two, three or more dead overboard every night." On the island the dead were buried in shallow mass graves. Tragically, Dunmore continued to draw fresh black recruits at the rate of six to eight each day, most of whom succumbed to the disease as soon as they arrived. Moreover, those who recovered from the inoculation fell victim to an outbreak of "fever," almost certainly typhoid fever. In this dreadfully weakened condition, Dunmore's force was easily driven from the island in early July 1776, and took refuge with the fleet once again, having lost up to 70 percent of the black recruits.

In late July, part of the fleet made a foray up the Potomac River to gather fresh water, where they were joined by a small craft that had come down from Fairfax County. The three men on board offering their services to the British were described as three of General Washington's servants. Lund Washington had always suspected that the general's white indentured servants would prove disloyal to him, and perhaps some had seized the opportunity offered by the proximity of Dunmore's fleet. Yet the three "servants" aboard the craft from Mount Vernon must have also included the enslaved hostler Harry, since he told authorities in New York in July 1783 that he had run away from General Washington seven years before.

Driven out of Virginia, Dunmore went to New York in August 1776 taking three hundred runaways, all that remained of his shattered dream. Harry was among them, and he appears to have been absorbed into a noncombat black army corps called the Black Pioneers, formed in May 1776. Three years later, he was a corporal in the Black Pioneers that was part of the seven-thousand-strong force General Clinton took from New York for the invasion of South Carolina. During the siege of Charleston, which began on 31 March and lasted till 8 May, the Black Pioneers were employed building the defensive earthworks, making grapeshot, and performing a myriad of support services. Some were armed and engaged in fighting. Once Charleston fell, runaways poured into the British lines, while a fratricidal guerrilla war on the Carolina frontier stimulated a wave of defections to the British outposts in the backcountry. One prominent patriot claimed to have lost 237 slaves in a mass defection. In May 1780, General Clinton had returned to New York, and few months later General Cornwallis marched north to Virginia, leaving Harry Washington at the British garrison in Charleston.

Early in 1782 news came from England that the British government had granted independence to the American colonies and opened negotiations for peace. Charleston was scheduled for evacuation in June that year. This raised the thorny issue of the British obligations to the black runaways, since promises of freedom made by successive British commanders had been contingent on the British winning the war and retaining control of the colonies. No one had a contingency plan for losing the war and leaving America. Confronted with a catastrophic defeat and an unanticipated evacuation of both his army and thousands of loyalist refugees, the British commander, General Leslie, could hardly be expected to concern himself with the runaway slaves, who had, after all, gambled with their future in taking refuge with the king's men. Yet to leave them behind was no easy matter. Every time he looked about, Leslie was exposed to the expectant faces of people who had taken monumental risks in their alliance with the British and who were not prepared to passively submit to reenslavement. By the same token, he had been served an ultimatum by the new governor of South Carolina, that Carolinians would default on debts to British merchants should any slaves be carried off from Charleston. A contest over the fate of runaways presented the humiliated British with the opportunity for a show of moral superiority over the victorious Americans. Weighing up the situation, Leslie concluded, "Those who have voluntarily come in under the faith of our protection, cannot in justice be abandoned to the merciless resentment of their former masters." In New York the commander in chief, General Carleton, was of the same mind.

Throughout November until the final evacuation on 14 December 1782, hundreds of runaways in Charleston queued up to be interviewed by the board established to assess their status. Slave owners, keen to retrieve their property, tried desperately to coax them away, to no good effect. Carolinians bitterly complained that the board had declared obnoxious "almost every Negro, man, woman and child, that was worth carrying away." Leslie stoutly defended his position to Carleton. "I have insisted . . . on the impossibility of delivering up, under any stipulation, a certain description of Negroes, who having claimed our protection and have borne arms in our service, or otherwise rendered themselves more peculiarly obnoxious to the resentment of their former masters," he wrote on 18 October. Men and women cleared by the board were allowed to choose their destination, though the availability of transport was a key determinant as to where they went. The largest evacuation fleet took British, German, and provincial troops to New York, and also carried several hundred of their black allies. Undoubtedly Harry Washington was part of this evacuation.

By 1782 there were at least four thousand black men and women living in the British zone in New York. Black artisans worked on rebuilding projects and in the naval yards; black teamsters hauled provisions and collected firewood; black nurses and orderlies staffed the hospitals; black laundresses and needlewomen did the washing and sewing; black pilots guided the ships safely in and out of the port; black musicians provided entertainment at social events; black jockeys rode the horses at the races; black cooks, servants, and valets ensured the comfort of the elite. Among this teeming black community were people Harry knew from his days of enslavement at Mount Vernon. Eighteen people had run off to the British in April 1781, including two of Lund Washington's slaves. While Washington recovered seven of his chattel, Deborah and Daniel certainly escaped to New York, and possibly Peter, Lewis, Thomas, Stephen, James, and Watty, all young men with skilled trades, found a niche for themselves in New York as free artisans.

Whether they lived in barracks or in the canvas town of the burnt-out districts on Manhattan, the black allies of the British formed a community, bound together by the struggle to survive and by forms of cultural expression that reached back to an African past. Central to this community were the black preachers, none more so than the Methodist preacher known as "Daddy Moses," who brought with him a large congregation from Virginia. Blind and lame, probably as a result of smallpox, Daddy Moses was a charismatic preacher who put great store by dreams and visions to reveal the will of God and the sure road to eternal happiness. Harry Washington was among his many converts.

At the time that Charleston was being evacuated, a peace treaty was being hammered out between the British and the Americans in Paris. Hastily included in the treaty was a clause in Article 7, to prohibit "carrying away any Negroes or other property of the American Inhabitants." For the black refugees in New York this was utterly demoralizing. Rumors that the British would be obliged to abandon them in America filled them with anguish and terror. Determined to maintain their freedom, the runaways were kept on constant alert against attempts to spirit them back to slavery. A senior Hessian officer reported that about five thousand people had come to New York to take possession of their former property. His figure may have been exaggerated, but there can be no doubt that a great many slave owners were gaining entry into the British zone, and they were not using sweet reason to reclaim their property. Without warning, runaways could find themselves knocked on the head, bound hand and foot, and kidnapped back to the place they had fled. As most of the runaways behind the British lines had experienced years of freedom, they were horrified at the prospect of reenslavement. Day and night they pressed their case with the British authorities to make good the promises of freedom and remove them from the reach of their vengeful owners.

The governor of Virginia was furious that the British consistently refused to hand over his absconded chattel. Alarmed by such a flagrant violation of the treaty, he complained to George Washington, who undertook to raise the issue directly with General Carleton. "I have but little expectation that many will be recovered," Washington warned the governor; "several of my own are with the enemy, but I scarce ever bestow a thought on them; they have so many doors through which they can escape from New York." Washington also engaged the army contractor Daniel Parker to recover the slaves for the governor and asked Parker to also keep an eye out for his property. "If by chance you should come at the knowledge of any of them," he wrote, "I will be much obliged by your securing them so I may obtain them again." Washington's choice of Daniel Parker was strategic. Parker had done personal errands for the general in the past; on this matter, however, he was uniquely positioned to help Washington locate his slaves. He was one of the Americans appointed as commissioners to inspect embarkations to ensure no American-owned property was taken away.

General Carleton was appalled by the terms of the treaty, but in apparent compliance he allowed the inspection of the departing ships, while at the same time making sure that all the runaways who had been with the British for a year were provided with certificates of freedom. He would not permit anyone who met that condition to be claimed as American property. So when Parker inspected the ships in the evacuation fleet that sailed from New York on 27 April 1783, he was impotent to stop the woman named Deborah who had run away from Mount Vernon in 1781 from leaving on the ship *Polly*, bound for Nova Scotia. When Washington protested a violation of the treaty, Carleton told him that the British government would never agree "to reduce themselves to the necessity of violating their faith to the Negroes into the British lines under the proclamation of his predecessors," and further that "delivering up Negroes to their former masters . . . would be a dishonourable violation of the public faith."

Under Parker's impotent gaze, Harry Washington embarked on the ship *L'Abondance* in July 1783, with 405 black men, women, and children going to Nova Scotia. He was said to be forty-three years of age and traveling alone. Despite the protest of Congress and Washington himself, Carleton had facilitated the evacuation of three thousand black refugees whose names were recorded by the commissioners, as well another two thousand whose departure from New York was not recorded.

Those on board *L'Abondance* were mostly followers of Daddy Moses, and they settled as a community in Nova Scotia at a place called Birchtown. The muster at Birchtown taken in July 1784 listed Harry Washington, aged forty-four, as a laborer with a wife, Jenny, aged twenty-four. No children were listed. To survive, Harry probably hired himself out to his white neighbors in nearby Shelburne, as most of the black settlers were forced to do. These labor agreements were highly exploitative, with the free blacks regarded as cheap labor by the white loyalist settlers. Sometimes the black workers were never paid at all. Nova Scotia proved hard for both white and black settlers, forced to create a new life in inhospitable weather and faced with innumerable delays in the allocation of the promised land grants. When the grants were made, the lots allocated to the black settlers tended to be smaller than expected and on poor, rocky soil. In many cases, black refugees were still waiting for their land allocation three years after their arrival. In addition to the bitter cold and grinding poverty, tension between the black settlers and their white neighbors ran high. Although the black community persisted, the people at Birchtown were in a pitiful state. A white visitor in 1788 was shocked by "their huts miserable to guard against the inclemency of a Nova Scotia winter and their existence almost depending on what they could lay up in the summer." In the opinion of this witness, "the wretchedness and poverty so strongly perceptible in the garb and continence of . . . these miserable outcasts" was as extreme as he had ever seen. Life was no better at the other black settlements.

Thomas Peters was a runaway from North Carolina who had been a sergeant of the Black Pioneers during the war. He was deputized to voyage to England in 1791 to put the grievances of his constituency in Nova Scotia to the British government. In his petition Peters requested that His Majesty's black subjects in Nova Scotia be resettled, or, should they chose to remain in Nova Scotia, they be given due allotment of the land they had been promised. In response to Peters's acutely embarrassing accusations of bad faith, Pitt's government undertook to pay the necessary expenses to transport as many black settlers as wished to leave Nova Scotia. The Sierra Leone Company, delighted with the prospect of new settlers in their colony on the west coast of Africa, offered free grants of land "subject to certain charges and obligations" to any who wanted to emigrate. New settlers were promised twenty acres for every man, ten for every woman, and five for every child.

John Clarkson, the young naval officer whose brother Thomas was a prime mover in the campaign for the abolition of the slave trade, was the agent appointed by the Sierra Leone Company to oversee the move from Nova Scotia. Harry Washington was among the hundreds of people who attended a meeting in Birchtown, at the church of Daddy Moses, to hear Clarkson explain the offer. Clarkson was adamant that the expression "subject to certain charges and obligations" did not signify that an annual rent would be levied on the land in Sierra Leone; rather it referred to "a kind of tax for charitable purposes such as for the maintenance of their poor, the care of the sick, and the education of their children." Harry and his fellow black settlers accepted Clarkson's explanation. They especially warmed to his assurance that, unlike in Nova Scotia, where they were barred from voting or serving on juries, in Sierra Leone there would be no discrimination between white and black settlers. Harry Washington was among a large group from Birchtown who decided to go, even though it meant abandoning his freehold land grants. In the list of settlers relocating from Birchtown, Harry was described as a farmer, born in Africa and aged fifty (although he was probably fifty-three), traveling with his wife, Jenny. He took with him an axe, saw, and pickax, plus three hoes, as well as two muskets and several items of furniture. He left behind two town lots, a house, and forty acres.

As a consequence of Clarkson's assurances, about half of the black refugees in Nova Scotia opted to leave. Nearly twelve hundred black settlers were relocated at a cost of 15,500 pounds to the British government. The directors of the Sierra Leone Company were so pleased with the response from Nova Scotia that they shelved plans to encourage white settlers to emigrate from England. Henceforth the only whites in Sierra Leone would be a handful of company employees. Company director William Wilberforce told Clarkson that he should call the new black settlers Africans, believing that this was "a more respectable way of speaking of them," but this was emphatically not how they conceived of themselves. In their eyes they were free British subjects, no less than Clarkson. Moreover, Clarkson ruefully conceded, they had "strange notions . . . as to their civil rights."

By the middle of 1792 Clarkson, who had been appointed the first governor of Sierra Leone, was finding that these strange notions were causing no end of grief. Since Clarkson had arrived in Sierra Leone, turbulent discontent he believed to be inspired by Thomas Peters had brought the governor to the end of his tether, yet he maintained a steely determination that he, and only he, would be in charge. Thomas Peters died, profoundly disillusioned, in June, and Clarkson's response was surprisingly rancorous, prompted by fear that Peters believed he should have been the appointed governor of Sierra Leone. Yet everywhere Clarkson cared to look was evidence that Peters was not acting out of personal ambition, but giving expression to a shared disillusion. As the settlers told him, finding themselves in Sierra Leone with no land, despite all the promises, "makes us very uneasy in our mind that we might be liable to the same cruel treatment as we have before experienced." On the very day Peters died, Clarkson received a petition from the large Methodist congregation in eccentric spelling that betrayed the authors as barely literate. They said they willingly agreed to be governed by the laws of England, but "we do not consent to gave it into your honer hands with out haven aney of our own culler in it" and reminded Clarkson he had promised them that "whoever came to Saraleon wold be free . . . and all should be equel," so it followed that they had "a wright to chuse men that we think proper for to act for us in a reasnenble manner."

By late July, the settlers were in a fever pitch of indignation, because the survey for the farm lots they had been promised had not yet begun. They had only the huts they had built on small town lots carved out of the jungle in Freetown, and the only basis for their subsistence was two days a week of work for the company, paid in credit at the company store. Their habit of trusting Clarkson was all that protected the company's handful of haughty, idle, and incompetent white employees from their collective wrath. Clarkson had been forced to persuade the settlers to accept only one-fifth of the land they had been promised, and a bitter grievance had been reignited when he indicated that the company directors would not allow the settlers to take land along the Sierra Leone River. Access to the water was an absolute necessity. There were no carts or horses in Sierra Leone; communication and transport were all by means of water. The settlers reacted with fury to the suggestion, pointing out this same trick was played on them in Nova Scotia, where white men had occupied the entire waterfront, built wharves along it, and then charged money for access. They had not crossed the ocean to suffer the same discrimination all over again, they said.

In deference to the settlers' fears of further injustice at the hands of self-interested white people, Clarkson hastily rescinded the company instructions concerning the waterfront. He also agreed that the settlers could elect their own representatives as peacekeepers. Clarkson chose not to act on his orders from the company directors to institute a quit rent of two shillings an acre on the settlers' land grants, rationalizing that the company would have to comply with the spirit of his promises. It was a high-risk strategy for a servant of the company who was due to go on extended leave in December 1792.

Clarkson never came back to Sierra Leone. He was dismissed by the company in May 1783 and was replaced as governor by William Dawes, who was in turn succeeded in 1796 by twenty-seven-year-old Zachary Macaulay. By 1796 the settlers were sending anguished appeals to Clarkson to come back as the governor and rescue them from the authoritarian regime of Governor Macaulay, who obliged them to pay the huge quit rent. The Sierra Leone Company was blithely determined to impose a tax that was a hundred times higher than in Nova Scotia, where the colonial government had been forced to abandon the quit rent because settlers, black and white, refused to pay two shillings for every one hundred acres. When Governor Macaulay cut the amount in half, requiring only one shilling an acre, he naively believed that he was being generous to the settlers and fully expected them to be grateful to him.

For more than twenty years, the defining issue for Harry Washington and his fellow black settlers had been to live as free people and not to submit to the indignities and deprivations that had marked their lives as slaves. Owning land—not renting it or working it for somebody else—was critical in their self-definition, as was regulating their own community. It was equally important that men should be responsible for the maintenance of their families and that the women and children should not labor as they had in slavery. For a time after their arrival, Harry had been prepared to endure the indignity of working for credit at the company store rather than monetary wages, even though this was a condition of labor the settlers believed akin to bondage, because he was waiting for the land allocation that would give him the capacity to be independent and self-sustaining. By 1796 land had been granted and he had already achieved the self-reliance that was now threatened by the quit rent.

On 5 January 1797 the elected representatives met to discuss how to get rid of the quit rent, determined never to submit to an imposition that reduced them to perpetual tenancy. When the demand for the first payment of the quit rent was proclaimed in June 1797, about thirty settlers reluctantly agreed to pay rather than face the governor's wrath, while the great majority held out against it. On 5 August, the settlers' representatives wrote to the governor reminding him that they had abandoned land in Nova Scotia in the expectation that they would receive land on the same conditions in Sierra Leone, and that they were never told that the land belonged to the company, for which they must pay quit rent. "Sir if we had been told that, we never could come here," they wrote; "we are astonished why the company could not tell us after three years we was to pay a shilling per acre . . . if the lands is not ours without paying a shilling per acre, the lands will never be ours."

About two weeks later, the governor called a public meeting of heads of households in which he denied that the black settlers had left freehold land in Nova Scotia and insisted that they had always known about the quit rent. The problem with ignorant people, he concluded, was that they were susceptible to "every prating, malicious, designing talebearer" who wished to misrepresent the good intentions of the company. "You have often been made to see the folly of acting thus," he told his stunned audience, "yet you still return like the sow to flounder in the same dirty puddle." For all his sardonic bravado, Macaulay could see that the quit rent could not be imposed without violence. He told the company directors it would be prudent not to collect the rent, at least in the short term.

In November 1798, an edict arrived from the company directors that the quit rent must be paid. Macaulay duly informed the settlers that new titles had been drawn up incorporating the quit rent conditions, for which they must apply by December. This time about a dozen families accepted the grants and the rest refused, even though the refusal meant their children were barred from the free company school. A new grants register excluded the names of all those who refused their grants and listed their allotments as unallocated land. Among those whose land was reallocated in this fashion were some of the colony's most successful farmers, including Harry Washington. The governor's action drove nearly every settler into a rebellious coalition against him. In the weeks before Macaulay's departure from the colony in April 1799, he told his fiancée that he felt the need to sleep with loaded muskets in his bedroom.

The moment Macaulay left Sierra Leone for good, the settlers took the matter into their own hands. Without consulting the new governor, a twenty-three-year-old stripling named Thomas Ludlam, they chose a judge and two justices of peace from among themselves. The elected representatives of the black settlers formed into a bicameral parliament, passing resolutions about the day-to-day management of the colony. In September 1799 they resolved that they were the proprietors of the colony, since it was to the black settlers that the local African chiefs had ceded the land. The settlers were not to know that in England at the same time the directors of the Sierra Leone Company had applied to the British parliament for a royal charter to give the company incontestable jurisdiction over the colony and the power to repress all dissent within the colony. As the directors explained in their subsequent report, "the unwarranted pretensions of the disaffected settlers, their narrow misguided views; their excessive jealousy of Europeans; the crude notions they had formed of their own rights; and the impetuosity of their tempers" made it imperative for the company to have means to "repress the turbulence and assumption of the colonists." There would be no more elections in Sierra Leone.

On 25 September, the settlers' own code of laws was displayed in Freetown, drawing curious crowds the following day. A witness later reported that "people being on farms, hearing of this news, gathered themselves together to hear and understand" at one of the settlers' houses. The frightened young governor overreacted. He sent to the house a group of loyal black settlers, whom he had armed and deputized as marshals, with warrants for the arrest of the leaders on charges of treason. The marshals burst into the house just as the meeting was breaking up. In the mêlée that followed, two were arrested and others were wounded. Those who had escaped from the meeting fled out of the town and set up camp about two miles away, where they were joined by Harry Washington, whose farm was nearby.

Later the Sierra Leone Company tried to portray these men as armed and dangerous rebels who wished to annihilate the company employees. Significantly, the men labeled as rebels were all past middle age—Harry Washington was sixty—and they were largely without arms. They had some guns, but no ammunition, which was almost all stored at Government House. On the third day they stole a gun and some powder from the governor's farm, as well as powder and shot from the farm of a white employee of the company, but that was hardly evidence of preparation for an armed coup; they were as likely to have wanted the arms for hunting game.

On 30 September, as if life was imitating fiction, a large British transport ship arrived in the harbor carrying over five hundred Maroons who had been deported from Jamaica after their surrender after the Second Maroon War in 1795. The Sierra Leone Company agreed to take the Maroons from their first place of exile in frigid Nova Scotia, in return for additional financial and military support from the British government. Accompanying the Maroons to Freetown was a detachment of forty-seven soldiers of the 24th Regiment. Ludlam could not have prayed for a more timely intervention. The Maroons were extraordinary warriors; for generations they had been used to repress slave rebellions and hunt runaway slaves. After weeks at sea they were desperate for some physical activity so were pleased to be invited to "stretch their legs a little," as one of the company's directors later joked, and hunt the rebels down.

Within a week, Ludlam had thirty-one supposed rebels in his custody, charged with engaging in unprovoked rebellion. After a hasty military tribunal, five men were banished to the slave forts of Goree and one to Rio Nunez, a sure sentence of death for men of their age. Two of the leaders were hanged. Harry Washington and twenty-three other men were banished across the Sierra Leone River to the Bullom Shore. The personal tragedy and appalling loss in human resources that resulted from these dubious and draconian decisions—over forty of the colony's most respected settlers dead or banished—was of no consequence to the directors of the company. They believed that Sierra Leone was much better off without these men and "the crude notions they had formed of their own rights." The runaway slaves from America had made "the worst possible subjects," William Wilberforce concluded in disgust, "as thoroughly Jacobin as if they had been trained and educated in Paris." They had, of course, been trained and educated in the American Revolution, and the radical notions about their rights as free men and women were forged in the tortuous negotiations to secure their freedom and to make it a tangible reality in their lives. These were notions that George Washington believed worth dying for. It should be no surprise that a man he once held as property believed the same.

Sources

American sources for this account of Harry Washington can be found in W. W. Abbot and Dorothy Twohig, eds., *The Papers of George Washington, Colonial Series*, Vol. 7–10 (Charlottesville: University Press of Virginia, 1990–1995); Donald Jackson and Dorothy Twohig, eds., *The Diaries of George Washington*, Vol. 3 (Charlottesville: University Press of Virginia, 1978); John C. Fitzpatrick, *The Writings of George Washington*, Vol. 26 (Washington, DC: Washington United States Gov. Print. Off., 1937).

British sources can be found in the National Archives of the United Kingdom in the series: PRO 33/55/100, PRO 30/55/43-60, CO 217/63, CO270/4; the Wray Papers in the Clements Library, University of Michigan (Ann Arbor); John Clarkson's journal at the New York Historical Society (New York); the Muster Book of Free Black Settlement in the Public Archives of Nova Scotia; the Clarkson Papers in the British Library (London); the journals of Zachary Macaulay in the Huntington Library (San Marino, CA).

~

CHAPTER FIVE

Rufino José Maria (1820s–1850s)

A Muslim in the Nineteenth-Century Brazilian Slave Trade Circuit

João José Reis, Flávio dos Santos Gomes,
and Marcus J. M. de Carvalho

Rufino José Maria's distinct trajectory in the first half of the nineteenth century crisscrosses the Atlantic and ties together many important themes in the history of the Black Atlantic. Rufino was a Yoruba Muslim who grew up during the decline of the Oyo empire, was taken through the African slave trade to Bahia in Brazil, and lived as a slave in times of slave rebellions in Bahia and political turmoil throughout the country. He gained his freedom, took part in the Pernambuco–Angola slave trade route as a crew member, and was eventually caught by British cruisers and taken to Sierra Leone. He used his stay in West Africa to advance his knowledge of the Quran. As far as we know, he ended up settling in Recife, in northeastern Brazil. Brazilian historians João Reis, Flávio Gomes, and Marcus Carvalho have joined together to recount the life of an unusual and powerful person who survived one of the most brutal aspects of Atlantic reality, the slave trade, and later engaged in it, and who was able to forge his own base of power to settle into Brazilian slave society. The Muslim presence in Africa and the African diaspora is often overlooked, but Rufino's story reminds us that Islam had a real and vital role in the lives of millions of people of African descent on all continents bordering the Atlantic Ocean.

In September 1853, Rufino José Maria was arrested in Recife, capital of the province of Pernambuco. Rufino was an African freedman who belonged to the Nagô nation, the term that identified Yoruba speakers in Bahia, Brazil. The Nagôs had waged a series of slave uprisings in the province of Bahia during the first half of the nineteenth century. Rufino was also a Muslim, and Yoruba-speaking Muslims (known as *malês* in Brazil) had been responsible for a major slave uprising in 1835, in Salvador, the captial of Bahia.[1] Rufino was arrested as the police investigated a slave conspiracy in a sugar plantation area in Pernambuco. Nothing was found in the houses of freed Africans, except in Rufino's home, where notebooks and papers written in Arabic were confiscated, the same kind of material that almost twenty years earlier had been found in great quantity with African rebels in Bahia. The so-called Malê papers were used by the police as the main proof of involvement in the 1835 uprising. However, the story Rufino told the police in 1853 was one of a peaceful Muslim, though not a story devoid of movement.[2]

Rufino was born in the early nineteenth century in Oyo, one of the most powerful states in the hinterland of the Bight of Benin in West Africa. Oyo controlled most of Yorubaland up until the last decade of the eighteenth century. Its decline began after a rebellion against the king in 1796 led by a powerful military commander named Afonja. The civil war lingered for many years and triggered a major slave rebellion in Oyo territory in 1817, led by a Fulani Muslim preacher. Rufino grew up in a time of turmoil in a family he declared to be Muslim. He said that he attended Quranic school in Oyo and that his father was himself an *Alufa* (a Yoruba Muslim cleric). His father was Ocoche, and his mother Bixoumi, according to the police scribe's understanding of Rufino's parents' traditional Yoruba names.

In the first half of the nineteenth century, Oyo had a sizable Muslim community formed by free immigrants, primarily Hausa slaves and local Yoruba-speaking people. Both local and foreign literate Muslims lived by making amulets, which were very popular. Harmony between Muslims and traditionalists in Oyo in general ceased after the 1817 slave rebellion and the support given by Muslim groups to the rebel forces of Afonja. But religion was not the only line of demarcation in the conflict. Even though he was a Muslim, Rufino declared he was made prisoner by the mostly Muslim Hausas.

Rufino arrived in Bahia when he was approximately seventeen years old, during the independence struggle against the Portuguese garrison, in 1822 and 1823. The Portuguese occupied the capital city of Salvador, while Brazilians controlled the surrounding sugar plantation region. In July 1823, the Portuguese surrendered, and Bahia joined the rest of the country to form the Brazilian Empire, under Pedro I. Rufino was bought in Bahia by a druggist, who trained the young slave as a cook. In the 1820s, he lived in Salvador, a city of fifty-five to sixty thousand souls, about 40 percent of whom were slaves, 60 percent of them born in Africa. Rufino witnessed the arrival of thousands of his countrymen in Bahia, victims of the civil wars in

Yorubaland. By the early 1830s they represented close to 30 percent of the African-born slaves in Salvador. The majority of urban slaves were either domestics—like Rufino seems to have been—or *ganhadores* (slaves-for-hire, literally "earners"), who worked on the streets, usually as porters and street vendors, contracting with masters for a weekly fee, the excess of which slaves were allowed to keep. Many slaves were able to save enough money to buy their freedom.

During the 1820s many slave rebellions took place in Bahia. The Yoruba were responsible for most of them. The typical rebels were recently arrived Africans, although their leaders tended to be seasoned or ladino slaves. At least three of those rebellions took place around the time Rufino arrived in Salvador. Others happened in 1826, 1827, and several in 1828. Nagô fugitive slaves were most conspicuous in the 1826 movement, when they gathered in a *quilombo* or runaway hideout where an Orisa cult house or Candomblé was found by the police.

We do not know what Rufino thought about those events or if he was ever involved in them. There is no evidence of direct Muslim participation until the 1835 Malê Rebellion, when the Nagô Muslims, like Rufino, were in the forefront of the insurrection. Until then they seemed to be gathering forces, and converting other Africans, mainly Nagôs. Our man probably belonged to a *malê* group and as such attended prayer sessions, Quranic lessons, ritual dinners, and celebrations of Muslim holidays. Thus he probably met and prayed with coreligionists who rose up in arms in 1835, and he could have rebelled were he then residing in Bahia.

Rufino lived in Bahia for eight years. Sometime between 1830 and 1831, he traveled south to the province of Rio Grande do Sul with his young master, the druggist's son, a cadet in the army, who had probably been commissioned to the frontier between Brazil and Uruguay, where Dom Pedro had waged an unsuccessful, three-year frontier war. We do not know the length of his master's residence there, but for reasons that are not clear he decided to sell his servant for a good price in the local market, which was a traditional buyer of slaves from the North. Rufino was sold to a merchant, who kept him for less than two years, or until he bankrupted and moved to Montevideo to escape creditors. As part of his master's business spoil, Rufino was auctioned and bought by a high court judge, José Maria Peçanha.

Slaves made up the majority of the labor force involved in the jerked beef and cattle industry of Rio Grande do Sul, where Rufino lived until late 1835, most of this time probably in Porto Alegre, the provincial capital. Like Rufino many slaves of Porto Alegre were born in West Africa and committed to classical strategies of slave resistance. Sixty percent of the fugitives announced in newspapers between 1828 and 1838 were African born; of 114 runaways sent to prison between 1856 and 1859, 43 percent were specifically West Africans. The latter also represented 25 percent of all Africans taken to court for different crimes between 1818 and 1833. The Nagôs were well represented in the larger towns of Pelotas and Porto Alegre. They were highly successful in purchasing their freedom. In Porto Alegre, West Africans represented 74.2 percent of all manumissions granted between 1858 and 1887. The Nagôs alone counted 60 percent of the slaves obtaining freedom during those years. African Muslims could also be found among them. There is evidence of an active Muslim prayer group that was dispersed by the police for suspicion of conspiracy in Porto Alegre in 1840.[3] This very group may have been active since 1835, or even before.

Like other countrymen, Rufino obtained his freedom in November 1835, for which he paid 600,000 réis (approximately 210 pounds sterling). That was the average market price for a slave in Rio Grande do Sul. He probably saved that money working as a slave-for-hire for Peçanha and his previous masters. Thus Rufino became a freedman after almost fifteen years as a slave, and as freedmen usually did in Brazil, he adopted his master's name to become Rufino José Maria. This fact, his ability to save money, and the terms of his manumission suggest that he was on good terms with Peçanha.

Rufino left Rio Grande do Sul for Rio de Janeiro, capital of the Brazilian Empire, between late December 1835 and January 1836. He said nothing about his life as a freedman in Rio. Most Africans in Rio had come from the Angola-Congo region, the Nagôs being a small minority—but again they were deeply involved in urban peddling. Their relative prosperity is reflected in the high number of manumissions among them. Although they represented 9 to 15 percent of urban slaves, they responded for 50 percent of paid manumissions between 1840 and 1859.[4] Such a large group of freed persons only increased police suspicion, for in Bahia freedmen had also joined the 1835 rebellion.

We do not know how long Rufino remained in Rio. All he said under interrogation was that, at some point, he became a cook in a small slave ship named *Paula*. The majority (55 percent) of African crews serving on Brazilian slavers came from West Africa, which means that Rufino probably met other Nagôs on the *Paula*.[5] We do not know exactly the port of destination of the *Paula* in Africa, but we know for sure that Rufino returned to Brazil from Angola in another ship, the *São José*. But instead of returning to Rio, the ship went to Pernambuco. The *São José* belonged to Joaquim Ribeiro de Brito, a well-known slave trader who lived in Luanda and had business connections in Rio, Recife, and Bahia. At this point, the transatlantic slave trade had been declared illegal by the Brazilian government since 1831. When one of Brito's slave ships was captured by the British navy, it was his business partner in Recife who represented him before the courts.

Thus the first time Rufino set foot in Pernambuco, he arrived in a ship that belonged to a highly active slave-trading network in the Atlantic circuit. The *São José* made at least six trips from Angola to Pernambuco between 1837 and 1841, being one of the many slave ships that smuggled close to 23,500 slaves to Pernambuco in these years. The vast majority of those slaves were imported from the Congo-Angola region, precisely the route covered by Rufino. Since the transatlantic slave trade was illegal, slave ships disembarked their cargoes on hidden beaches, and then proceeded to the harbor. That was exactly the strategy employed by the *São José* while Rufino worked on it.

In the early 1840s Rufino embarked on a trip to Africa aboard the *Ermelinda*, a larger vessel than the *Paula* and the *São José*. It belonged to José Francisco de Azevedo Lisboa, a well-known slave dealer in Pernambuco, and a partner of the Angolan slave dealer who owned the *São José*. Therefore, Rufino continued to work for the same slave-trading group. In June 1841, the boat left Recife bound for Luanda loaded with traditional goods used to barter for slaves. Its sixteen crew members and fourteen passengers were of Brazilian, Portuguese, Angolan, and Nagô origin. One of the passengers was a lieutenant in the African Portuguese army, and the others were merchants, traders, and their clerks. They all had shares in the cargo of the *Ermelinda*, including Rufino, who had become a small slave trader, for he also owned 180 boxes of guava sweetmeat, which amounted to 2 percent of the goods embarked in Recife.

After the *Ermelinda* left the coast of Pernambuco, a serious leak was discovered before it reached the high seas, and it had to anchor in Bahia. We have no record of Rufino's whereabouts during this visit to the place where he had first landed in Brazil twenty years earlier and where he had lived as a slave for about eight years. On October 27, almost three months after leaving Bahia, the *Ermelinda* was seized off the coast of Angola by a British ship. It had no slaves on board, but according to the British, it was equipped for the slave trade. The *Ermelinda* was first taken to St. Helena to obtain a supply of water and then to Sierra Leone, where it arrived on December 9, 1841.[6]

The British colony of Sierra Leone was founded in 1787 by rich philanthropists, as a settlement for poor blacks living in England and blacks who had served the English during the American war of independence; later it also received imprisoned Maroons from Jamaica. All these groups had been promised land and protection, which they did not fully obtain. After the abolition of the British slave trade effective in 1808, Sierra Leone became a Crown Colony of England, and the place where Africans who had been rescued from slave ships captured in their antislave trade crusade in the Atlantic Ocean were taken. Thousands of Africans were relocated to Sierra Leone this way. In addition, its capital, named Freetown, became the seat in West Africa for mixed commission courts for the suppression of the slave trade, tribunals composed of British judges and representatives of the countries that had celebrated treaties favoring the abolition of the slave trade: Portugal, Spain, the Netherlands.

The forced reunion of tens of thousands of people from different regions of Africa made Sierra Leone a true ethnic melting pot—"more than two hundred different tribes and countries," according to missionary and linguist Sigismund Koelle, writing in 1854.[7] Among these the most numerous group were Yoruba speakers, Rufino's countrymen. While in Sierra Leone, Rufino decided to improve his knowledge of Islam. He said to the Pernambuco police in 1853 that he attended school in "Farobê" (Fourah Bay), a district near Freetown where a Muslim Yoruba community existed in the 1840s. There, he said, "he continued to learn Arabic, of which he already knew the principles, with a black man who taught there." Rufino studied in Fourah Bay while he awaited the trial of the *Ermelinda* by the Anglo-Brazilian mixed commission. The commission was acting on the basis of Anglo-Brazilian treaties that considered "good prizes" ships either loaded with captives or fitted for slaving purposes. The *Ermelinda* had no slaves, shackles, or handcuffs on board. But the British argued that they found several other objects, such as irons, siphons used by captives to drink water, a small cabin suspected of being mounted to accommodate slave women, and an amount of food and kitchenware that far surpassed the needs of the crew. The equipment employed by Rufino in his job called the attention of the British officer who captured the *Ermelinda*: "A very large cooking apparatus, fitted for large boilers and having on board more boilers than required for the use of the crew of any merchant vessel." Besides, there was "a quantity of manioc flour stowed in bulk not entered in any manifest," and "a large quantity of firewood."[8]

One piece of indirect evidence, however, the British held up very high: The *Ermelinda* papers indicated its ownership by Francisco Lisboa, a notorious slave trader. "This person," the British wrote, "has already been reported . . . to be the treasurer of an extensive Slaving Company established in the Brazils, and it is also there remarked that an arrangement had been made by the parties forming that company, for Lisboa's name to appear in the papers of all vessels belonging to them as the ostensible proprietor: accordingly he appears in that capacity in the Imperial passport of the *Ermelinda*."[9]

Rufino was one of the few crew members to be interrogated. Unfortunately there is no transcript of his deposition. There is a record of an accusation he made against a British officer of insulting, hitting, and wounding him with a stick, and falsely accusing him of stealing kitchenware from the ship.[10] Unfortunately, here again we do not have the words of Rufino but those of his opponent:

> Having been informed by one of the prize crew (a Krooman) that the said cook had given away some of the saucepans belonging to the said Barque, this deponent went forward to ascertain the correctness of his statement, and the said cook refused to let this deponent see the number of saucepans in the galley, this deponent then taxed him with being the thief, when the cook called this deponent a dog. This deponent then told him if he did not at once muster the whole of the saucepans he would send him on shore and have him put in gaol, and as he still refused, this deponent seized him by the shirt to pull him out of the galley, when the cook laid hold of this deponent, and this deponent did then strike him with his hand, and not with a stick as stated by the said cook and that in the scuffle the cook's head struck against the corner of the galley, which caused a slight cut, and further that upon counting the number of saucepans in the galley two were found missing.[11]

Though certainly distorted in favor of the aggressor, this account gives a glimpse of Rufino's character. He was not easily intimidated and could firmly react to arrogance. It is also relevant that the officer complained that Rufino called him a dog, which is a typical Muslim insult.

The *Ermelinda* became a cause célèbre in the annals of the Brazilian slave trade as the first ship to be acquitted by the Sierra Leone mixed commission. This happened because the Brazilian judge did not consider the evidence against the ship good enough to declare it guilty as charged, and a Brazilian arbitrator won the toss, the legal decision method when there was disagreement between the two parties. After the acquittal, the *Ermelinda*, under the command of a British master, returned to Pernambuco on May 5, 1842. It carried "no passenger and a cargo of general merchandize." Rufino was again on board as a cook, after spending exactly 139 days in Sierra Leone.[12]

The trip had been a commercial disaster for Rufino, for his guava sweetmeats rotted in Sierra Leone while the *Ermelinda* was being tried. On his return to Pernambuco he spent a few months working as a cloth seller while still in the payroll of his former employers. In the beginning of April 1843, he returned to Sierra Leone with the documents listing losses and damages incurred by the unlawful detention of the *Ermelinda*. However, this time his main purpose was religious. He went back to the Fourah Bay community to attend Quranic classes for one year and seven months. In his words, that's when "he finished learning to read and write Arabic."[13] On his way back to Brazil, he spent three months in Rio de Janeiro, where he spent two and a half months before proceeding to Recife with a stop in Bahia. At this point of his narrative to the Pernambuco police, we are informed that Rufino had a son in Bahia, Nicolau, whom he took with him to Pernambuco. Nothing is said about Nicolau's mother.

In mid-1845 Rufino settled with his son in Recife, a city of about fifty thousand inhabitants, one-fifth to one-fourth of them slaves. We know nothing of his life until he was arrested by the police in 1853. He was then described as a "fat and old man" approximately fifty years old. According to an eyewitness, Rufino carried a respectable and intelligent semblance. In spite of his strong accent, he could speak Portuguese fluently. He was very calm during his interrogation, but frowned at ironic remarks made against his religion, and smiled dryly as he answered some of the questions, showing that he had nothing to hide or, otherwise, that he felt no fear. He clearly stated that he was a fortune-teller and a healer, and that his clients included people from several African ethnic groups, local blacks, mulattoes, and even whites. He also said that clients paid for his services according to their possessions and to what they sought to obtain "by means of his power and science." However, he concealed any proselytizing activity that he may have engaged in, and his participation in any Muslim prayer group.

The kind of Islam Rufino professed was similar to magical practices of priests of traditional African religions. He prepared written amulets containing passages of the Quran, popular prayers that were worn around the neck to protect against or cure witchcraft. He also cured diseases with water used to wash Muslim writing boards. The same board served as an instrument to promote union between men and women by writing on it "their names turned one towards the other and praying on the other side [of the board]." And he divined. All of these "magical" practices, including divination, are known in many parts of the Islamic world, and they were especially popular in West Africa.

A major contrast to African, non-Muslim priests was his control of the written word. The police found in his house an old manuscript copy of the Quran that he had brought from Sierra Leone, prayer books, Arabic language manuals, and a notebook that he declared "teaches the medicines." There were also loose manuscript papers that "contained prayers, songs and other things, even sermons" written or copied by him. According to Rio de Janeiro's newspaper *Jornal do Commercio*, where this episode was reported, he explained "that his religion was the one preached by Mohammad and included in the al-Koran, and explained with great knowledge and intelligence the full doctrine of that religion, which . . . he said he would not give up even if he were to be sent to the gallows."

When a judge told him that Catholicism was the "true religion," he answered that "some learn one religion when they are born, others [learn] others, and on which [religion] was the best that was a question to be decided only when the world ends." And he criticized Catholic priesthood by saying that in Brazil it was "an occupation learned with a purpose, but that in his homeland . . . the most knowledgeable ones directed the others." Asked why he did not use his power to improve his own lot, he said he was satisfied with what he owned because "some people asked God for wealth but he only asked for knowledge; and the two precepts did not fit in the same bag."[14]

Rufino also drew attention from the press in Recife because his attitude reminded them of a Christian black religious leader, Agostinho José Pereira, known as the Divine Master. Pereira had been arrested by police in 1846 and accused of promoting a religious schism and conspiring against the slaveholding order while teaching other blacks to read and write.[15] Just like Pereira, Rufino belonged to the world of the written word, which was supposed to be reserved for whites only. Rufino was called the Divine Teacher II by the press, and the authorities further linked his religious practices with those of the 1835 Bahian rebels. However, very soon it would be clear that Rufino's activities were quite different from Pereira's, and that his brand of Islam was quite different from that of the Bahian Malês.

Being a Yoruba speaker, Rufino's ethnic background was exceptional in Pernambuco, where most Africans, like those in Rio, had come from the Angolan or West Central African coast. Nevertheless, there was a less regular but significant influx of slaves from West Africa to Pernambuco in addition to reexports from Bahia. In the mid-1840s, when Angola's coast was under severe surveillance by the British navy, slavers intensified imports from Lagos and Whydah. At least six ships brought slaves from that region in 1844 alone. The presence of Nagôs among slaves in Pernambuco is evident in the advertisements of runaways. Inácio, a Nagô slave of a local merchant, fled in 1844. In 1848, Joaquina, a Nagô woman, also fled in Recife. It seems, therefore, that although Rufino was part of an ethnic minority, he was not alone in Recife.

Rufino had been arrested on the trail of investigations of a slave conspiracy in a sugar plantation parish near Recife. The late 1840s and early 1850s were a time of social tensions in Pernambuco, with the Praieira Rebellion in 1848, when the Conservative and Liberal parties fought against each other for power followed by armed personal retinues. After the civil war, groups of armed men roamed the countryside, and some included runaway slaves. In January 1852, the imperial government decided to enforce a civil registry and start a national population census. Nobody ever knew how rumors started, but within a few days armed crowds of free and freed blacks occupied public buildings in several rural parishes in Pernambuco and Paraíba to protest against the law that would "enslave all the colored people." The movement was controlled with great difficulty and a lot of persuasion by priests and local authorities. The imperial government suspended the census and the civil registration.

In the following year, rumors spread of a slave conspiracy involving several plantations. The rebels argued they had been freed and their manumission papers were being held by the priests. They were quite organized, with leaders dispersed in different plantations. It seems that the police feared not just a slave rebellion, but the possibility that disgruntled free and freedmen would join to act together. Thus, in September, when fourteen slaves in Pau d'Alho stole weapons, money, and other property and fled to the bushes, the local authorities panicked. There were widespread rumors that the rebels were supported by freedmen not only in the area but also in Recife. Actually two free men were among the fourteen slaves arrested. Plantation owners immediately sent troops to pursue the runaways. The government supported them with more troops. Two slaves were arrested and confessed their plans. The rebels allegedly planned to kill their masters, destroy the bridges, and incite slaves from several plantations to rebel. In a plantation invaded by police free workers accused slaves of planning a rebellion against the suppression of some Christian holidays.

Unfortunately, we did not find the slaves' interrogation records. All we know is that some of the suspects fled to the bushes or to Recife. According to a local newspaper, Africans like Rufino who were arrested in Recife were accused of vagrancy and, presumably, of attending secret meetings. The police authority who broke into their homes also suspected they were hiding runaway slaves.

The calm attitude of Rufino and other Africans arrested in Recife, most of them elderly freedmen, led police authorities to believe they were not involved in the 1853 conspiracy. Less than two weeks after his arrest, Rufino was released under the obligation of showing himself every week to the local police authority. According to a newspaper, it had been proved that he was just a harmless, old Muslim preacher, who earned his daily bread reading other people's fortunes. At this point, we lose track of our character.

Having traveled widely in Brazil and Africa, Rufino had certainly acquired a worldview that made him quite different from most freedmen of his time.

As a cook and a small-time merchant in a slave ship he had access to inside information about, and personal experience with, the Atlantic mercantile connections that linked Brazil, Europe, and Africa. He could speak several languages—such as Portuguese, Yoruba, probably the slave-trade pidgin and some Arabic—which made him a polyphonic and multicultural interpreter of the world in which he lived. His story is even more extraordinary because of his experience as a worker in the slave trade; he was a Muslim who, unlike other Muslims enslaved in the Americas who managed to return to Africa to stay, went to Africa to improve religious training, and he returned to live the rest of his life in the land where he had once served as a slave. In sum, Rufino's story allows historians to glimpse the range of possibilities Africans could experience in spite of the heavy pressures imposed by the slave system.

~

CHAPTER SIX

Buenaventura Lucumí (1820s–1872)

African Slave, Head of a Household, and Lottery Winner in Cuba

Aisnara Perera Díaz and
María de los Ángeles Meriño Fuentes

The nineteenth-century Atlantic World was marked by the abolition of the slave trade by European powers, yet also by the growth of plantation agriculture and consequently by a renewed demand for African slaves. Cuba and Brazil received hundreds of thousands of African slaves through the illegal slave trade, and Buenaventura Lucumí was one of them. Buenaventura lived not in the plantation sector, but in a district of Havana, Cuba, devoted to the production of foodstuffs and other crops destined for the local markets. Recent historiography has shown that family and community life were considered of foremost importance for slaves and freedpeople of African descent in the Americas. Cuban historians Aisnara Perera Díaz and María de los Angeles Meriño Fuentes carefully reconstituted Buenaventura's family life to explore his choices and constraints within Cuban slavery, demonstrating that slave lives were marked by hard work, but also by chance. This chapter was translated from Spanish by Karen Racine.

In 1820, the Anglo-Spanish treaty to suppress the slave trade came into effect. Paradoxically, in the spring of that very same year, a young Lucumí boy was baptized in the Church of San Felipe and Santiago in Bejucal, a town located twenty-seven kilometers south of the capital city of Havana, and had his liberty taken away from him. According to the terms of the international convention, which had been signed three years earlier in 1817, all those Africans introduced into any Cuban port after January 1, 1820, were to be seized, then declared free. Nevertheless, due to the inaction and even the complicity of Spanish colonial authorities, the traffic in slaves continued, and its volume attained new heights in following years. Men who acquired these now-illegal slaves were not at all disturbed by the offense that they were committing, because the government never undertook any action to determine the fate of those Africans introduced into the island after the treaty went into effect. In fact, these illegal sales were so brazen that the slaves were registered in public books, and officially baptized into the Christian community in full view and awareness of the Cuban populace, including civil and religious authorities.

The young Lucumí boy was undoubtedly among the first Africans smuggled in as contraband after the Anglo-Spanish treaty went into effect, following an Atlantic slave trade route that had been established for centuries. The act of baptism initiated several features of the youth's new life and identity in Cuba. He was introduced into a new Hispanic culture through the grace of the Holy Spirit, and received the new Christian name of Buenaventura; this is the only name by which we know him today, his original African name having been lost to the historical record. At his baptism ceremony, Buenaventura was assigned a godfather, a man named Rafael who shared his West African heritage, and with whom he maintained a lifelong friendship. Finally, the baptism and registration served as a central act in the creation of the African youth's new Cuban identity. In the New World, he became the property of a young entrepreneur named Tomás Acosta Tabares, who was just beginning to make his own fortune by buying a few slaves and setting up his own small farm.

According to the 1817 census, Cuba's population was calculated to be 630,980 inhabitants, of whom 291,021 were classified as whites, 115,691 were considered to be freed persons of color, and 224,268 were slaves. On a local level, the census indicated that 36 percent of Bejucal's population were slaves, which represented one of the lowest percentages of slave populations of any town in Havana Province. From a demographic point of view, this atypical social structure reflected the relatively light presence of agro-industrial sugar in the region, and never varied much over the course of the town's history. Significantly, in Bejucal itself, and in its environs, where Buenaventura Lucumí built his family and spent his life, the number of slaves never exceeded that of the free population. Although the area had been one of the pioneering frontiers of commercialized agriculture in the western part of the island, as the nineteenth century progressed, it slowly became a zone of less-intensive agriculture geared mainly toward the domestic market. Acosta and his Lucumí slave, therefore, operated outside the exploitative and brutal structure of the export-oriented sugar mills.

Marked by hundreds of small farms and cattle ranches, the rural landscape of the Bejucal region was characterized by the modesty of its enterprises. These small farms, separated from each other by low walls made of stones and subdivided into various types of crops, typically comprised just one and one-half *caballerías* of land (a *caballería* was a measure equivalent to thirty-three acres in Cuba) and employed only one or two slaves. The slaves' work was essentially the same as that of the region's free peasants: the cultivation of staple foodstuffs and garden vegetables, and the raising of pigs and cattle.

In Bejucal, however, the terrain best suited for cultivation was in the power of the wealthiest landowners. Rising prices made it impossible for most poor peasants to acquire their own small farms. As a result, the majority of the free population had to make due as tenants, typically paying an annual rent of 250 pesos for the right to reside on and cultivate a small plot that was often not large enough to provide subsistence for their own large families. Tomás Acosta, the eventual master of Buenaventura Lucumí, came from one of these families who lived on a rented plot, one that had been established in the city since the middle of the eighteenth century but without many economic resources. Acosta was the youngest of eight brothers, who were not permitted to remain in the bosom of the impoverished family household as the five sisters were. In fact, Acosta had to go out in search of work as a day laborer, offering his services to the area's large landowners, known as *hacendados.*

According to a will drawn up much later in his life, when Acosta contracted marriage with Nicolasa Delgado in 1815, they were so poor that neither of them brought assets of any kind into their union. The couple's deep desire to improve their material conditions, however, eventually brought them much material success. Although they were not able to purchase land in the beginning, they were able to scrape up enough money buy a couple of *bozales*, as the recently arrived African slaves were known, and then rent them out to work on nearby farms. It was in this context that they acquired the young African man now known as Buenaventura Lucumí. The first few years of Buenaventura's life as an enslaved person in Cuba were spent in constant movement. He and his enslaved mates spent much time in the towns of Quivicán, Batabanó, and La Salud working at a variety of jobs that had been arranged through their entrepreneurial owner Acosta. In this way, Buenaventura Lucumí became familiar with the region and its people, became used to personal mobility, and worked on his own quite often.

In 1826, Tomás Acosta was already in possession of five slaves (four Africans and one Creole) when he bought the woman who very shortly afterward became Buenaventura's common-law wife: It was a woman from the region of Calabar in West Africa, identified in Cuba as from the Carabalí nation, who was baptized as Maria Josefa. Three years later, the couple contracted a formal marriage in the church of San Pedro de Quivicán, which they swore was undertaken as a result of their own free will and informed consent. Buenaventura Lucumí had begun to absorb some of the values of his new environment as he sought to build a successful family in Cuba. By the time of their marriage, the happy couple had already produced their first child, a daughter. Two other girls were born to them while they resided in Batabanó. Their only son, José Lucio, arrived while they were living in La Salud in 1836, and their last daughter was born in Bejucal in 1837. The fact that all of these children not only survived such difficult conditions but reached adulthood strong and healthy is a true testament to the care and attention that their parents paid to their well-being. Indeed, it was a felicitous situation in which the master's and parents' interest in providing a healthy childhood coincided.

Acosta bought his first property in the fertile region of Aguas Verdes in 1834. Later, he went on to purchase an additional coffee farm of three caballerías in size, which he gave the name of Santo Tomás, in gratitude to the guiding figure who he believed had watched over his business successes. As Acosta's enterprise expanded, he was anxious to increase the number of slaves who could work for him and produce value. The price of bozales, however, was rising dramatically now that the effects of the Anglo-Spanish ban were starting to be felt; because slaves could no longer be legally imported, slave owners started to look toward any augmentation of slave numbers through natural reproduction. While the large sugar plantations traditionally had maintained their stock supply of slaves by a continuous importation of new bodies, the situation in the jurisdiction of Bejucal had operated quite differently. As a small entrepreneur without much land himself, Acosta took a long-term view of his slaves' wellness, paying particular attention to their reproductive health. This economic incentive mean that Acosta had a self-interested motive to ensure healthful childhoods for his slaves' offspring. In addition to Buenaventura and Maria Josefa's young family, many other children were born to enslaved families on his farm. For example, the children of Buenaventura's godfather Rafael and his wife, Concepción Conga (from Congo), were born and grew to adulthood under Acosta's control. Besides this natural growth in his slaveholdings, Acosta bought two other Creoles and eight Africans who then became part of his workforce.

Buenaventura, or Ventura as he was commonly called, took great pride and pleasure in the confidence that his master Acosta placed in him. That Acosta considered them to have an amiable relationship can be seen in a document dated 1857 in which he expressed gratitude for more than thirty years of his Lucumí slave's faithful service. The master recognized that his slave had carried out all tasks with a remarkable fidelity and efficiency, even taking pleasure in doing his work well and exhibiting those marks of character and physical strength that so many contemporary observers attributed to Africans of Lucumí origin. Acosta entrusted difficult jobs to him, and Ventura Lucumí won further esteem through his hardworking dedication, his impressive physical endurance, and a keen intelligence. It is less clear how Lucumí perceived their relationship.

Ventura Lucumí clearly understood how the system worked, and had developed a plan for himself and for his family, which in 1859 consisted of his wife, four children, and three grandchildren. One of his most important desires, quite obviously, was to secure their freedom. Yet when given the opportunity to spend some of his saved money, personal freedom often was not the first item on his agenda. He had internalized the way a capitalist economy worked, and made the assessment that his funds might be more profitably spent on property that would bring in greater wealth down the line, and thereby provide something more substantial for his family in the longer term. Although he was a slave, Lucumí's work on Acosta's coffee farm brought with it access to a small portion of land that he could cultivate for his own benefit. Interestingly enough, when given this resource, he did not devote his land and time to subsistence agriculture, or to the cultivation of special crops intended to complement the meager diet that his master provided for the slave family, but rather he set out to achieve a commercially viable crop, the sale of which could be done through a small store near Acosta's coffee farm. He understood the value of short-term sacrifice for long-term gain. Lucumí the entrepreneur was constantly on the lookout for other opportunities to enhance his private income. For example, Sundays and holidays were times that legally belonged to slaves themselves to rest or to work on their own behalf. On those days, Lucumí would offer his labor to neighbors to do odd jobs, including digging wells; shucking corn; cleaning seeds; searching for lost animals; helping to construct or repair corrals, stables, or domiciles; or picking fruits and vegetables. In this way, the head of the slave household was able to use his initiative to bring additional income into his family's coffers.

Strategies of this type permitted Ventura Lucumí to amass the significant fortune of four hundred pesos, with which he bought a small slab stone house with a tiled roof in the town of Bejucal. This transaction was endowed with a singular importance for him. He was a slave, meaning he could not accumulate goods according to the Spanish laws, and neither did he have the juridical standing as an actual person who was able to enter into contracts legally. In Lucumí's case, however, his master Acosta granted the favored slave his authorization to make the purchase. To do so, Lucumí had to resort to the use of a representative, in this case a *procurador judicial* (a solicitor) named José Gervasio Valdés, whom he had met in the course of various legal affairs undertaken on Acosta's behalf. Once again, Lucumí's careful strategizing and his clear-thinking ability to utilize the various provisions available to him in the restrictive colonial legal context were impressive and indicate a certain degree of mobility for those who were determined to achieve it.

If we condemn Lucumí's decision to purchase a house rather than secure his own personal freedom or that of a child or grandchild, we fail in our effort to know the soul (if that is even possible) of a man who until that moment had lived the majority of his life in slavery. With four hundred pesos, Ventura Lucumí was aware that he could have freed himself, the proof of which can be found in the fact that he had paid for his wife's freedom some years earlier. He also could have chosen to use the money to purchase the freedom of his third grandchild, a little boy named Nazario who had been born in July 1858. Acosta would not have asked more than one hundred pesos for the boy, the standard sum for a child under two years of age. Similarly, he could have chosen to invest in the eventual freedom of children by placing a sort of down payment that would guarantee that their price would be held at current levels until the full amount could be earned, even though the value of a slave was steadily increasing over time. Yet none of these things happened. Lucumí instead opted to invest in real estate and thereby assure his family's future income through the monthly rents that he charged for the use of the Bejucal house. Well aware of its excellent location on a street with good circulation and easy access from outside, Lucumí had no doubt that he would be able to demand fifteen or twenty pesos per month. In this way, the savvy entrepreneur figured he could recover his investment in just two years, and then begin to make a profit, which could be used to benefit his family in myriad ways. While the investment in real estate reliably brought in money for the family, the petty capitalist head of a slave household continued to spend his own time meeting his duties on Acosta's coffee farm and traveling to town, where his wife, Josefa, had found employment as a domestic servant in the household of the Díaz de Aguiar family.

In accordance with his upwardly mobile aspirations for his family, Ventura Lucumí demanded certain sacrifices from his daughters to contribute to the unit's well-being. A crucial one of these requirements was to control their fertility in order not to add to the family's burden by increasing its numbers. This command would seem strange among a class of women to whom was attributed a total absence of sexual morality and a gross self-indulgence in lustful behaviors; without any pressure to maintain their virginity before marriage, and no one to monitor their chastity, early and frequent pregnancies were common among African women. If we compare, however, the reproductive behavior of Ventura Lucumí's daughters with that of their enslaved peers, we can see that Juliana and Gertrudis both dutifully complied with their father's dictates, which were in direct contradiction to and in defiance of their master Acosta's wishes to augment his slaves' numbers. Controlling their reproductive lives was both a mode of resistance and a tangible contribution to the well-being of their family household. Lucumí's daughter Lutgarda was the only one of the three who seems to have broken the agreement. When she turned sixteen years old, the impetuous girl began a relationship with a fellow slave and gave birth to three boys between the years 1854 and 1862. Despite Buenaventura Lucumí's initial irritation with the additional burden placed upon him as head of household, his disgust quickly disappeared when his first little grandson smiled and gurgled his way into the older man's heart. According to the era's normal practices, he soon consented to become the baby's godfather, and assumed the same role for the ones that followed.

Up until that moment, Lucumí had resisted taking on the responsibilities of a godfather. To assume such a role implied promises and the creation of ties of shared parental affinity with other families, and he preferred to focus his time and scarce resources on his own household's needs. Before Lucumí's grandchildren arrived, he had agreed to take on those significant responsibilities only on two previous occasions, including the time in 1829 when he stood in as the godfather for the son of his own beloved godfather Rafael. After he consented to assume this important role for his grandsons, he never again agreed to become a godfather for any other children for the rest of his life. Clearly, he preferred to limit the extent of his responsibilities to his immediate circle of the Lucumí family, which is to say that he felt more comfortable adopting a type of godfatherhood less visible but more typical of his cultural roots.

Ventura Lucumí did, however, participate in the larger Afro-Cuban communities and local self-help organizations that had emerged over time. For example, the presence and activities of African *cabildos de naciones* (ethnic brotherhoods) in Cuba dated back as far as the end of the sixteenth century. In Havana, that great swirling economic enclave, many *cabildos de naciones* organized themselves and reflected the cultural origins and geographic diversity of the Africans brought to the island. These confraternities provided some solidarity and solace for the diasporic population, and provided a site at which information could be shared and identities fortified. Over time, these *cabildos* spread throughout Cuba. After 1810 or so, Bejucal's African residents—identified as Congo, Carabalí, Gangá, and Lucumí—began to meet just as their brethren had done in the capital. Ventura Lucumí, like other Yoruba-speaking residents in Bejucal and its environs, affiliated himself with the *cabildo* of his ethnic group and considered himself to be a participant in a new community of Afro-Cubans acting on their own behalf despite restrictive social conditions and a disadvantaged legal status.

The festivals, balls, and drumming sessions held in their official headquarters were the most visible activities of those voluntary associations. Their leaders were often mediators between their slave members and the established powers. At the same time, they were also mutual-aid organizations that collaborated in whatever form was needed to attain their slave members' freedom. One of the most common strategies of these associations was the group purchase of Royal Lottery tickets. The participation in such raffles—promoted and controlled by the colonial state—was a means of speculation, because so little money was invested but the promise of a large payoff held out great hope for a quick return and, therefore, a change in status. One could buy a whole ticket or only a small share. In this way, anyone could join in the speculative enterprise simply by paying according to his or her means. If their lucky number was drawn, the prize was then distributed proportionately to each person's investment.

The authorities customarily gave much publicity to the times when one or more slaves won the lottery because it held up a good example of one way in which a slave could achieve freedom without resorting to flight or robbery or social violence; furthermore, these stories also encouraged further sales of lottery tickets to hopeful enslaved persons. Ventura Lucumí, like the rest of his mates, learned about the "lucky ones." In fact, he even knew someone who had won the lottery; Tomás Acosta's brother had a slave whose number had been called. The hope of a large return on a small investment led Lucumí to participate in the state lottery, year after year.

Then, in 1862, the fates smiled on the hardworking man whose very name, Buenaventura, means "good fortune." It took no time at all for the news to spread throughout Bejucal and reach him at Acosta's coffee farm. Lucumí had won the Royal Lottery's grand prize. The amount was a fabulous sum for the period: five thousand pesos! Negotiating his own and his children's freedom with Acosta was not conflictive. Unlike other cases in which slaves attempted to buy their freedom, acrimonious negotiations that often ended up being mediated by *síndicos procuradores* (local justices), Lucumí had no conflicts when negotiating the purchase of his and his children's freedom with Acosta. No doubt the slave owner intended to take advantage of Lucumí's windfall and demanded excessive prices. He asked for, and received, six hundred pesos for Ventura's freedom and one thousand pesos for each of his children: Juliana (aged thirty-nine), Lutgarda (aged twenty-eight), José Lúcio (aged twenty-six), and Gertrudis (aged twenty-five). The prices were dramatically higher than the ones they had been willing to accept a few years earlier in 1857, when Acosta and his wife had offered to let the adult children be conditionally manumitted "for 500 pesos for being born under our power and in return for their good services" while promising Ventura that he would be freed in their wills when both were deceased. Acosta believed he had the right to participate in and profit from his slave's good fortune. It is useless to debate whether the master had perverse feelings or bad intentions, or even to consider that he might have forgotten the offer made five years earlier. Putting it simply, economic calculations superseded any others. If the household was to become free, if the master was to lose four young able-bodied slaves, he considered it fair that he obtained from his faithful Lucumí slave a price that would compensate his loss.

On November 18, 1862, Ventura appeared before Bejucal's public notary, a man named Justo Baronal. His letter of manumission was the first to be registered. With that document in hand, he could finally enter into legally binding contracts as a free person. Lucumí's first act as a free man was a gesture of love and honor as the head of a household. In the papers that granted their children's manumission, he made sure that his wife Josefa's name was also inscribed on the documents for her constant exertions on behalf of their family. It was his express recognition that such a profound victory belonged to them both, even if he had been the lucky one to win the lottery. It was the clear acknowledgment that without her, his life's work would have been more difficult and his days more disheartening in a foreign land. Ventura's intimate desire to make public and immortal through "the power of writing" what he was feeling after forty-two years of captivity was understood by the notary who identified them as "the parents" who had deposited in Acosta's hands "in full and cash" the price that the master had demanded for the one thing that really mattered to them: their children.

The new legal condition did not mean a dramatic change of activity for the African man. His relationship with Acosta continued, not only because the former master allowed Ventura and his family to stay on his property and cultivate the provision grounds that he had been allocated, but also because his grandchildren had remained there. Lucumí's daughter Lutgarda herself had also stayed on for a while in the Aguas Verdes property to care for her little boys Crispín, Nazario, and Celestino. Buenaventura continued to walk a distance of several miles between the city and the rural property every day, something that did not change when the roads became increasingly dangerous in the mid-1860s because of the presence of bands of armed robbers and the emergence of bands of independence-minded rebels.

After gaining their freedom, the adult children finally felt secure enough to form their own families. Gertrudis had a conflict-ridden relationship with a colored (*moreno*) slave named Francisco Gonzáles, with whom she had three children born between 1864 and 1871. Juliana, the oldest daughter, had her only child, a girl, at age thirty-five. Meanwhile, José Lucio married a woman from Quivicán named Matilde, also identified as *morena* whose mother and father, coincidentally enough, were Africans of Lucumí and Carabalí ethnic identity just like his own parents. Sharing common ancestors no doubt contributed heavily to their decision to engage in a relationship.

Tomás Acosta died in 1869. With this sad event, not only did the Lucumí family experience the loss of a friend and patron, but they also lost access to the small plot that they had cultivated for decades on his Aguas Verdes property. Acosta's widow, Nicolasa Delgado, his only heir, could not manage on her own and decided to sell their Santo Tomás coffee farm, and another property of four *caballerías* that was located in Quivicán. She also reduced the number of the slaves under her direct care, among them Ventura's grandchildren, keeping only a few for her private service and permitting others to hire themselves out and then pay her a portion of their weekly earnings. The farm's new owner did not grant Lucumí's request to remain on the lands that he had labored on as a slave first, and then as a free laborer.

So, at an advanced age, Lucumí was forced to establish himself in Bejucal town for good. He had no choice but to do so, and we have his name recorded in a neighborhood roll taken in those years. It may have been his own conscious self-identification when he declared his occupation to be a peasant, or it is possible that the clerk knew him personally and attributed to him the occupation of most freedmen of African origin. The conditions that in other places combined for the rise of a black peasantry were not present in Bejucal, so that men like Ventura Lucumí lived the paradox of being a peasant with no access to land. So it was a good thing he had had the foresight to invest in a house in the town; it was the ideal place to which he could retire and reunite his family.

The town had changed a lot since Lucumí had bought himself the small wooden house on Vestry Street. All sectors of the population had grown.

So-called coolies from China and the Yucatán had arrived and joined whites, free people of color, and slaves in a complex labor force. The small Creole elite had mobilized to found a *Liceo Artístico* (an Arts Lyceum) to advance the cultural life of the citizenry. The press had taken a long time to arrive, but a famous printer named Murtra began to publish and circulate a periodical. For that time period, Bejucal had the third-smallest proportion of slaves to free people among the urban centers of Cuba. That is to say, the free population grew considerably, and there was a certain social mobility. To a certain point, this flexibility contributed to a diffusion of the fear of racial conflicts. The old Lucumí man perceived those changes, and slowly came to embrace those attitudes that arose from the political confrontation that put Cuba on its long road to independence. Those were difficult times for the *cabildos de nación*. The city dusted off an old ordinance that prohibited the existence of buildings made of precarious materials such as thatch palm in downtown Bejucal. The measure showed the good intention, at first sight, of preventing a fire from spreading to the rest of the population, but its essence was segregationist because it ordered the poor population to live in the south of the city. The headquarters of the *cabildos de nación* were relocated there.

For Ventura the move meant the loss of the social space he had attended most often, because his humble house—the only property he managed to acquire in his entire life and that since he became free constituted his family's home—was located on the extreme opposite side of the city from the *cabildo*'s headquarters. To reach it, he had to cross the whole city. Beaten by time and sadness, he died days after his daughter Gertrudis. It was March 1872, the same month he had been registered as Tomás Acosta's slave fifty years earlier. On his death certificate, this circumstance was remembered, as were the facts that he was a free man of color (*moreno libre*) of the Lucumí nation, the widower of Josefa Carabalí, and had died before sunrise receiving his final sacraments from the priest Rodrigo Delgado Cienfuegos. At peace with his gods, with the memory of the dead and in the presence of his only male child, José Lucio, Buenaventura Acosta Lucumí, or simply Ventura, died. Like hundreds of African men and women he had been capable of saving himself and saving others through the simplest of means: the family.

Sources

This reconstitution of Buenaventura Lucumí's life is based on baptismal, marriage, and death records from Iglesia Parroquial de Ascenso de San Felipe y Santiago del Bejucal, from Iglesia de San Pedro de Quivicán, and from Iglesia del Santo Cristo de La Salud (1810–1890); and on notarial

(*Protocolos notariales*) and municipal records (*Libros de Actas Capitulares del Ayuntamiento*) from San Felipe y Santiago del Bejucal (1810–1889).

Suggested Readings

Casanovas, Joan. *Bread or Bullets: Urban Labor and Spanish Colonialism in Cuba, 1850–1898*. Pittsburgh: University of Pittsburgh Press, 1998.

Ferrer, Ada. *Insurgent Cuba: Race, Nation and Revolution, 1868–1898*. Chapel Hill: University of North Carolina Press, 1999.

Gutman, Herbert. *The Black Family in Slavery and Freedom: 1750–1925*. New York: Pantheon Books, 1976.

Howard, Philip A. *Changing History: Afro-Cuban Cabildos and Societies of Color in the Nineteenth Century*. Baton Rouge: Louisiana State University Press, 1998.

Kiple, Kenneth. *Blacks in Colonial Cuba, 1774–1899*. Gainesville: University of Florida Press, 1976.

Knight, Franklin. *Slave Society in Cuba during the Nineteenth Century*. Madison: University of Wisconsin Press, 1970.

Manzano, Juan Francisco. *The Life and Poems of a Cuban Slave: Juan Francisco Manzano,1797–1854*, edited by Edward J. Mullen. North Haven, CT: Archon Books, 1981.

Martinez-Alier, Verena. *Marriage, Class and Color in Nineteenth Century Cuba*. Ann Arbor: University of Michigan Press, 1989.

Pérez, Louis A. *Slaves, Sugar and Society: Travel Accounts of Cuba 1801–1899*. Wilmington, DE: Scholarly Resources, 1992.

Scott, Rebecca. *Slave Emancipation in Cuba: The Transition to Free Labor 1860–1899*. Pittsburgh: University of Pittsburgh Press, 2000.

———. *Degrees of Freedom: Louisiana and Cuba after Slavery*. Cambridge, MA: Harvard University Press, 2005.

CHAPTER SEVEN

~

Blaise Diagne (1872–1934)

Senegal's Deputy to the French National Assembly

Hilary Jones

Throughout the nineteenth century, citizenship was a contested terrain. It entailed individual and public rights and marked the belonging to a political entity. Both in independent nations and in colonies, the political participation of the majority of the population was either prohibited or highly regulated. In French Senegal, the residents of the old districts of the Four Communes enjoyed special status among French colonial subjects in West Africa, yet were not considered French citizens until World War I. Blaise Diagne was the first black African deputy to the French National Assembly, and fought for the recognition of black Africans as French subjects. At a time of heightened scientific racism, Diagne insisted Africans could be assimilated into French society. Drawing from her research on French West Africa, historian Hilary Jones shows how Diagne's life represents the struggles and dilemmas of people of African descent at the turn of the nineteenth to the twentieth century.

As early as the decade following the French Revolution, local inhabitants of the Senegalese towns of Saint Louis and Gorée fought for the right to be recognized and treated as citizens of France rather than subjects of the empire. In the 1790s, prominent Afro-European residents of the town sent a statement of grievances to lawmakers in Paris calling attention to the problem of free trade along the Senegal River. This marked the beginning of a tradition in which inhabitants of Senegal's colonial towns sent petitions to Paris lawmakers arguing for the right to participate in electoral politics. In the late nineteenth century, mulatto or *métis* inhabitants of the towns joined with black Muslim and black Catholic city dwellers in the struggle to assert their power through democratic political institutions. At the same time, however, military conquest established authoritarian colonial rule throughout the vast interior of the nation that is today the Republic of Senegal.[1] The life history of Blaise Diagne, who was born into this world, offers important insight into the establishment of colonial rule in Senegal, the politics of race in France and her empire, and the meaning of French citizenship for urban Senegalese in the late nineteenth and early twentieth century.

French Colonialism and Urban Politics in Senegal

Today the Republic of Senegal is strategically located where the Sahara Desert meets the savanna lands of sub-Saharan Africa. The town of Saint Louis (called Ndar by the Wolof people) is located where the Senegal River empties out into the Atlantic Ocean. Saint Louis du Senegal and Gorée Island, farther south on the Atlantic coast, served as convenient locations for the establishment of fortified trading posts in the era of the transatlantic slave trade. France built her first permanent settlements in Saint Louis in 1659 and in Gorée in 1677. These towns gave rise to a multicultural community of Africans from neighboring states, an enterprising class of African women called *signares* who owned property and married European men, and the mixed-race products of these unions. The towns, however, remained distant outposts in French mercantile trade relations until the early nineteenth century. As the Atlantic slave trade gave way to "legitimate" commerce after 1820, French interests turned to the export of raw materials. *Métis* and black African residents of Saint Louis, in particular, filled important roles as intermediary traders and as cross-cultural brokers between French military officers and Wolof, Pulaar, and Serer aristocrats in the Senegal River valley and the peanut basin to the south.

From the perspective of Paris lawmakers, Senegal became relevant to imperial expansion only in the 1880s. Although French military officers appointed as governors of the colony began to launch wars of conquest in the 1860s, Paris considered the creation of a territorial empire in West Africa only in the 1880s. As France recovered from defeat in the Prussian War and a new generation sought to strengthen French power in the world, lawmakers in Paris turned to colonial conquest. Saint Louis acted as the administrative capital of Senegal and the place from which advocates of imperialism imagined the French civilizing mission would spread to West Africa.

By the 1890s, French military officers succeeded in eliminating most of the legitimate heads of local kingdoms and suppressing resistance in the interior of Senegal, called the "Protectorate." In 1895, Paris established the Federation of French West Africa. In 1905, the capital of the federation moved from Saint Louis to Dakar, a burgeoning administrative and commercial center farther south along Senegal's Atlantic coast. Dakar and the town of Rufisque emerged in the late nineteenth century as key locations for the lucrative trade in peanuts. As a result, Senegal under French rule consisted of a vast area subject to French overrule, taxation, and systems of arbitrary justice, as well as a small enclave of African residents in the four colonial towns called the Four Communes (Saint Louis, Gorée, Dakar, and Rufisque) who had access to participation in democratic political institutions.

The theory of assimilation provided an ideological justification for French imperial ambitions in West Africa. Proponents of overseas expansion rationalized French imperialism in terms of its unique ability to spread enlightenment values associated with the French Republic. The idea gained momentum in France after 1871 when France did away with the government of Louis-Napoleon and ushered in the Third Republic. In metropolitan France, this era marked a return to the values of "liberty, equality, and fraternity," and a desire to forge a new republican citizenry that would embrace the universal values embodied by the French Revolution. For advocates of colonialism, French expansion acted as a logical mechanism for spreading French republicanism to areas of the world believed to be ruled by tyranny and aristocracy and defined by oppressive social institutions such as slavery.

In the 1880s, the Ministry of Colonies followed a policy of assimilation with regard to her territories in Senegal. Like older colonies such as Martinique and Guadeloupe in the French Caribbean and the Indian Ocean island of Réunion, Paris instituted a series of political reforms. All adult male residents of Senegal's colonial towns, regardless of race or religion, had the right to elect representatives to city councils, a departmental assembly that had control over part of the colonial budget, and the Chamber of Deputies of the French National Assembly in Paris. Recognition of voting rights and the ability to participate in urban politics, thus, furthered the struggle by Senegalese in the towns for full legal rights as citizens of France.

Blaise Diagne learned politics from growing up amid the electoral campaigns and political meetings that took place regularly in Senegal's colonial towns. He belonged to the population of urban residents known as *originaires*.

The *originaires* claimed permanent residency in one of the Four Communes and viewed themselves as entitled to the same privileges and responsibilities that French citizens enjoyed. This segment of the urban population consisted primarily of African Muslims and a smaller population of Catholics. Gorée residents tended to include more Catholics, whereas the majority of *originaires* in Saint Louis, Dakar, and Rufisque were Muslim. Historically, the *originaires* came to the towns as workers (some as slaves), and played key roles as middlemen traders along the Senegal River valley and in the burgeoning peanut basin to the south. Some served as foot soldiers in the colonial army.

By the early twentieth century, a new generation of Western-educated elites emerged from within this group. They worked as letter writers, interpreters, employees of large French commercial firms in the interior, and lower-level civil servants for the colonial administration. In this capacity, many *originaires* traveled throughout Senegal and French West Africa. Outside the towns they insisted on retaining their "special" status as city dwellers with access to French courts rather than residents of the Protectorate who were subject to the arbitrary laws of the colonial state. Of the Four Communes only Dakar had a small but significant French settler population. This group of small businessmen, professionals, and administrators for the federation increasingly sought political power in urban politics despite being outnumbered by *originaire* voters.

Born in 1872, Blaise Diagne came of age in this era of changing political, social, and economic realities for people of Senegal. As a child of the communes, he certainly experienced and understood the contradiction between French republican ideals and imperial control. Before 1900, urban politics was dominated by French and *métis* residents of the towns. Access to Western education through Catholic schools, literacy in French, and conformity to French civil laws that looked down on polygamy prevented the vast majority of *originaires* from holding political office. While elections depended on the ability of leading political figures to mobilize black African voters through extensive patron-client networks, few actually held political office until 1914. French authorities recognized *originaire* voting rights in the colony but remained ambivalent about granting growing numbers of urban Senegalese full legal rights as French citizens. Moreover, at the turn of the century more *originaires* found their mobility curtailed by a colonial administration more intent on maintaining control over the interior and a French settler population increasingly hostile to *originaire* rights. Blaise Diagne's entry into this debate proved a turning point in establishing citizenship rights for African residents of Senegal's colonial towns.

Blaise Diagne: The Struggle for Equality

Diagne was born and raised on Gorée Island. His mother, Gnagna Preira, worked as a domestic. She traced her maternal line to the Lebou ethnic group of Rufisque and her paternal line to the Afro-Portuguese population of today's Guinea-Bissau. Diagne's father, Niokhar Diagne, came from the Serer ethnic group and grew up in the town of Joal, a key railway depot for the peanut trade. The elder Diagne worked as a cook for a family on Gorée. The Diagnes belonged to the Catholic Church and raised their son as part of the Catholic community. Blaise Diagne spent his early childhood in Gorée and Saint Louis. He attended the elementary school run by a Catholic order on Gorée.

At a young age Diagne's parents entrusted him to Adolphe Crespin, a member of a prominent *métis* family in Saint Louis. This common practice allowed some African children from less-privileged backgrounds to enter into networks of social and economic mobility in the towns. Diagne's affiliation with Crespin may have facilitated his entry into the secondary school in Saint Louis and influenced his decision to further his studies in France like a number of mixed-race children at that time. Yet higher education in colonial Senegal was not equal to that of France, prompting *métis* families to seek government-sponsored scholarships for their children to study in metropolitan France. Few *originaire* families had the opportunity to pursue higher education for their children abroad. After a short time in Saint Louis, Blaise Diagne left Senegal to attend a lycée in Aix-en-Provence. Finding it difficult to adjust to the new environment of southern France, Diagne failed the high school examination. He returned to Senegal in 1890, passed the exam, and graduated at the top of his class from the new secular lycée in Saint Louis.

Diagne's introduction to politics probably came from his exposure to the workings of electoral campaigns in Saint Louis and Gorée and observation of *métis* representatives to these institutions in the late nineteenth century. Métis families such as Crespin, Devès, and Carpot used the council as a forum for debating colonial policy, scrutinizing the policies of the administration, and upholding the principles of equality and democracy that the Republic claimed to stand for. His affiliation with the Crespin family certainly shaped his outlook on the importance of Senegalese participation in urban politics. Adolphe Crespin's brother, Jean Jacques Crespin, garnered a reputation as a skilled lawyer and representative in electoral politics. Known for his radical perspective, he challenged the French to fulfill their claim of fostering democracy by championing a free press and fair elections. As a Freemason, Crespin argued for secularism in education and social services provided by the colonial administration. The dynamic nature of electoral politics and the activities of black, white, and *métis* men and women who used their position to speak out against injustice must have made an impression on the young Diagne.

In 1892, Blaise Diagne decided to compete with other recent graduates for a post in France's colonial customs service. At the time, few black Africans attended French schools or had the opportunity to take the civil service exam for the customs service. No overt measures barred black applicants from competing with white applicants for the position, although we must acknowledge that very few had the opportunity or preparation at the time. In November 1892, Diagne passed the exam and entered the customs service as a second-rank clerk. His career in the customs service proved to be an eye-opening and somewhat tumultuous experience. He began service in Benin, West Africa, and occupied a series of posts in French Congo and Gabon, then the Indian Ocean locations of Réunion and Madagascar. He ended his career in the customs service in French Guiana, South America. As a civil servant, Diagne earned a reputation as an outspoken individual who fought against racism and discrimination and defended the rights of Africans and people of African descent everywhere that he went. Historian G. Wesley Johnson, a biographer of Diagne, noted that one inspector referred to him as well dressed and enthusiastic but very pretentious and that he pushed his superiors to the limit of their endurance. Consequently, Johnson reports, after every post Diagne received the same notation in his personnel file: "Never to be sent to this colony again."[2]

Blaise Diagne did not fit the model of the docile and dutiful *assimilé* that French colonial authorities had in mind. Instead, he viewed himself and other Senegalese as equal to Frenchmen in every respect. In 1898, Diagne faced two months' suspension for insubordination and was forced to take a six-month leave in Paris. Interestingly, while Diagne was sanctioned for his actions, he never faced termination. Some historians have speculated that his ties to the Freemasons in the colonies may have contributed to his professional survival. In addition, Diagne's ties to Crespin, a Freemason who now lived in Paris, where Diagne reportedly was a frequent visitor, may also have helped him to navigate the challenges of being Senegalese in French institutions largely closed to black Africans.

After being denied entry into the Masonic lodge in Dakar, Diagne succeeded in becoming initiated in a lodge in Réunion. He believed in the ideals of fraternity, liberty, secularism, and human progress that the Masons stood for. Masonic lodges in the colonies tended to hold significant influence in colonial affairs because their members often came from high positions in the administration, the military, or the commercial sector. In 1908, when Governor General Augagneur of French Equatorial Africa tried to fire Diagne, his fellow Masons intervened on his behalf. Augagneur did not fire Diagne but instead ordered him to take a leave of absence from his position in Madagascar.

Diagne spent the next fifteen months recuperating from an illness in France. He used this time to become more involved in metropolitan politics and the activities of colonial lobbies. Diagne became a friend of Senator Alexandre Issac of Guadeloupe, whom he probably met in Saint Louis in the late 1890s. Issac often defended the rights of Senegalese against the colonial administration. He first came to Saint Louis at the request of the Devès family, one of the most prominent and influential mulatto families in urban politics. In addition, Blaise Diagne came to know Gratien Candace, a member of the Chamber of Deputies from Martinique. Candace and Issac both gained reputations as human rights activists and as critics of the abuses of colonial rule. During this time in France, Blaise Diagne also met his future wife. In 1909, he married Mlle Odette Villain, a French woman from Orléans. One year later Diagne resumed work with the customs office.

In 1910, Diagne and his wife arrived in French Guiana, South America. He began the post well having received the Cross of the Order of Agricultural Merit for his service in developing public gardens to beautify the penitentiary city of Saint Laurent du Maroni. Yet once again, Diagne found himself embroiled in conflict with his superiors when a group of drunken French sailors insulted him. Diagne first antagonized his colleagues by insisting that they punish the sailors. Then he faced complaints from the French merchant community in Guiana because he did not accept the common practice of bribery to influence customs officials. The merchants accused Diagne of violating his contract when he served as an advisor to the Saint Laurent municipal commission while working for the customs service. Although the merchants asked officials in the capital, Cayenne, to suspend him, his superiors agreed to grant Diagne a twelve-month leave in France instead.

This period marked the crystallization of Diagne's interest in electoral politics. Although he obtained a high level of French education, accepted French religious and political values, and even married a French woman, Diagne continued to face exclusion and rejection wherever he went, within the institutions of the French Empire. Moreover, France began to abandon the concept of assimilation in favor of a policy of association. Association suggested that Africans could never be equal to Frenchmen and, therefore, should develop along separate lines. Diagne certainly experienced frustration as the climate of racism in France and its overseas colonies increased significantly in the years before World War I. While on leave in Paris, he began contributing editorials expressing his ideas on the problem of racism in a number of newspapers. He also began lecturing about France's colonial problems. Diagne even challenged Governor Augagneur, his former nemesis in Madagascar, and other popular French writers to debates on colonial affairs. At this time, Diagne's name began circulating as a candidate for the upcoming 1914 race for the deputy position from Senegal. The only problem was that while Diagne was known in France and in other parts of the empire, few Senegalese knew anything at all about the Lebou customs officer from Gorée.

Senegal's First Black African Deputy

This moment marked a turning point in Blaise Diagne's life. He returned to French Guiana and began studying for the qualifying exam for customs inspector, the highest position available to a career civil servant. In September 1913, he requested a six-month leave to take the qualifying exams in France. Increasingly frustrated by being silenced by his superiors, he considered leaving the civil service to run for electoral office. Gratien Candace and Galandou Diouf, the leader of a new youth movement among young men in Senegal's towns, encouraged Diagne to enter the upcoming legislative race. In January 1914, Diagne left France and returned to Senegal to launch his candidacy for the colony's seat in the Chamber of Deputies.

Having made a name for himself in metropolitan France and its overseas empire, Diagne found himself faced with the challenge of convincing the various interest groups in the communes to vote for him. The established mulatto families and agents of metropolitan French commercial houses generally controlled the electoral machine in the communes. François Carpot, a member of the *métis* elite, held the deputy position since 1902 and had a strong base of support among commune voters and key leaders in the interior. Certain of the support of the small voting population of his hometown, Diagne began the race by courting the leaders of the Lebou community of Dakar and Rufisque. This group traditionally voted for the chosen candidate of the small French settler population. Second Diagne turned his attention to Saint Louis, the most populous of the Four Communes. To gain a base of support in a region controlled largely by the old mulatto families, Diagne had to convince a new group of young and politically astute black African men in Saint Louis of the viability of his candidacy. The group that called themselves the Jeunes Senegalais brought together young French-educated men angered at the injustice of French politics and interested in breaking the French and *métis* hold on electoral politics.

After some debate, the group decided to back Blaise Diagne over the incumbent and the candidate supported by the Devès family. The Jeunes Senegalais found Diagne appealing because he could fight for their rights as French citizens by speaking to the French on their own terms while appealing directly to African people on their own terms. The issue of citizenship rights for the *originaires*, thus, became the hallmark of Diagne's campaign. He attacked the administration and proposals backed by other candidates that sought to reduce or possibly eliminate the legal and political privileges of *originaires* in the colony. Diagne also appealed to the small community of metropolitan French businessmen by citing his extensive experience in the customs office. He assured them of his intention to follow the "rational evolution" of the political process rather than engage in a "brutal revolution."

In an effort to reach Senegalese voters beyond the communes, Diagne traveled to railway towns and small villages to meet with local people in their villages and homes. He promised to address dissatisfaction among peasants and *originaires* in the countryside over unjust and racist policies by the administration. In the communes, Diagne followed the established tradition of electoral campaigns. He relied on public meetings organized according to French law but infused with local African tradition of *palabres* or community gatherings for public speech. Each person had the right to address the group, state his or her position, and debate the issues. Holding the principle of freedom of speech in high regard, these gatherings were staples of the electoral campaign season. The lively meetings allowed the candidates to introduce themselves and their ideas to the voters. At the same time, family politics, neighborhood quarrels, and interest group politics could enter into the debate. Diagne, a native Wolof speaker, managed to hold his own in these assemblies that were conducted in Wolof, the lingua franca of the towns.

Finally, the growth of local newspapers provided another avenue for disseminating information about candidates. Diagne benefited from editorials in support of his candidacy by *La Democratie*, the newspaper of the Jeunes Senegalais. From these sources we know that Diagne defined his platform on the fight to guarantee the political and legal rights of *originaires*. In addition, he argued for the abolition of the head tax, compensation for Lebou whose land had been confiscated to build Dakar, and an improvement in social services. He supported the establishment of a medical school in Dakar, a full lycée in Saint Louis, pensions for elder workers, and the recognition of labor unions. To appeal to French businessmen in the towns, Diagne maintained that he would fight for customs rates favorable to small businessmen, not monopoly merchant firms.

Although the April 1914 election proved contentious, Diagne garnered the highest number of votes in the first round of elections. In the second round held in May 1914, Diagne defeated Carpot and the Devès candidate by winning the majority of votes. His victory was significant on a number of levels. First, it broke the long-established hold that *métis* families and French merchant firms held on commune politics. Second, it marked a moment in which young men of the communes defeated the older more conservative generation. Finally, Diagne's victory raised the issue of citizenship for black African commune residents to the forefront of colonial politics. The colonial administration held the power to dissolve elections suspected of being unfair. Yet despite some complaints by his opponents, the Ministry of Colonies and the administration in Dakar did little to prevent Diagne from assuming his position in the Chamber of Deputies.

The Path to Full Citizenship

The greatest test for Diagne came as World War I escalated from a regional conflict to a global war encompassing western Europe and its colonial territories. Politically, it brought the issue of full legal status for *originaires* who served in the French military to the forefront. Since the late nineteenth century, Muslim *originaires* had petitioned for the right to serve in the regular French army rather than the segregated African units. Like African American soldiers in World War II, service in the military offered *originaire* men the opportunity to prove their loyalty to France and demonstrate their equality as men. In the run-up to the war, Diagne's predecessor François Carpot and members of Senegal's General Council called on Paris to allow *originaires* to perform military obligations by mobilizing for the war. Although these requests were denied, the French military began recruiting more and more Senegalese from inland regions of the colony to serve. Although this effort initially met with some success, by 1913 recruitment fell significantly, and administrators noted that young men were moving to the communes to avoid serving in the colonial troops.

Realizing the manpower shortage faced by France in the first year of the war, Diagne mobilized key leaders among the *originaire* population to encourage young Senegalese men to enlist. On April 1, 1915, Diagne argued on the floor of the Chamber of Deputies for the right of *originaires* to enlist in the regular French army. He maintained that his election confirmed the status of *originaires* as citizens, and as citizens they had to fulfill the same military obligation of all Frenchmen. After some debate on July 8, 1915, the chamber approved a bill acknowledging the right of *originaires* to serve in the regular French military. Gratien Candace and Diagne's allies in the socialist party in the chamber cosponsored the legislation.

Once the bill became law, Diagne faced the daunting task of persuading *originaires* to join the regular French army and Africans in the countryside to join the colonial troops. Although the first Diagne law resolved the question of *originaire* military service, the citizenship question remained unresolved. After a successful recruitment effort, Diagne again brought the issue of *originaire* citizenship before the chamber. In September 1916, Diagne proposed a second resolution that stated, "The natives of the four communes of Senegal and their descendants are and remain French citizens subject to the military obligations imposed by the law of Oct. 19, 1915." It passed both houses of the assembly without debate and was entered into law.

The 1916 Diagne law not only affirmed the legal status of black African commune residents, regardless of religion, but also confirmed over a century of arguments by commune residents for recognition of their unique role in the expansion of French influence in the region and their loyalty to France in times of war. In addition, Diagne's presence in the legislative body reversed proposals by administrators in Dakar and Saint Louis to deny *originaire* rights in the colony and upheld the principles of assimilation over association. Yet this victory also placed Diagne in an ambivalent position with regard to the colonial administration. In 1917, when France found herself in desperate need of colonial troops, the minister of colonies organized a special recruiting mission to Senegal headed by Blaise Diagne. As a result, Diagne led an effort to recruit masses of African subjects to serve on the front lines for the French. Before leaving for this assignment, Diagne secured special concessions for French West African soldiers from the minister of colonies. The government agreed to exempt them from taxation, and provide veterans hospitals, new job opportunities, and the opportunity to apply for French citizenship in order to have the same rights as *originaires*.

Back in the communes, the war disrupted electoral politics. The governor suspended electoral campaigns until the end of the war. A number of Diagne's key supporters in the communes enlisted and served in the front lines in France as well. Diagne, however, shored up his role in the local assemblies by creating a network of supporters on the General Council and municipal councils of the towns. Galandou Diouf, the Saint Louis leader of the Jeunes Senegalais, and Louis Guillabert, the son of an influential *métis* family and supporter of Diagne, served as his liaisons on the Colonial Council, which replaced the General Council after the war. He even founded the first

Western-style political party in the country called the Republican Socialist Party of Senegal. The shift in commune politics after World War I reorganized electoral politics for Senegalese and stimulated new debates about the future of assimilation, association, and colonialism.

The Ambiguities of French Citizenship

Blaise Diagne carried out the rest of his career in the Chamber of Deputies in Paris. He won reelection to the legislative seat in 1928 and again in 1932. During this time, Diagne enjoyed friendlier relations with Bordeaux merchants and the colonial administration. Yet he walked a fine line between supporting French interests and defending African rights. Diagne approved of W. E. B. DuBois's idea for an international organization to champion the rights of black people in Africa and the diaspora but disapproved of Marcus Garvey's concept of Pan-Africanism. He maintained that Pan-Africanism treated all people of black descent as a monolith and didn't account for those who had a special relationship to France and the francophone world. Instead, Diagne focused his attention on advancing the interests of the francophone African community rather than fighting for racial unity between Africa and its worldwide diaspora.

In 1924 Diagne sued René Maran, an award-winning Caribbean novelist and former colonial administrator, for libel. An unsigned article published in the newly established newspaper of the growing *movement noir* called Diagne an agent of French imperialism and accused him of accepting bribes for each soldier he recruited to fight for France in the war. As vice president of the newspaper and head of the tiny but vocal group of West African veterans and Caribbean intellectuals who became radicalized in France during and after the war, Maran became the target of the lawsuit.

Diagne won the case. The trial, which captured the attention of the mainstream press in Paris, however, symbolized the shifting politics of black identity and politics in the post–World War I period. Blaise Diagne's position appeared more conservative vis à vis this increasingly radical and anticolonial black movement.

Once again, Blaise Diagne found himself in a position not simply to represent Senegal in France but to represent France in Africa. In 1931 the Ministry of Colonies named Blaise Diagne undersecretary of state for colonies. Two years later the ministry called upon Diagne to lead a delegation of French and African officials on a tour of French West Africa. Ironically, this position made him an official member of the French government and its colonial administration. Blaise Diagne died in 1934, in the middle of his third term as deputy from Senegal. He left behind his wife and three sons. His oldest, Adolphe, perhaps the namesake of his former mentor, became an inspector general in the French army. Raoul, his middle son, gained fame as a soccer star for the French national team, and Roland, the youngest, returned to Senegal, where he lived permanently.

Blaise Diagne's life embodied the inherent contradiction in French colonialism, which espoused universal rights on the one hand while practicing racial exclusion on the other. His passion for equality corresponded to the most important principles of the Republic, which claimed as its moniker the universal values of "liberty, equality, and fraternity." Yet he faced prejudice and discrimination that sought to deny black people entry into the French Republic. He used his connections to influential individuals in politics in Senegal and Paris as well as his association with fellow Freemasons to enter institutions and fields in France and her colonies that were normally closed to black Africans. Blaise Diagne's public life in the colonial customs service, the French legislature, and the colonial ministry not only broke barriers for people of color in France and its overseas empire but also transformed the nature of French politics.

At the same time Blaise Diagne changed the nature of electoral politics in Senegal. He not only witnessed the rise of a new generation of Senegalese politicians in the country but also affirmed the rights of full-blooded Senegalese, Muslim or Christian, to obtain French citizenship. While he faced an internal contradiction of claiming the privilege of French citizenship for urban residents over those of the countryside, he sought ways to reconcile the division between the two groups. In his lifetime the notion of political participation in Senegal moved from the preserve of the elite populations of the towns to that of the larger country. As a result, Blaise Diagne paved the way for the rise of nationalist leaders like Lamine Guèye and Leopold Sedar Senghor who negotiated Senegal's independence from France in the decade after World War II.

Suggested Readings

Biondi, Jean-Pierre. *Saint Louis du Senegal: Mémoires d'un métissage*. Paris: Denoel, 1987.

Colvin Phillips, Lucie Gallistel. "Blaise Diagne." In *Historical Dictionary of Senegal*, edited by Lucie Colvin Phillips. Metuchen, NJ: Scarecrow Press, 1981.

Conklin, Alice L. "Who Speaks for Africa? The René Maran-Blaise Diagne Trial in 1920s Paris." In *The Color of Liberty: Histories of Race in France*, edited by Sue Peabody and Tyler Stovall. Durham, NC: Duke University Press, 2003.

Dieng, Amady Aly. *Blaise Diagne: Député noir de l'Afrique*. Paris: Editions Chaka, 1990.

Diouf, Mamadou. "The French Colonial Policy of Assimilation and the Civility of the *Originaires* of the Four Communes (Senegal): A Nineteenth Century Globalization Project." *Development and Change* 29, no. 4 (1998): 671–696.

Johnson, G. Wesley. *The Emergence of Black Politics in Senegal: The Struggle for Power in the Four Communes, 1900–1920*. Stanford, CA: Stanford University Press, 1971.

Zuccarelli, François. *La vie politique sénégalaise*. Paris: CHEAM, 1987.

CHAPTER EIGHT

~

Phyllis Ann Edmeade (1920s)

Caribbean Migrant Worker
Deported from the United States

Lorna Biddle Rinear

The migration of workers in search of salaried occupations and better living condi-tions is not a contemporary phenomenon. The experience of failure, however, is rarely described as perceptively as in this article. Caribbean workers have looked at the United States as the "promised land" since the wide gap opened between their home economies based on the export of agricultural crops, and the fast industrial-ization in America in the second half of the nineteenth century. Phyllis Edmeade, a young woman from the British Caribbean island of Montserrat, followed a com-mon path: She went to live with relatives in Boston and found work as a domestic servant. Yet, as historian Lorna Rinear shows, after being jailed for a petty crime, she was caught in the U.S. judicial and immigration systems that, guided by mod-ern, seemingly objective yet highly skewed psychological testing, ultimately deemed her unfit to stay in the country.

Described in immigration records as a nineteen-year-old African black female, standing five feet four inches tall and at 120 pounds "moderately developed and nourished," with black hair, brown eyes, and a scar on the right side of her chin, a large mouth with two front teeth missing, an oval face, and a flat nose, Phyllis Ann Edmeade was admitted into the United States on April 25, 1924. At the time of her entry, records show she could read and write, her health was good, and she had one hundred dollars. Five years later, she was deported.

When Phyllis was returned to Montserrat, British West Indies, for violating Section 19 of the Immigration Act of 1917, her deportation was based on her conviction for petty larceny, a crime considered to involve "moral turpitude," for which she was sentenced to one year in jail. The Act of 1917 was the culmination of a series of statutes that reflected America's growing xenophobia, and concerns about unassimilable immigrants, the uncertain economy, gender roles, and urban crime, including prostitution. In this period, anti-immigrant feelings were expressed in the revival of the Ku Klux Klan; the Red Scare, and the deportation of Emma Goldman and 248 other alien radicals; the Palmer Raids, and almost six hundred deportations; the deportation of Marcus Garvey; and the trial and executions of Nicola Sacco and Bartolomeo Vanzetti. The federal judges in *Tillinghast v. Edmead* chose to interpret the law very narrowly in keeping with the mood of the times. While it seems unbelievable and unjust that a woman could be deported for stealing ninety-five cents, Phyllis's treatment in the American judicial system and the subsequent administrative deportation proceedings were entirely legal. In 1929, she was just one of the 12,907 aliens deported by the United States government.

Phyllis had left her grandmother's home on Gages Estate, St. Anthony's Parish, near Plymouth, Montserrat, to live with her aunt and uncle, Mr. and Mrs. Henry James of 762 Shawmut Avenue, in the Roxbury section of Boston. Traveling from Montserrat, British West Indies, to St. John, New Brunswick, Canada, on the SS *Chignecto*, she proceeded from Canada to the port of Vanceboro, Maine, and on to Boston by train. An only child and the illegitimate daughter of Margaret West and Stephen Edmeade, Phyllis was born July 23, 1904, at the home of her grandmother Sarah Edmeade. Phyllis's mother died when she was three, and her father emigrated to Cuba, leaving Phyllis with her grandmother. Growing up, she attended the Plymouth public school and St. Anthony's Church. Before leaving Montserrat, she worked on W. H. Wilkin's 172-acre sugar plantation, Gages Estate, as a domestic.

Although Phyllis must have known a little bit about Boston before her arrival, Uncle Henry's letters could not have prepared her for a city like Boston in the 1920s. The population of Boston was greater than the entire population of Montserrat, and the majority was white. Phyllis was assaulted by new experiences that included New England weather; the sights, sounds, and smells of a large urban center; modern conveniences; and strange American customs. In Boston, life was artificial in its disconnection from nature, and was structured by unfamiliar customs and laws and machines. The pace and rhythm of Boston must have amazed her. Coming from a rural agricultural community, she may not have been used to marking time by clocks and calendars, but instead by the sun and seasons. She needed to acclimate herself to the cold weather and snow of Boston winters, as well as to wearing heavy clothing, including scarves and gloves, shoes and boots.

In Montserrat, the semitropical climate with hurricanes, the volcanic topography, and earthquakes had structured her life. A small, rocky island, one of the Lesser Antilles, also known as the Leeward Islands, Montserrat has always provided a marginal existence to its population. While the volcanic soil is rich, many parts of the island are too vertical for human habitation, and boulder-strewn hillside fields are difficult to clear and subject to erosion. Modern conveniences and public utilities were unknown on Montserrat in the first half of the twentieth century. Donkeys provided transportation for goods and people. Although Plymouth, the capital, had telephone and telegraph capabilities by 1919, service was not widespread. Until the middle of the twentieth century, Coleman gas lamps, Tilley lamps, Aladdin lamps, and hurricane lamps lit the streets of towns.[1] In homes, people heated irons on coals before pressing clothes, and stoves and refrigerators used kerosene. Water was carried in pails from streams and rivers. Some women still washed their clothes in these natural waterways, although it was against the law to do so.

A blend of English, Irish, and African cultures, Montserratian society had customs, values, and laws that differed from those in the United States. British products were in the stores; British terms were used for common items; and cricket was the most popular sport. In Montserrat in the 1920s, a woman could be arrested and sentenced to seven days' hard labor for "abusive language," and men were still flogged for criminal offenses such as "wandering abroad." As many as half the children born on Montserrat were illegitimate. Marginal economics meant that many young people formed relationships and had children while both partners still lived at home with their families. In both small and large ways, Phyllis experienced the abrupt change that many immigrants experienced when they arrived in the United States.

Fortunately, her aunt and uncle provided a mediating force. Born on Montserrat, they had immigrated to Boston separately: Henry James in 1912, Anna in 1914. After their marriage in 1917, when he was thirty-two and she twenty-two, Anna stayed home with their growing family. Henry worked as a laborer in a stable in 1920. Ten years later, still a laborer, he worked for the railroad, a career trajectory reflective of the differences between life in Montserrat and life in the United States. In 1920, Henry's twenty-one-year old sister-in-law Sarah Allen, who had arrived in 1918, lived with the family and was employed as a maid. Then, in 1924, Henry paid Phyllis's fare and probably supplied the one hundred dollars that she had with her upon entry.

This money paid her eight-dollar poll tax and assured officials that she had enough money to support herself until she could find a job. Without this cash, she could have been excluded as a person likely to become a public charge.

A recognized economic option for young people on Montserrat, migration was viewed as the best means to achieve an improved standard of living. The pattern began at the end of the apprenticeship system in 1838 when large numbers of former slaves began to leave Montserrat. At first, migrants like Phyllis's father looked for work within the Caribbean, including the coast of South America and later in Panama during the building of the canal. When transportation improvements made it easier and cheaper to look for work in the United States, almost 230,000 black West Indians immigrated to the United States between 1891 and 1910, but only 566 West Indians resided in Boston by 1910. The first major wave of immigrants arrived during World War I when wartime disruption stemmed the flow of European workers, and employers looked to the West Indies for laborers. Higher wages pulled immigrants from the larger, more prosperous islands, while overpopulation and the failing economies of the smaller islands pushed other immigrants to the United States. Making up 12.5 percent of the black population, approximately 12,000 foreign-born blacks lived in New England between 1920 and 1930.

In the 1920s and 1930s, 90 percent of the black immigrant population in the United States lived in New York, Boston, and Florida. West Indian immigrants knew that Boston, like New York, would provide jobs. Yet there is some evidence that West Indians felt that Boston was a better choice because it was a cultured city, unlike brash, commercial New York. In the complicated identity of West Indians, anglophilia is a significant factor, and some immigrants believed that Boston was the next best thing to England. Montserratians, in particular, may have felt at home in a city with a distinctly Irish flavor. Additionally, for immigrants who prized education, Boston's many institutions of higher learning provided alternatives to English universities such as Cambridge and Oxford.

Boston was a city of neighborhoods. In the 1920s, the black community in the Boston area was not one community, but rather a number of smaller groups living primarily in the South End and lower Roxbury. The South End was convenient, close to the docks and the business district. In general, West Indians resided along three main streets, Massachusetts Avenue, Tremont Street, and Columbus Avenue, and their side streets. While there were clusters of West Indians living near each other, there was no visible center to the West Indian community, although St. Cyprian's Church functioned as both a religious and a social center. The Caribbean immigrants in Boston were not as visible, nor nearly as influential, as New York's West Indians. Prior to 1965, their numbers never exceeded six thousand. Although the black population composed 3 percent of the total population of Boston between 1920 and 1930, it grew six times faster than the white population as two migrant streams responded to the growing needs of industry. Three-quarters of the black population were not Boston born in the 1920s. Boston-born blacks had as neighbors Southern-born African Americans as well as foreign-born blacks from various parts of the British Empire, especially Canada and the Caribbean.

Boston's West Indian community, composed of sojourners, laborers who wanted steady jobs but expected to return to their island homes eventually, numbered about three thousand individuals aged twenty to fifty in the 1920s. As a minority within a minority, and as a result of their strategy to return to the West Indies eventually, West Indian immigrants did not buy houses, start businesses, or form a neighborhood identity of their own until the 1930s. Although Caribbean families rarely emigrated as a unit, immigration was a family venture. In a pattern of chain migration, men and women, in almost equal numbers, came as individuals. A young man or woman moved to the United States, sending money home until a spouse, sibling, cousin, nephew, or niece, could afford to emigrate. Young children were often left behind with relatives, and money sent home supported them until their passage could be paid for, or until they were old enough to contribute to the family economy by joining their parents.

While formal, church-sanctioned, Christian marriages, especially among the young, were rare, family units existed, consisting of collateral kin, immediate and distant relatives, and even close friends, who pooled their resources together to provide economic stability for the group members, raise the children, and transmit cultural values. Important to West Indians at home in the islands, family relationships became even more valued by those living in Boston, away from familiar foods, customs, and climate. Family members, friends, and other West Indian immigrants helped new immigrants acclimate themselves to Boston by referring them to jobs and places to live, or by taking them in as boarders. Over time, Caribbean immigrants either recomposed their family units or married and started new families in the United States. Few families brought older parents to the United States. This migration pattern was a young person's strategy.

West Indian immigrants moved from a society where they were the majority to a new culture where they joined a low-status minority, whose members were identifiable to the white majority by visible, physical, biological features, rather than cultural factors. Within the black community, however, subgroups existed based on class, occupation, education, and place of birth. The advent of immigrants from the West Indies introduced new problems of social status and social process that throw light on many aspects of the inter-racial pattern. West Indians were lumped together with black Americans by most white Americans, although West Indians had different life experiences, values, customs, and traditions. In Boston, West Indians held on to their ethnic identity, tending to feel superior to American-born blacks. Proud that slavery had ended earlier in the British colonies, many had held better jobs at home in the Caribbean than American blacks did in the United States in the 1920s. In Boston, competition for the same jobs fostered some intergroup antagonisms. Marcus Garvey, among others, tried to make the two groups understand their common cause and their need to unite. Although this did not work well on an organizational level, on a personal level, individuals born in the West Indies and blacks born in the United States worked to-gether, socialized, and intermarried.

One thing all West Indian immigrants remarked upon was American rac-ism. African-descended immigrants like Phyllis experienced a racial discrimi-nation that white immigrant groups did not face upon their entry, such as the daily insult of entering an apartment through the back door instead of the front. West Indians often tried to deny that they experienced racism or dis-crimination. Focused on work and family, and as temporary sojourners, at first they ignored things that American blacks noticed immediately. For example, the segregated black areas of Boston were composed of rental properties that looked run-down and ill-kept, and stores and restaurants in white neighbor-hoods did not always welcome black clientele. Occasionally, ethnic tensions in Boston were expressed with verbal and physical harassment that the National Association for the Advancement of Colored People (NAACP) and others, including the Jewish Anti-Defamation League of B'nai B'rith, tried to record and address. In the United States, the idea that one drop of African blood made a person nonwhite resulted in a binary society. West Indians were unused to this brand of racism. As a result, West Indians employed several strategies to define themselves as British subjects, dressing in tropical styles in the sum-mer and self-consciously speaking English with a Caribbean accent. Strategies such as playing cricket and celebrating British holidays proclaimed that they were not American-born blacks. In the face of racism, West Indian immigrants developed a new race consciousness and a pan-Caribbean identity.

With American-born blacks, West Indian immigrants were on the low-est rung of the ladder economically and politically. Boston's economy in the 1920s was based on shipping, commerce, and manufacturing. These industries provided steady but low-paying jobs to blacks. While virtually all of them could read and write, West Indian men were limited to jobs in manufacturing, transportation, and the growing service sector, while unmarried women usually worked as seamstresses and domestic servants. Their conviction that their stay in Boston was temporary helped them deal with the racism and occupational stagnation they experienced. Although these early West Indian immigrants had middle-class aspirations, most were not professionals or members of the middle class. The 1920 census reports six doctors, three dentists, and two ministers from the West Indies, but no lawyers, teachers, or engineers.

Although as part of the effort to extend rights and citizenship to freed slaves the Naturalization Law in 1870 was amended so that people of African descent could become U.S. citizens, several factors kept immigrants from the West Indies from applying for citizenship. In the 1920s, most still expected to return to the islands eventually. Pride in their West Indian origins, especially during the peak of Garveyism, may have also prevented West Indian immigrants from naturalizing. Unlike European immigrants, West Indians did not gain status by becoming Americans; instead, they joined American-born blacks on the lowest rung of the social and economic ladder. These immigrants saw no advantage to American citizenship at a time when lynchings of black Americans went unpunished and segregation was legal. Becoming American citizens meant that West Indians lost the social status that accrued to them as British subjects. In fact, acquiring American citizenship sometimes attracted criticism from fellow immigrants. Yet black newspapers published in New York City in the 1920s castigated West Indian immigrants for their refusal to naturalize, charging that they impeded the progress of the black community when voting was so crucial to political power. Since universal adult suffrage in the West Indies did not exist until 1951, West Indian men were not accustomed to the rights and responsibilities that citizenship granted. As for women, prior to 1920 they could not vote in most state or federal elections, so officials, settlement house workers, and reformers saw no reason to encourage immigrant women to naturalize.

Living in the community of West Indians in Roxbury, Phyllis watched her cousins Helen (born in 1919), Margaret (born in 1921), and baby Herman (born in 1924) for her aunt Anna. Later she found a job as a live-in maid. As a domestic, Phyllis filled a low-level gender-specific job that few American-born women or white immigrant women were willing to take. As a result, Irish women and black women found an uncontested niche for their services. Live-in domestic situations were safer and provided better living conditions than industrial work and a room in a tenement. In some homes, domestics could organize their own day and chores. At the Hoffenburgs', Phyllis lived in a clean, uncrowded, middle-class home, with good heat and food and few living expenses. Moreover, domestic employment was not subject to seasonal adjustments. For women who had migrated for economic reasons, domestic service was an ideal situation. However, the negative aspects of domestic work meant that most working-class women chose any occupation over domestic service. Isolated, domestic workers were poorly treated by employers, who expected a level of feudal obedience and personal devotion akin to slavery. Long, irregular hours provided little private time or a sense of independence for a domestic worker. Literally they were available to be called upon seven days a week, twenty-four hours a day, especially if they lived in, which is why most preferred day work. Under a private agreement between two parties, domestic workers had little recourse in disputes about duties, hours, and wages; as a result, the average length of tenure for domestic servants was a year and a half.

After working for the Hoffenburgs in Roslindale for three weeks, Phyllis took two of Mrs. Hoffenburg's dresses to her room with the intent of taking them to show her uncle that she was working, and holding them for ransom until she was paid her wages. Caught before she could remove the clothes from the house, Phyllis was arrested. Without a lawyer to represent her, she confessed her plan to the West Roxbury court and pled guilty on the advice of an officer but maintained that the Hoffenburgs were in arrears with her salary. Although she had not removed the dresses from her employers' residence, legally they were considered under her control, and she was sentenced to three months, and admitted to the Charles Street Jail on April 12, 1926.

If her food, shelter, and possibly a uniform were supplied by the Hoffenburgs, Phyllis should not have needed her salary as badly as taking Mrs. Hoffenburg's dresses indicates she did. Several possible interpretations explain Edmeade's actions. She may have felt responsible for sending money back to her grandmother or repaying her uncle. In her testimony, Edmeade claimed that she told Fannie Hoffenberg, "I would have to get my money to carry home to my uncle, or I would have to take him something, and if she did not pay me I would take two of her dresses home to show my uncle I was working and holding these dresses until she paid me. But before I could get the dresses she had me arrested."[2] The pressure exerted on immigrants to pay back loans that could support the migration of additional family members and to send money back to those left behind shaped the lives of sojourners from the Caribbean islands.

Phyllis's problem may have been that she spent her wages instead of repaying her uncle. No longer living with her grandmother in the intimate community of Gages Estate, Phyllis had the chance to escape the traditional controls of family and community in Boston. Living in a large city during the Roaring Twenties, she may have frequented public entertainment spots with other young people, going to shows and amusement parks. Certainly, by September 1925, Phyllis had met Norman Branly and developed an intimate relationship with him, because she was five months pregnant when sentenced to jail. It is also possible Phyllis was preparing for her baby's birth. Knowing that a midwife or a hospital stay would be expensive, Phyllis may have been buying things for her baby or saving money for when she would no longer be able to work.

One plausible explanation for the Hoffenburgs' harsh treatment of Edmeade is simply that Fannie Hoffenburg, an inexperienced housewife of twenty-six, but a new mother, discovered that Phyllis was five months' pregnant. No good housewife would have kept a pregnant maid, thus seeming to condone immoral behavior. Perhaps the two women simply miscommunicated about how and when Phyllis would be paid. It is impossible to know whether Phyllis was a satisfactory maid for Fannie Hoffenburg. Both women brought prejudices, as well as personal history, to this intimate situation. Cultural differences may have exacerbated the terms of employment between Phyllis and Fannie.

Samuel Hoffenburg, listed as a manufacturer in the Boston city directory, had achieved a certain level of success, since he was able to provide his wife with a servant. His wife needed help because she was a first-time mother with a four-month-old baby daughter, Dorothy. Phyllis may have been hired because she could claim experience helping her aunt with the James children. Servants were usually required to provide references, but records do not indicate that Phyllis had any work experience in Boston other than watching her cousins before she worked for the Hoffenburgs. Perhaps Fannie was willing to hire Phyllis without references, or maybe Phyllis was recommended through an informal network of acquaintances and referrals. With her mother living in New York City, Fannie probably liked the idea of hiring a maid who had experience and was close to her own age. A trained baby nurse would have warranted higher wages than Phyllis and might have been harder to find. She might also have been more rigid and intimidating, threatening a new mother's place in her baby's life.

Having come to the United States from Russia in 1904 as a child, Fannie Hatoff Hoffenburg was an immigrant herself. Fannie's and Phyllis's decisions to emigrate from their original homelands could have provided a common ground for understanding and even friendship, but it is more likely that these two young women came from such disparate backgrounds that they could not bridge their cultural differences. Virtually an orphan, Phyllis had made the decision to emigrate as a young adult responding to economic conditions. Like her aunt and uncle, Phyllis took no steps toward becoming an American citizen, probably because she planned to work in the United States during her most productive years and then return to Montserrat to retire. She spoke English, yet she belonged to a racial minority and had lived in the United States only two years when she went to work for Fannie Hoffenburg.

Fannie had entered the United States with her family, which included her father, mother, two brothers, and a sister. In a pattern of chain migration, the two oldest siblings emigrated one year earlier than the rest of the family. Going to school and working in retail forced the Hatoff children to learn English. As a Jew, Fannie was a member of a religious minority, and the Hatoff family probably emigrated due to religious persecution, rather than for economic betterment. However, the Hatoffs intended to become American citizens; they had already started the process of naturalization in 1910. As a white, English-speaking child, Fannie blended into American society after twenty-two years' residence. In Boston in 1926, the girl from Montserrat and the Jewess from Russia met. Cultural, racial, religious, and class differences limited any female solidarity. Probably both women had expectations that were not met.

When the physical exam conducted at the beginning of her incarceration in April revealed that Phyllis was pregnant, she was transferred to Long Island Hospital in Boston Harbor, where she had a hearing with immigration inspector Martin J. Leonard. When offered the chance to have a lawyer present, she admitted she did not have the money to hire one. In her interview, Phyllis claimed that Norman Branly, who worked at a training school in West Newton, was the only person she "ever had relations with" and that he had promised to marry her. Perhaps naïve, and hoping that she would not be sent back to Montserrat, she told Leonard that she believed the young man responsible for her condition would marry her. In his report, Inspector Leonard highlighted the salient points that made Phyllis an undesirable alien. Deportation procedures were initiated based on his evaluation that Phyllis Ann Edmeade was "a person likely to become a public charge (LPC)." Often a charge made against female immigrants, LPC descended from the poor laws of England and reflected the fear that American society would be forced to support immigrants who could not support themselves. Women, limited to menial, poorly paying jobs, often fit this very general category. A warrant pursuant to deportation was issued April 27, 1926. However, the Board of Review recommended that the warrant be canceled since neither her conviction for a misdemeanor nor her out-of-wedlock pregnancy was sufficient to prove that Phyllis was LPC.

On June 21, 1926, Phyllis gave birth to John Stephen Edmeade at Long Island Hospital in Boston Harbor, at the expense of the State of Massachusetts. Released on July 10, she worked to support herself and the baby, but her son limited her employment opportunities. No longer able to find a live-in position, she worked for forty cents an hour, making about eight dollars a week at a time when social workers' studies indicated that at least nine dollars was the minimum needed to survive. Employment was sporadic; at one point when she had not worked for a week, she was forced to apply for help to a private charity, the Family Welfare Society, where she was given about three dollars in aid. It should have been easy for Phyllis to find work. Domestics were always in demand, even in times of economic downturns. Yet in her testimony, Edmeade stated that she needed to apply for charity because she was having trouble finding work.

Phyllis had several choices at this point. If she could have found work as a domestic, she would have needed to either take her baby with her or locate someone to provide child care. As a matter of convention, convenience, and cost, no doubt Phyllis was nursing her baby, so taking him with her was necessary. While it is somewhat feasible to take an infant to work, and hope that it sleeps most of the day, by the time John Stephen was learning to stand and walk, the logistics became much more difficult. No longer content to sleep, he needed to be restrained in some way so that his mother could work uninterrupted, and without worrying that he would make a new mess as she cleaned. Child care has always been an extremely difficult issue for working women. When a reliable person or institution can be found, it often eats up most of the mother's salary. At this point, Phyllis may have been somewhat estranged from her aunt and uncle since the obvious solution would have been for her to leave John Stephen with her aunt, who already had three children at home. However, the same year that John Stephen was born, Anna James gave birth to Josephine. Anna James may not have been physically or mentally able to care for five children under the age of seven.

To Phyllis's credit, she did not take the "easy" way out and become a prostitute at this time, although this was a pattern that reformers saw repeated again and again. Domestic servants who were unwed mothers and could not find jobs turned to the streets to make their living. Prostitution offered women a way to make more money than could be made by legitimate work, as well as a way to survive independent of families or men. Prostitutes saw themselves as making a conscious choice to pursue their new occupation. Phyllis made the choice not to follow that path.

Instead, in the spring of 1927, Phyllis was again arrested for larceny. On March 5, when she needed money to buy milk for her baby, she took ninety-five cents from the mantelpiece at the house where she was living. Phyllis felt she had not committed a crime because she had taken the money while her land-lady Annie Dale was looking right at her. Phyllis admitted taking the money, but she had not anticipated the consequences. Apparently she believed that Dale would be more lenient toward someone with whom she shared race and gender. Phyllis justified her action by saying she had promised to repay Dale the next day when she went to work, that Dale was "a colored woman like myself," and "was holding some of my baby's clothes."[3] Despite this defense, the judge in the municipal court of the Roxbury District of the City of Boston sentenced Phyllis to nine months' incarceration at the Reformatory for Women in Framingham.

When she took the ninety-five cents from Annie Dale's mantelpiece, Phyllis again expressed a desperate need for money. "I was living with a lady and I hadn't worked for several days and I had no money to buy milk for my baby."[4] In 1925, the purchasing power of a dollar was approximately thirteen dollars today and bought more than milk for the baby, but claiming she took the money for her baby provided a sympathetic reason. She may have needed food for herself or money for her grandmother or uncle. The larger question is why Annie, a black nurse and social worker, called the police when Edmeade "borrowed" the ninety-five cents. Obviously Dale did not trust Phyllis to repay the loan. Had this happened before? Did Phyllis already owe Annie money? Why did she have some of the baby's clothes? In a clash of cultures, in both situations where she was accused of larceny, Phyllis did not understand her actions as theft because she had used clothing as collateral, a common practice in places like Montserrat where cash was rare.

Some sort of deeper conflict must have existed between the two women prior to this incident. Of course, Dale may not have realized what the repercussions would be for an immigrant. Born in North Carolina, Annie Dale represented the other community of migrants in Boston, the million black Southerners who moved north between 1915 and 1925. Cultural differences probably made it difficult for the two women to be friends, despite the fact that both were single, young, black women. Annie Dale was thirty-two and Phyllis Edmeade was twenty-one at the time of the theft. The eleven-year gap between their ages represents a huge difference in emotional maturity and life experience. As a nurse and a social worker, Annie Dale was more educated. Perhaps she saw Phyllis as unlettered and uncultured, and there-fore someone who was an embarrassment to her race. Also, while there is no evidence to indicate that Phyllis drank liquor, Dale may have been a teetotaler with a strict sense of Christian morality since she later lived in housing founded by the WCTU. The records do not provide an answer, but the conflict between the two women appears to be deeper than the theft of ninety-five cents.

The conduct of this second larceny case was vital to Phyllis's ability to stay in the United States. Without a lawyer, she pled guilty. Sentenced to nine months' incarceration at the Women's Reformatory in Framingham, Phyllis was advised by an officer to appeal the sentence. As a result of her appeal, she was sentenced to one year in the Suffolk County Jail, Charles Street, Boston, Massachusetts. There, the Massachusetts Department of Correction administered an IQ test on the prisoner on September 8, 1927.

In Montserrat, Phyllis had attended the Plymouth Public School for four years. The history of education on Montserrat reveals the lack of both funding and government commitment to universal education. At the beginning of the twentieth century, thirteen primary schools with religious affiliations and one private school educated the 1,822 girls and 1,774 boys of Montserrat with little aid from the government. Few parents could afford to buy school supplies or clothing for their children. Schools were crowded, and equipment and supplies were inadequate. Sometimes classes were held outside under trees, but chronic absenteeism mitigated the most severe overcrowding problems. Many children missed school because they were needed to work. In 1900, for example, only 45 percent of the children attended classes at any time. Rote learning and memorization were the methods of instruction. With spelling, reading, and Bible classes, the objective of these schools was a moral and spiritual education.

Noting that her school knowledge was limited, the report indicated that although Phyllis had trouble doing mathematical problems, she could count to twenty. Phyllis could read and write, but she did not know the name of the president of the United States or the governor of Massachusetts, and she had a poor grasp of geography and current events. As a British subject, Phyllis probably knew the name of the reigning monarch of Great Britain, and she may even have known the names of the governor of Montserrat and the governor of the Leeward Islands Federation; however, it is not surprising that she was unable to name American officials. Further, Phyllis had not studied geography, although if she had, it would have been the geography of the British Empire. This does not seem to have occurred to the questioning officials. While the level of her education may have been similar to that of American-born black children in the rural South in the early twentieth century, most of them would never be subjected to the scientific analysis of an IQ test that would determine their suitability to remain in the United States.

During the interview, Phyllis was "reasonably pleasant and cooperative, but not altogether truthful in statements regarding her general conduct." She was unemotional, and claimed that she was neither quick tempered "nor subject to excitement or depression." The interviewer noted that no "delusions or hallucinations" were in evidence, and that she was "fully oriented" with a fair memory. Moreover, the report states that Phyllis appeared to have "some insight into her defect. . . . She should not have taken things without permission." In sum, despite appreciating "the need of steady employment and the location of a permanent home," Phyllis had displayed poor judgment, and was judged to have an IQ of sixty-two and a mental age of ten years. Her mental age may have been based on Phyllis's demeanor, described as "reasonably pleasant and cooperative," but making "no emotional display" or "variation of mood."[5] This passive demeanor usually worked as a protective shield, a façade displayed in the face of white authority by a scared, young, black woman, but immigration officials saw it as a lack of intelligence. They concluded that because she was "unreliable," and sexually promiscuous, she would "make a much better adjustment in her native country."[6]

The seemingly objective IQ test was one facet of the science in this period that supported theories about eugenics, racial nativism, and the hierarchy of races with Anglo-Saxons at the pinnacle of civilization. At a time when Mendelian genetics suggested that most personality traits were inheritable, immigrants like Phyllis were perceived to be able to pass on criminality and feeblemindedness to their children. Articles in scientific as well as popular publications argued in a gendered component that women, like all female mammals, exhibited the older, more primitive traits of the race to which they belonged.

Phyllis's case was further complicated by middle-class gender expectations. As a woman, she was held to higher standards of behavior. In this period of social change, amidst concerns about women entering the workforce, flappers and women adrift, Americans tried to legislate morality. Phyllis's illegitimate baby was a strike against her, although not an overt cause of her deportation. Immigrant women, because of their potential as mothers, became the focus of anti-immigrant consternation. Nativist rhetoric about women and childbearing in this period was supported by statistics that showed white, married, middle-class women were having fewer children. It appeared that immigrant women were having more children than native-born white women, that immigrant women were more fecund, and that their large families would overcome the white, Protestant, northern European population. Concerned about "race suicide" and the reproductive rate of immigrants, few Americans wanted Phyllis to stay in the United States with the likelihood that she might have more children who might need public support.

In jail, Phyllis also submitted to a physical exam, including a Wasserman test, a recently developed blood test for the venereal disease syphilis. Reticent about talking to their female patients about sex or ordering a test for a venereal disease, physicians treated few women for this disease. Yet no such reticence prevented immigration officials from ordering a blood test that would reveal the presence of promiscuous sexual activity. At this time of tremendous social and economic change, syphilis became a rallying point for sex and gender anxieties that revealed American society's mounting concerns about the health of individuals as well as the health of the nation. Moral crusaders and anti-immigrationists saw syphilis as an infectious disease as well as a genetic disorder. A "dirty" disease, syphilis was associated with prostitutes, immigrants, and African Americans. In particular, it was associated with women who crossed boundaries and did not meet the moral standards of female purity—women who were loose, uncontrolled, dangerous, and threatening. The assumption was that an immigrant woman who had syphilis was guilty of immoral behavior, and perhaps a prostitute.

Since syphilis could be transmitted from mother to child, it was seen as a hereditary disease. Transmitted from sex partner to sex partner, it was also a contagious disease. In both situations, women were the vector. Since syphilis caused neurological damage, it appeared similar to feeblemindedness, and therefore, an alien with syphilis could be labeled LPC and deportable. Many Americans believed that the solution for this serious social and medical problem was the eradication of prostitution and the exclusion or deportation of syphilitic immigrants. Phyllis's Wasserman test was negative. A positive result would have added another negative mark against her, for the presumption would have been that she was a prostitute. The Progressive Era had fostered a belief in the use of quantifiable, scientific data to solve social problems. As a result, these new tests, the IQ test and the Wasserman, were credited with the ability to answer questions about Phyllis's character and suitability for remaining in the United States.

In addition to the scientific tests, Phyllis also had a hearing with Ida B. Collins of the immigration department on November 19. Although she had the right to be represented by counsel during the interview, she waived it with the explanation that she was "not a bad girl" and would ask her uncle and a lawyer to help her later. Collins noted in her report that Edmeade's reputation was bad, although she provided no specific information or the source of her judgment. In addition to the charge of moral turpitude, Collins asserted that Edmeade, at the time of her entry, had been a person likely to become a public charge. This was based on the fact that Phyllis had not paid for her hospital stay when her baby was born, and on the psychiatric exam that had computed her IQ as sixty-two. This time, looking at the records and Collins's report, the Board of Review recommended deportation. A warrant of deportation was issued November 22, 1927.

On March 5, 1928, Phyllis was discharged from jail with her baby, having served 330 days. At this point she acquired a lawyer, John T. Lane, a black graduate of Suffolk Law School. It is likely that Lane was hired by Phyllis's family or through the West Indian community, perhaps by the West India Aid Society, or by St. Cyprian's Church. On March 12, with Phyllis out of jail on five hundred dollars bail, Lane initiated a petition for a writ of habeas corpus that resulted in a hearing in federal court with Judge James Madison Morton Jr. Habeas corpus protects people from illegal detention or imprisonment by the government.

In his habeas corpus petition, Lane argued that the allegation that Edmeade was a person likely to become a public charge was not sustained, and that the hearing with Inspector Collins was unfair; however, the legal case rested on several other important points. First, deportation was an administrative matter initiated by the federal government through the Bureau of Immigration, part of the Department of Labor in the 1920s. An immigrant in these proceedings does not possess any of the rights guaranteed in criminal proceedings. Lane's writ of habeas corpus, requiring that the court decide whether Phyllis was imprisoned lawfully, moved her case from the administrative setting of the Bureau of Immigration into the federal court system. Such a petition must show that the imprisonment was based on a legal or factual error. The elements or facts of the larceny conviction could not be tried de novo, that is, anew. Forced to assume that the conviction was just, Lane could argue only that it was a legal error to assert that petty larceny involved moral turpitude. This position challenged the accepted understanding that larceny always involves moral turpitude as argued by Sir William Blackstone in his *Commentaries on the Laws of England*, written between 1765 and 1769, and still used today as an important source on classical views of the common law and its principles.

On June 11, Judge Morton issued his opinion in *Ex parte Edmead*, releasing Phyllis on five hundred dollars bail pending an appeal by the government. In his decision, Morton emphasized that in understanding the term "crime involving moral turpitude," law and morality are not the same thing. Noting that crimes involving moral turpitude are ones in which the perpetrator's conduct is "inherently base, vile, or depraved, contrary to the accepted rules of morality," he ended by saying that "I am not prepared to agree that a boy who steals an apple from an orchard is guilty of 'inherently base, vile, or depraved conduct.'" Extending this to the case before him, Morton stated, "The evidence as it stands about the crimes for which Edmead was convicted does not seem to me to prove moral turpitude."[7] Morton's decision argued that the immigration bureau's proceedings were based on an error of law. This meant that the federal courts, rather than the immigration bureau, had jurisdiction over Phyllis's right to remain.

At this point, Phyllis's case was no longer just about her. It became legally significant. Morton had asserted that not all acts of theft were moral turpitude, and that courts had the jurisdiction to reexamine the circumstances of a conviction that could lead to deportation. The government could not let this judgment stand. The decision suggested that immigration officers should examine the facts of the conviction of each and every case. Time-consuming, cumbersome, and costly, this interpretation was not what the legislators had meant when drafting the Act of 1917, according to many federal officials. As a result, Frederick H. Tarr, the United States attorney, and John W. Schenck, the assistant United States attorney, appealed the decision in an assignment of errors dated September 10, 1928. On February 18, 1929, in the First Circuit Court of Appeals, Judges George Hutchins Bingham and Charles Fletcher Johnson reversed Judge Morton's ruling that Phyllis had violated the Immigration Act of 1917 and was, therefore, deportable. The Act of 1917 mandated deportation of an alien who, within five years of arrival, was found guilty of a crime that incurred a one-year jail sentence and involved moral turpitude. The law was clear, unequivocal, and uniformly applied to all immigrants.

Phyllis was desperate to stay and unsure her grandmother would take her back. Having exhausted all legal remedies, in the days before her deportation, she acted out by threatening the matrons at the detention center, announcing she would escape, and calling her lawyer. On October 31, 1929, having been transported from Boston to Ellis Island in New York Harbor, Phyllis Edmeade and her son, John Stephen, were deported back to Montserrat, on the SS *Dominica*. At this point, she disappears from the records. Although Phyllis could never legally return to the United States, her son, as a U.S. citizen, could have and might have.

Phyllis's case played out against a background of rhetoric about immigration and race, morality and gender, dependency and criminality, fueled by the new sciences of the times, including social work, psychology, and genetics. The judges' strict interpretation of moral turpitude and larceny in *Tillinghast v. Edmead* reflected the anti-immigrant animus present in the general public, in popular magazines and newspapers, in scholarly works, in cartoons, and in political speeches. The deportation of Phyllis Ann Edmeade for the theft of ninety-five cents was not an isolated incident but one expression of the mood in the United States in the 1920s. That mood was revealed in both small, individual acts as well as in the laws of the land. It provides the answer to why a Russian immigrant housewife would have her West Indian immigrant maid arrested for almost stealing her dresses instead of just firing her with no references. It explains the negative report of a second-generation German American immigration inspector. It solves the riddle of why a black woman from North Carolina would call the police when she watched her black boarder from Montserrat take ninety-five cents from her mantelpiece. It justifies the judges' strict interpretation of petty larceny as moral turpitude.

The decision in *Tillinghast v. Edmead* quickly became well known. Useful because it was short, clear, and harsh, it provided generations of judges with a way to expunge "bad" elements from American society. Into the 1970s, the precedent set in *Edmead* was usually followed, engendering little criticism or dissent. As recently as 2003, as American society once again becomes more intolerant of immigrants and crime, Edmeade's case has resurfaced as a way to deport undesirable immigrants. Beyond the legal precedent, however, the heart of *Tillinghast v. Edmead* is the tradition of human migration in the Atlantic World.

Sources

City Directory. Boston: Sampson & Murdock Co., 1924–1930.

Ex parte Edmead, 27 F.2d 438 D.C.Mass., 1928.

Martindale-Hubbell Law Directory. January 1935, Vol. I. New York: Martindale-Hubbell, Inc., 1935.

National Commission on Law Observance and Enforcement. *Report on the Enforcement of the Deportation Laws of the United States.* No. 5, May 27, 1931. Washington, DC: GPO, 1931.

Tillinghast v. Edmead, 31 F.2d 81C.A.1, 1929.

U.S. Census Records: http://ancestry.com/.

U.S. Department of Labor, File 55617/96. National Archives, Washington D.C.

Who's Who in Massachusetts: A Biographical Dictionary of Important Living People in the Commonwealth, Vol. Two: 1942–1943. Boston: Larkin, Roosevelt & Larkin, Ltd., 1942.

Suggested Readings

Aiken, Katherine G. *Harnessing the Power of Motherhood: The National Florence Crittenton Mission, 1883–1925*. Knoxville: University of Tennessee Press, 1998.

Bredbenner, Candice Lewis. *A Nationality of Her Own: Women, Marriage, and the Law of Citizenship*. Berkeley, Los Angeles, and London: University of California Press, 1998.

Clark, Jane Perry. *Deportation of Aliens from the United States to Europe*. New York: AMS Press, 1968. (Reprinted from Columbia University Press, 1931.)

Diner, Hasia R. *Erin's Daughters in America: Irish Immigrant Women in the Nineteenth Century*. Baltimore: Johns Hopkins University Press, 1983.

Deutsch, Sarah. *Women and the City: Gender, Space, and Power in Boston 1870–1940*. New York: Oxford University Press, 2000.

Fergus, Howard A. *History of Alliougana: A Short History of Montserrat*. Plymouth, Montserrat: Montserrat Printery, 1975.

———. *Montserrat in the Twentieth Century: The Trials and Triumphs*. Manjack, Montserrat: UWI School of Continuing Studies, 2000.

Gabaccia, Donna, ed. *Seeking Common Ground: Multidisciplinary Studies of Immigrant Women in the United States*. Westport, CT: Frederick A. Praeger, 1992.

———. *From the Other Side: Women, Gender, & the Immigrant Life in the US 1820–1990*. Bloomington: Indiana University Press, 1994.

Higham, John. *Strangers in the Land: Patterns of American Nativism, 1860–1925*. New Brunswick, NJ: Rutgers University Press, 1994.

Hull, Elizabeth. *Without Justice for All: The Constitutional Rights of Aliens*. Westport, CT: Greenwood Press, 1985.

Hutchinson, E. P. *Legislative History of American Immigration Policy 1798–1965*. Philadelphia: University of Pennsylvania Press, 1981.

Irish, J. A. G. *Alliouagana in Agony: Notes on Montserrat Politics*. Plymouth, Montserrat: n. p., 1974.

———. *Alliouagana in Focus*. Plymouth, Montserrat: Montserrat Printery, 1973.

Jacobson, Matthew Frye. *Whiteness of a Different Color: European Immigrants and the Alchemy of Race*. Cambridge, MA: Harvard University Press, 1998.

Johnson, Violet Mary-Ann. "The Migration Experience: Social and Economic Adjustment of British West Indian Immigrants in Boston, 1915–1950." PhD diss., Boston College, 1992.

Kline, Wendy. *Building a Better Race: Gender, Sexuality, and Eugenics from the Turn of the Century to the Baby Boom*. Berkeley, Los Angeles, and London: University of California Press, 2001.

Lowenstein, Edith. *The Alien and the Immigration Law: A Study of 1446 Cases Arising Under the Immigration and Nationalization Laws of the United States*. New York: Oceana Publications, for the Common Council for American Unity, 1958.

Luibheid, Eithne. *Entry Denied: Controlling Sexuality at the Border*. Minneapolis and London: University of Minnesota Press, 2002.

Philpott, Stuart B. *West Indian Migration: The Montserrat Case*. London: University of London, Althone Press, 1973.

Reid, Ira. *The Negro Immigrant: His Background, Characteristics and Social Adjustment, 1899–1937*. New York: Columbia University Press, 1939; repr. New York: AMS Press, 1970.

Smith, Jessie Carney, and Carrell Peterson Horton, eds. *Historical Statistics of Black America: Media to Vital Statistics*. Detroit, MI: Gale Research Inc., 1995.

Sokal, Michael M., ed. *Psychological Testing and American Society, 1890–1930*. New Brunswick, NJ, and London: Rutgers University Press, 1987.

∽

CHAPTER NINE

C. L. R. James (1901–1989)

The Black Jacobin

Jerome Teelucksingh

Painfully aware of racial discrimination, colonial domination, and economic exploi-
tation, writers and activists of African descent became some of the most brilliant
minds of the twentieth century. Through their critical eyes and sharp pens (and
typewriters) the Western world was confronted with dissent over the outcome
of modern industrialism. Debates on racism, colonialism, and social inequalities
dominated the political as well as the intellectual arenas throughout the world dur-
ing this century, giving rise to independence movements in Africa, Asia, and the
Caribbean, Pan-Africanism, civil rights movements in the United States, and the
antiapartheid struggle in South Africa. C. L. R. James, a Trinidadian-born intel-
lectual, activist, and public speaker, was one such brilliant critical mind whose ideas
irradiated far and wide through the Black Atlantic. Historian Jerome Teelucksingh
explores his long life of activism, showing that the cultural diversity of Trinidad
inspired him to propose the union of the working classes, regardless of race or ethnic
background, to overcome exploitation that was common to all.

Cyril Lionel Robert James was born on January 1, 1901, in the British West
Indian colony of Trinidad and Tobago. He was fondly known as "Nello" by
his mother and close friends. His political colleagues referred to him by the
nickname "Jimmy." As a precocious teenager James attended the prestigious
Queen's Royal College in the colony's capital of Port of Spain, and later
briefly taught there. James was a voracious reader of literature and an excited

cricket journalist and gradually underwent an intellectual reformation that would serve as a powerful impetus in his quest for life's meaning. His multifaceted career encompassed diverse activities and fields, as he was simultaneously or at turns intellectual, novelist, avid cricket analyst, occasional politician, newspaper correspondent, cultural theorist, brilliant historian, and eloquent speaker.

As a young adult, James displayed traits of both a rebel and idealist. He found it difficult to accept the yardstick used by the colonial society to judge success and failure. For instance, the overwhelming majority of the Caribbean society believed that respect and success could be achieved only by becoming a doctor, a lawyer, or a politician. Indeed, James never sought to conform to the established order in which the black man was considered inferior. Instead, he conceptualized the need for society to be classless and acknowledged the equality of all human beings.

Interestingly, James's style was unorthodox, and he did not separate the issues of culture, identity, and race from the material struggles. This allowed for the incorporation of Marxism/Trotskyism and Pan-Africanism in a flexible and unique ideology. He conceptualized an autonomous black movement that was socialist in nature but not influenced by the predominantly white trade unions and political parties. One of the crippling colonial legacies was the racial division between the colony's two major ethnic groups—East Indians and Africans. Throughout his life, James promulgated the dire need for racial harmony.

The formulation of his Pan-African paradigm originated in Trinidad. As a boy in Tunapuna, James frequently heard stories of the work and life of Henry Sylvestre-Williams, the island's respectable lawyer and foremost Pan-Africanist. While a teenager, James witnessed a major strike in 1919 among black dockworkers in Port of Spain who were protesting over low wages and deplorable working conditions. The protest received support from the island's major working-class organization—the Trinidad Workingmen's Association (TWA). Though James did not participate, he knew some of the strikers, who were staunch disciples of Marcus Garvey, a charismatic and fearless Jamaican Pan-Africanist residing in the United States. James was a regular reader of the Garveyite publication *Negro World*, which had been deemed seditious by the local colonial authorities and banned in 1920.

Garveyism, with its problack consciousness, outright condemnation of colonialism, and pride in Africa, struck a chord among the black working class in Trinidad and the rest of the Caribbean. James credited Garvey's monumental work in making African Americans more conscious of their African origins and promoting a feeling of solidarity among the people of the

African diaspora. However, James was skeptical of Garvey, particularly of his collaboration with American racists and imperialists, which James saw as an inability to grasp the virtues of industrial organization and as the promotion of a limited racial outlook.

In 1932, James departed for England. This was a watershed as he embarked on a life of activism, writing, and public speaking. While in London he wrote cricket commentaries for the *Manchester Guardian*, and his love for cricket eventually materialized in the timeless masterpiece *Beyond a Boundary* (1963). This study was an in-depth analysis of the early development of West Indian cricket and the complex interaction of ethnicity and class.

Undoubtedly, James was a prodigious writer and dealt with a diverse array of topics. During the 1930s, he contributed fiction and book reviews to the *Beacon*, a literary publication, which was circulated mainly in Trinidad. His literary and historical classics included *Minty Alley* (1936), *Notes on Dialectics* (1948), and *State Capitalism and World Revolution* (1950). Additionally, his repertoire included a historical play on the role of slaves in Haiti's independence entitled *Toussaint L'Ouverture*. It was initially performed in England in 1936, and Paul Robeson, a talented Afro-American actor, played the lead role of Toussaint L'Ouverture. It was a brilliant and provocative analysis of the San Domingo Revolution and declaration of the Negro Republic of Haiti after France failed to subdue the slaves in 1802. The critically acclaimed play would later be published as *Black Jacobins: Toussaint L'Ouverture and the San Domingo Revolution* (1938). The seminal work not only depicted revolutionary politics but also emphasized the significance and interaction of ethnicity, color, and class in the outcome of events in Haiti.

It was primarily during the formative years in England and the United States that James began to comprehend his power to influence persons through radical writings. He documented sympathy for the colony's black working class in *The Life of Captain Cipriani*, which was published in London. This was the first indicator of the potential of James to incite the working class. In highlighting the deplorable working and living conditions among the East Indians and Africans, James had a major impact in radicalizing the Caribbean working class. Not surprisingly, Britain blamed the circulation of the book for the outbreak of the riots during 1937 in Trinidad. Tubal Uriah Butler, an Afro-Grenadian who migrated to Trinidad to work in the oil fields, led a strike in the oil fields in protest of working conditions, wages, racism, and exploitation. The movement later spread to the sugar factories. James openly praised Butler's leadership and radicalism in the social manifestations of 1937. Furthermore, James believed that not only the labor movement but the Trinidadian society was supportive of Butler's anticolonial challenge to the status quo that the upper class and whites attempted to maintain.

The first major display of James's activism was his response to the Italian invasion and occupation of Ethiopia during the mid-1930s. James founded the International Friends of Ethiopia with such prominent members as Jomo Kenyatta, Amy Garvey, I. T. A. Wallace Johnson (a Sierra Leone national-ist), and George Padmore, one of James's childhood friends. Padmore was an ardent Pan-Africanist with a vision for a liberated Africa and improvement of the African diaspora. After the crisis subsided, the group was transformed to a permanent organization, the International African Service Bureau (IASB). This proactive group became the bulwark against imperialism and highlighted the struggles for African liberation. James continued to display concern for African affairs, and from July through October 1938, he edited its monthly journal, *International African Opinion*. In England, James estab-lished a network of friends and forged alliances with groups who influenced his ideology. Among his comrades were T. Ras Makonnen (a Guyanese) and Duse Mohammed Ali (an Egyptian), who was the founder of the *African Times and Orient Review*.

James was involved with the black workers in trade unions and radical working-class groups throughout Europe and the United States. The bet-terment of workers was always on the priority list of James's activities. His activism was not confined to organizing anticolonial and anti-imperialist groups. For instance, in 1934, James agreed to submit a regular column to the magazine *African Review*. While in England, until 1936, James was a member of the Independent Labour Party (ILP). He occasionally addressed their meetings and joined the Marxist group within this organization. James also regularly submitted short articles for the ILP's publications *Controversy* and *New Leader*. In 1936, James helped form the Socialist League and was the editor of its newspaper, *Fight*.

During the years from 1936 to 1951, James resided in the United States. This was a renaissance phase in which James was intellectually powerful, filled with creative energy and very confident. In 1938, James accepted an invitation of the Socialist Workers Party (SWP) to undertake an extensive lecture tour in the United States. James's volatile personal life was evident from the exchange of more than two hundred letters with Constance Webb, an aspiring model and actress, from 1939 through 1948. Most of this torrid correspondence revealed a crucial phase in his life when he began to appreci-ate the interrelation among culture, ideology, and ethnicity.

Due to his radical ideas, James decided to go "underground" in December 1939 and adopted the pseudonym J. R. Johnson in many of his articles that were published in *Labor Action* and *New International*. However, in 1940, James split with the SWP and assisted in the formation of the Workers Party. By 1943 he led a small group, the Johnson-Forest Tendency, within the Workers Party. In 1952, he was deemed a rabble-rouser and Communist threat by the U.S. authorities, briefly interned on Ellis Island, and subsequently expelled from the United States. Despite the public humiliation and expulsion, James believed the fifteen years he spent in the United States were the most important for his political and intellectual evolution. Traumatized but still undefeated, James found solace in England during the next six years.

James's vast and unrivaled knowledge of world events and the intricate contours of his political and literary landscape were largely a result of his extensive travels. Among these international trips that broadened his intellectual horizons were visits to Greece and Italy in 1954, to Italy again in 1956, and to Spain in 1958. His seminal work *A History of Negro Revolt* had a brief chapter, "Revolts in Africa," that analyzed the conditions in Sierra Leone, Gambia, Congo, and South Africa. An increased black consciousness was identified at the time of Ghana's independence, in 1957. During Nkrumah's inauguration, James is reported to have said that the development of Africa was more interesting than that of the Caribbean.

There were numerous requests for James as a speaker on issues relating to Africa. For example, in December 1953, the secretary of the Cambridge University Students' Club invited James to deliver a lecture on an African-related topic. Eventually James agreed to speak on the topic "Africa and the Crisis of Modern Civilization" in January 1954. In September 1958, Présence Africaine, a problack group, invited James to deliver a presentation at this prestigious conference of Afrocentric writers, which was held in Rome.

In 1958, after spending more than two decades in United States and Europe, James, the prodigal intellectual, decided to return to Trinidad. Prime Minister Eric Williams, who was of African descent and leader of a predominantly black political party, the People's National Movement (PNM), gladly welcomed James to Trinidad. James was given the task of editing the PNM's paper the *Nation*. In 1958, James became immersed in regional politics and was elected to serve as secretary of the Federal Labour Party, the governing party of the newly formed West Indies Federation. However, this nascent Caribbean integration experiment soon collapsed.

The commitment of James to revolutionary politics and his history of being embroiled in ideological feuds would haunt him during his sojourn in Trinidad. James and Williams disagreed over a number of issues including the organization of the PNM, and James resigned as editor and bitterly departed from the PNM. The rift with Williams widened as James brazenly criticized the tactics and hypocrisy of the ruling regime.

In August 1965, James and Stephen Maharaj, an East Indian, formed a political party, the Workers and Farmers Party (WFP), which was launched in October 1965. James was also the founder and editor of the WFP's paper *We the People*. The party had its headquarters at Woodbrook in Port of Spain. Emerging from the bowels of the Oilfield Workers Trade Union (OWTU) the political party envisioned a government that was controlled by the working class. The party hoped to establish a sound and scientifically based farming community that would result in labor being enlightened on its rights and its contributions to social progress. The executive of this working-class political party included James, who served as its general secretary and opted to contest the elections on a WFP ticket.

The contribution of James to the trade union movement in Trinidad and Tobago was not infallible. Despite the WFP's idealistic ambitions and claims at being representative of labor, the party never developed comprehensive and necessary links with the island's working class. The grandiose plans of the WFP failed to materialize at the polls. The party received only 3 percent of the votes, and all their candidates lost deposits. In Tunapuna, James was soundly defeated as he received only 2.8 percent of the vote. One of his major shortcomings was the failure of the WFP to gain political power. James contended there was "no sense of direction" of the PNM because Williams had "depoliticized" and "miseducated" every aspect of the country.

The electoral defeat was a blow to James's ego and damaged his political credibility. He soon left Trinidad and never contested any elections. A possible reason for the defeat was that James spent the best years of his life abroad and did not devote sufficient time for building a sturdy political foundation among trade unionists in Trinidad and Tobago. Despite this setback, the reputation of James among the working class remained intact.

James was among the few indefatigable black personalities who made a genuine effort to transcend the racial barriers and unite the colony's working class. Being African, East Indian, Chinese, or Syrian did not pose an obstacle for James, whose outlook was class based. Among his nonblack friends in the trade union movement and politics were Arthur Cipriani, Adrian Cola Rienzi, Stephen Maharaj, and Basdeo Panday. During the 1960s and 1970s, there were other East Indians who publicly expressed admiration and support for James. These included Walter Annamunthodo of the National Union of Sugar Workers, who, at a meeting at Waterloo, launched the Bring Back

CLR James Committee to raise funds for James to visit Trinidad and lecture on the political and social conditions there.

By 1962, a frustrated James returned to England and became actively involved in the revival of Pan-Africanism during the late 1960s. This era marked the onset of black studies at colleges and universities in the United States and black power marches in the Caribbean. During the mid-1960s, Walter Rodney, a Guyanese student at the School of Oriental and African Studies at the University of London, came under the influence of James. Both West Indians were anti-Stalinist, had an interethnic ideology of socialism, and were radically democratic. Rodney later returned to Guyana, formed a political party, and was murdered by the oppressive political regime of Forbes Burnham.

During 1966 and till his death in 1989, James spent time lecturing and working in England, the United States, and Trinidad. His fame had grown, and by the 1960s he was an internationally renowned speaker and advocate for the liberation of Africa and rights of blacks. In the United States, he taught at Federal City College in Washington, D.C. During the following year he came into contact with radical black nationalists, and they founded the Drum and Spear bookstore and a community college, the Center for Black Education. While James was in the United States, his residence served as a meeting place for discussion on issues such as black liberation. James was in constant demand as a magazine writer and was a regular presenter on radio and television programs that dealt with blacks. On November 23, 1964, the British Broadcasting Corporation (BBC) in London thanked James for his cooperation in a program that focused on Kwame Nkrumah of Ghana and Jomo Kenyatta of Kenya. It was obvious that James was well respected by both academics and activists.

In 1967, Tony Martin, president of the West Indian Society at Hull University in England, heard a fiery James denouncing imperialism and racism at a black power rally at Conway Hull and at Speakers' Corner in London. Martin, impressed by this fellow Trinidadian's oratorical skills and vast knowledge, arranged for James to speak at Hull University on the topic of "Black Power and the Third World." The audience thoroughly enjoyed his presentation. In 1968, Rosie Douglas, another West Indian and chair of the Congress of Black Writers at Montreal, invited James to be a guest speaker at their gathering.

He was among the visionaries who initiated plans for the sixth Pan African Congress that was held in Dar es Salaam, Tanzania, in 1974. However, James decided to avoid attendance and involvement because participating

African leaders were interested in regional independence rather than unity for the African continent.

During the 1980s, James continued to be in high demand as a speaker due to his oratorical fame and vast knowledge. In March 1982, James spoke on the topic "Memories of Kwame Nkrumah" at the Africa Centre in London. A few months later, in May, the Sussex African Student Association invited James to lecture to their group. Also during this month, the Oxford University Africa Society expressed their appreciation for James's provocative discourse to the students. In these presentations, James played an important role and made a monumental contribution in sensitizing the next generation of blacks to the existing problems in Africa and promoting black consciousness. The Pan-African Association Uhuru Project, formed to address the problems of Africans in London, had James as a speaker on the topic of "Pan-Africanism: The Present and the Future." In 1983, the program organizer of the Africa Centre thanked James for initiating their lecture series Africa and the Forces of Change. James spoke at the cultural evening of the Hackney Black Alliance of London. In December 1983, James spoke in a seminar on Kwame Nkrumah and Pan-Africanism held at the Commonwealth Institute.

Undoubtedly, James identified with and supported organizations and individuals in the cause of Pan-Africanism. In February 1984, he was invited by the Zimbabwe African National Union (ZANU) to witness their annual congress in August. During this month, James participated in an international conference on Namibia entitled "1884–1984: 100 Years of Foreign Occupation, 100 Years of Struggle." The conference was organized by the Namibia Support Committee in London. In mid-1984 the Tower Hamlets Afro-Caribbean Association in London was instrumental in having James address the students pursuing an Afro-Caribbean history course.

During 1986 and 1987, James made financial contributions to Pan-Africanist activities such as a London-based project dubbed Repatriation of Africans from Jamaica to Afrika. Furthermore, James made a substantial donation to cover the expenses of missions to England, Jamaica, and the United States. Additionally, in January 1987, he made a pledge to the Land Rover Fund. Other prominent personalities in the African diaspora, such as singer Jimmy Cliff, were involved in plans for the return trip to Africa. Persons and organizations expressing interest and support for this idea were John Henri Clarke, the National Black United Front, and the Organization for African-American Unity.

The OWTU was one of the few organizations whose respect and admiration for James never diminished. On February 25, 1980, George Weekes, president of the OWTU, appointed James as Labour Relations Officer of the union. Undoubtedly, the OWTU valued the presence of this international speaker and was delighted when James accepted its offer to visit Trinidad in October 1982. By late 1984, the charismatic James had begun to decline speaking engagements due to deteriorating health.

His impact on the international stage and the influence of his works in the Caribbean did not go unnoticed. For his contribution to the OWTU and trade unionism in Trinidad and Tobago, James received the OWTU's highest and most prestigious award, the Labour Star. Subsequently, in 1987 James received the prestigious Trinity Cross, Trinidad and Tobago's highest national award. As he approached the final years of his life, James's mental capacities had not dimmed, and he continued to pursue his love for writing until his death in 1989.

The public persona of James could be epitomized as the activist par excellence and one of the gifted orators of the twentieth century. His genius assumes even greater proportion when one considers the fact that he possessed only a high school education and never received a university education. His vast literary output whetted the appetite and stimulated the imagination of numerous academics, students, and activists throughout the world. For him the rationale of life was both a historical narrative and a progressive movement. The enigma and legacy of James's thought rest largely upon a paradoxical class-based Afrocentrism and faith in the ability to overcome seemingly overwhelming obstacles. James risked reputation and life as he sought the free and full expression of individual personality.

Suggested Readings

Buhle, Paul. *C. L. R. James: The Artist as Revolutionary*. London: Verso, 1988.

Cripps, Louise. *C. L. R James: Memories and Commentaries*. London: Associated University Presses, 1997.

Dhondy, Farrukh. *C. L. R. James*. London: Weidenfeld & Nicolson, 2001.

Farred, Grant, ed. *Rethinking C. L. R. James*. Oxford: Blackwell, 1996.

Grimshaw, Anna, ed. *Special Delivery: The Letters of C. L. R. James to Constance Webb, 1939–1948*. Cambridge, MA: Blackwell, 1996.

Henry, Paget, and Paul Buhle, eds. *C. L. R James' Caribbean*. Durham, NC: Duke University Press, 1992.

James, C. L. R. *Beyond a Boundary*. London: Stanley Paul, 1963.

————. *The Black Jacobins: Toussaint L'Ouverture and the San Domingo Revolution.* 2nd ed. New York: Vintage Books, 1963.

Laughlin, Nicholas, ed. *Letters from London: Seven Essays by C. L. R James.* Port of Spain: Prospect Press, 2003.

Worcester, Kent. *C. L. R. James: A Political Biography.* New York: State University of New York Press, 1996.

∼

CHAPTER TEN

Robert Robinson (1930s)

Celebrity Worker in the USSR

Meredith L. Roman

Harsh economic crisis and pervasive racism affected the lives of black workers in North America in the 1930s in different ways. After moving to the United States from Cuba in search of professional development and feeling his future as an industrial worker limited, Jamaican-born Robert Robinson chose to migrate again, this time to the Soviet Union. Historian Meredith Roman draws a detailed portrait of African Americans' interests in the Soviet Union in the interwar period and explores the sharp contrast they perceived between their racialized lives in the United States and the absence of racialized prejudice against people of African descent in the Soviet Union. Robinson's trajectory in many ways exposes the complex consequences of racialization that spread in the West in different degrees but also brings up the search for alternative social structures in the interwar period.

On August 22, 1930, Robert Robinson, a twenty-four-year-old black worker, sat in an overcrowded courtroom in Stalingrad, USSR. Just a few months earlier Robinson had been working at the Ford Motor Company in Detroit, Michigan. At that time, he was unaware that Stalingrad even existed, and could not envision that he would be there in August at the center of a trial organized to avenge his honor. In fact, Robinson had been in the southern Russian provincial town for barely a month, yet had already been afforded a celebrity status to which he, as an extremely modest young man, was uncomfortable. Not only were his name and picture circulated widely in the central Soviet press, but his name also appeared in papers across the Atlantic including the *New York Times*, *New York Amsterdam News*, *Pittsburg Courier*, *Chicago Defender*, and *Afro-American*. Glaring at him from across the room and seated at the defendants' bench were Lemuel Lewis and William Brown. These two white American men, also recent migrants to the USSR and former employees of the Ford Motor Company, were his coworkers at the Tractor Factory in Stalingrad. Inadvertently, they had helped propel Robinson to this celebrity status by physically assaulting him on July 24 simply because he was black.

In the month that followed, Robinson, via the all-union newspapers, received numerous telegrams, protest resolutions, and letters from workers around the USSR expressing solidarity with him as their "brother" and demanding that his white American assailants be expelled from the country. Robinson even received an invitation from workers at a major electric factory in Moscow asking him to move to the capital to join their "worker family." He responded by thanking them for their gracious invitation but explained that he must remain in Stalingrad; otherwise, he would only be giving the American racists what they wanted. Although it was not his intention, Robinson's staunch response further solidified his ascendancy as a worker-hero in the country. Robinson's complex feelings about his experiences in the Soviet Union during the 1930s, precipitated by the racially motivated assault and court proceedings in Stalingrad, are emblematic of a larger, indeed, very important story about the relationship between racism, migration, labor, and masculinity during the interwar era.

In May 1930, Robert Robinson boarded the *Majestic* in New York City and began his fully funded journey to the Soviet Union, which would ultimately lead him to the courtroom in Stalingrad. This was not the first time that Robinson had assumed migrant status or boarded a vessel with the explicit purpose of exploring employment opportunities in another land. Robinson was born in Jamaica in 1906, but as was common among other Jamaicans during the late nineteenth and early twentieth centuries, his father had moved the family to Cuba when he was only a toddler to search for work. Since his father abandoned the family a few years later when he was only six, Robinson began working at an early age. He quickly developed a passion for science and inventions, and received four years of formal training as a universal toolmaker. In 1923, at the age of seventeen, Robinson assumed the status of migrant again—this time as a result of his own decision and desire to pursue potential employment opportunities. Like many other men and women from the Caribbean he chose New York City as his destination—the reputed Mecca of black American society.

Having grown up in Cuba, where racial inequalities existed but where racism did not shape every aspect of life, Robinson was completely unprepared for the pervasive racial prejudice and segregation that he confronted in the United States. Over the course of four years, Robinson was routinely denied consideration for advertised positions as a toolmaker even though he was highly qualified for them. Exasperated at being unable to cultivate his skill, Robinson, who became a naturalized U.S. citizen, decided to risk leaving Harlem and migrate yet again in 1927. On this occasion, his destination was the Detroit Ford Motor Company, where he hoped to advance his career and technical skill, in spite of its reputation as a hostile preserve of white male labor. After three years, Robinson had finally worked his way up from floor sweeper to toolmaker. His indefatigable diligence had even convinced factory leaders to enroll him in classes to receive additional technical training.

Yet Robinson's situation was by no means ideal. Although he exercised extreme humility, which included feigning that he had never received any previous formal training, his white coworkers and supervisor constantly harassed him. They tampered with his machine on a daily basis, intending to either physically harm him or, at the very least, cause him to lose his position. The onset of the Great Depression in early 1930 threatened to exacerbate the precarious conditions under which Robinson as a black laborer was forced to work at the Ford Motor Company. Faced with these grim prospects, Robinson signed a one-year, renewable contract to work in the Soviet Union. Representatives of Amtorg, a U.S.-Soviet trading company based in New York City, had offered him a high-paying position as a toolmaker.

Robert Robinson was not the only person of African descent in the United States who decided to travel to the USSR in the decades between the two world wars. Instead he represents the hundreds of black Americans of diverse political and socioeconomic backgrounds who journeyed to the Soviet Union for short- or long-term periods during the interwar era. Similar to Robinson, many of these black American migrants to the USSR had a history of prior migration. They had either migrated from the Caribbean to the United States (primarily to New York City) as part of the flow of some 88,000 individuals to the country from 1900 to 1932, or were part of the great migration of African Americans, an exodus of roughly 1.75 million people from 1910 to 1940, who moved largely from southern regions of the United States to northern cities. To be sure, this previous experience with migration imbued these black men and women, including young Robinson, with the necessary confidence, decision-making skills, and courage to again consider moving—even if for a short-term period—to explore another potential land of hope.

It is important to note that even though all forms of migration required serious contemplation, this was especially imperative in regard to journeying to the USSR. Unlike travel to France, which constituted the other popular European "promised land" of this era, there was considerably greater personal risk and sacrifice involved in deciding to explore Soviet Russia. First, the USSR was logistically more difficult to reach. Second, it entailed dealing not only with a foreign language but also with the Cyrillic alphabet. Third, it necessitated at the very least a tolerance of atheism and Communist ideology. And lastly, individuals who made the trek risked being ostracized by their own families while also invoking additional stigmatization from a U.S. government that already treated black people as second-class citizens. Suspicion and stigmatization were particularly grave prior to 1933 before U.S. leaders officially established diplomatic relations with the Soviet Union. Hence, for those individuals who consciously sought to protest the U.S. racial regime through travel or exile, there was arguably no more powerful political statement at the time than choosing Communist Russia as the destination. This meant that even though Robinson, like some other black Americans, did not necessarily conceive of his travel to the USSR as a political statement, his employment and residence there during the interwar era nonetheless constituted a symbolic boycott of racialized life in the United States where most blacks were divested of their civil rights, denied a livable wage, and subjugated to racial terror.

Certainly, Robert Robinson and all other black migrants to the USSR were motivated to journey there from the United States for a variety of complex, interrelated reasons. Yet these temporary and permanent migrants can be divided into three broad groups based on the principal factor that mitigated their decision to go abroad. The first and most obvious group excludes Robinson because it was composed of African American members of the U.S. Communist Party. These men and women traveled to the Soviet Union for primarily political purposes: to participate in congresses organized by the Communist International (Comintern) or to enroll in one- or three-year programs at either the Communist University of the Toilers of the East (KUTV) or the more prestigious International Lenin School (ILS). One of the most well-known figures from this first group was James Ford, a major speaker at international congresses in Moscow and the American Communist Party's vice presidential candidate in the 1932 and 1936 U.S. presidential elections. Another was Harry Haywood, who played an instrumental role in the Comintern's declaration of black Americans as a nation at its Sixth World Congress in 1928. Haywood attended KUTV and ILS from 1926 to 1930, and emphasized the pride and confidence that sojourns in Moscow conferred upon him and his black colleagues. When he returned to the United States to work in Birmingham, Alabama, fellow African American Communists Hosea Hudson and Joseph Howard admonished him to stop walking quickly with his head held high. They reminded Haywood that he needed to start slumping his shoulders and shuffling his feet to avoid trouble in the Jim Crow South.

Likewise, Robert Robinson was not impervious to feelings of increased confidence that accompanied living in the USSR. But his renewed sense of self-worth stemmed not from Communist ideology, participation in major international congresses, or attendance at Comintern universities. Rather, it was rooted primarily in his ability to engage in and excel at the work that he enjoyed and for which he received a respectable salary. Robinson, therefore, represents the second broad group of migrants whose motivations for traveling to the Soviet Union were predominately economic; that is to say they were black workers who pursued employment in the USSR. As mentioned briefly above, by the early 1930s the United States was reeling from the economic devastation of the Great Depression. In contrast, the Soviet Union was simultaneously experiencing a severe labor shortage that was precipitated by the state's decision in late 1928 to launch a massive industrialization campaign. The large number of jobs available in construc-tion and industrial production for engineers, technical specialists, and skilled and unskilled workers made the Soviet Union an attractive destination not only to white American laborers but especially to their African American counterparts who suffered disproportionately from the Depression's unprec-edented levels of unemployment. Robinson emphasized that in making his decision to leave the United States he had to seriously consider how his strong Christian beliefs placed him squarely at odds with the atheistic tenets of Marxism. But the greater opportunities, higher salary, and job security that employment in the USSR offered allowed him to reconcile that ideological contradiction. Robinson's desire to move his mother to the United States from Cuba and, subsequently, support her financially gave him greater in-centive to subordinate his Christian sensibilities to take advantage of these benefits in Communist Russia. After working in the Soviet Union for only two years, Robinson had settled his mother in Harlem and was sending her $150 each month.

Representatives of this second group of African American migrants did not just pursue positions in factories or at construction sites; they also accepted positions to help modernize Soviet agriculture. Noteworthy among them was a team of agricultural experts from the Tuskegee Institute in Alabama, who traveled to Uzbekistan in 1931 with their wives to assist in the development of the cotton industry. The group's organizer, James Oliver Golden, was unlike the fellow members of the Tuskegee team in that he was a former KUTV student and Communist Party member. Golden was also one of the group's few members who stayed in the country beyond the expiration of their three-year work contract. Golden and his wife, Bertha Bialek, a Polish-born Jewish American woman, decided that in light of the birth of their daughter, Lily, in 1935, it was in their best interest to remain in the USSR. Although the interracial married couple contemplated returning to the United States and settling in one of the more progressive enclaves in the country like Greenwich Village in New York City, Golden's occupational specialty rendered this impossible. To support his family in the economically depressed United States, this cotton specialist needed to live in the rural South, which would have endangered the lives of his entire family. In deciding to stay, Golden and Bialek, like Robinson, faced the many trials and tribulations that living in the politically repressive Soviet Union encompassed for all its citizens. Yet in at least one significant way, their courageous decision to remain in the Soviet Union had an extremely positive impact on their granddaughter, Yelena Khanga, who was the only child of their daughter Lily and her husband, a Tanzanian diplomat. Khanga, who ascended to celebrity status in the early 1990s as the host of a television talk show, emphasized that unlike black children in U.S. schools, she was "never made to feel less intelligent, less capable, less likely to achieve than my white schoolmates."[1]

In addition to Communists and industrial or agricultural workers, there was a third broad group of African Americans who journeyed to the Soviet Union during the interwar era. These men and women were not seeking to study in universities, participate in political conferences, or pursue employment. Instead, they were driven by a desire to engage in a more informal form of study: to examine in person the only country that claimed to have discovered the cure for racism. These included famous intellectual and cultural figures like Paul Robeson, Langston Hughes, and W. E. B. DuBois, as well as common middle-class or professional people who were able to finance the journey to satisfy their curiosity. When an American newspaper reporter asked Raymond Alexander, a Philadelphia lawyer, why he traveled to Moscow, he retorted, "I would go to the Antarctic circle to see the breakdown of the abominable system which holds the Negro in social and economic bondage."[2] Langston Hughes poignantly explained his own and other black Americans' curiosity in regard to the Soviet Union. He emphasized that because the U.S. leaders who sanctioned routine violence against blacks were the same men who tirelessly denounced the Soviet experiment as evil, he, as well as many African Americans, had concluded that Soviet Communism "whatever else it might be—was not unfriendly to the African American."[3] Hughes traveled to Moscow in June 1932 with twenty-one other African Americans to shoot *Black and White,* a film that was designed to explicitly expose U.S. racism. After the film was canceled for reasons that will be addressed below, Hughes further satisfied his curiosity by extending his stay in country and exploring Soviet Central Asia. As he recorded in the NAACP's *The Crisis,* it was on the train ride south from Moscow that he was able to think and feel again as an equal. Hughes became most cognizant of this feeling of equality on the Moscow–Tashkent Express because it was as a young boy riding on the train from New York to the southern United States that he had first learned that his skin color rendered him a "Negro" rather than a full human being. During this trip to Central Asia, Hughes was pleasantly surprised to find Golden and the other Tuskegee cotton technicians, with whom he then celebrated Christmas.

Like so many other African American migrants to the USSR, permanent and temporary alike, Robinson's feelings about his experiences in this "land of hope" during the 1930s were complex. The Stalingrad trial most effectively illustrates this. Robinson had neither anticipated the amount of attention that the attack had precipitated nor asked that his two white American assailants be tried in a court of law. However, he quickly realized that it was highly advantageous for Soviet leaders to pursue this course of action because it allowed them to assert, in a profoundly powerful manner, that racists belonged in a racist country. Accordingly, on August 30, 1930, the court in Stalingrad condemned Lewis and Brown to expulsion from the Soviet Union, a sentence that distressed both workers because it meant returning to the depression-ridden United States. While fully aware of the trial's enormous propagandistic value, at the same time, Robinson conceded that the court proceedings had an immediate, unexpected tangible effect on him. After the sentence of expulsion was issued, Robinson left the courtroom and embarked on what had by then become his routine evening stroll along the Volga. For the first time in his life, he emphasized that he was not on vigilant guard against any potential attackers. Robinson elucidated: "Everything looked the same, but I felt different. Breathing seemed easier, my heart felt lighter, and the tension that was always a part of me was gone. I was floating. 'This must be what freedom feels like,' I thought." Robinson added that the next morning he continued to experience the same new, welcomed tranquility: "As I was putting my clothes on, I even tried to think of things to worry about, so unnatural was this feeling of peacefulness."[4]

Robinson's forthright testimony in the immediate aftermath of the trial, in which he explicitly connected his feelings of freedom with physical safety, exemplifies one of the primary appeals of Soviet society during the 1930s for black migrants, and for black men in particular. The lynching of African American men—a brutal ritualized form of murder that sought to demasculinize the victim and, by extension, black people as a whole—increased steadily during the interwar era. The white male perpetrators typically claimed that the lynched black man had raped a white woman, when in reality the actual victims were African American males who had been so bold as to carry themselves as men. That is, they had held their heads high in dignity, had become relatively prosperous through hard work, and had been so audacious as to insist upon their rights as equal men. Although this form of extralegal justice and terror intensified during the 1930s, the U.S. government repeatedly refused to pass any legislation to end it. The fact that Soviet leaders would never allow the lynching of black American men to occur in the USSR—a guarantee that was made blatantly clear in the swift prosecution of Robinson's white American assailants—cannot be underestimated as an incentive for black American men to consider journeying there and perhaps staying as did James Golden and his white wife. While this guarantee of freedom from bodily harm was rooted to some degree in opportunism—a point that Robinson himself and other black migrants to the Soviet Union readily acknowledged—in reality it still translated into a physical security for African American men that was alien to them in the United States.

It is unsurprising therefore that Robinson was not alone in equating safety with his feelings of freedom in the USSR. Since the early 1930s many African American men experienced what they publicly portrayed as a freedom previously unknown to them as a result of their ability to simply associate with or marry white women (i.e., Russian, European, or American) in the Soviet Union without any threat to their physical safety. Paul Robeson described how in 1934, while on his way to Moscow through Berlin, he was deathly afraid he was going to be lynched. Police had surrounded him on the train platform merely because he was speaking with Marie Seton, a white American woman with whom he and his wife, Essie, were traveling to the Soviet Union. Robeson contrasted his experiences in Germany with those in the USSR. Having originally been reluctant to travel there, Robeson emphasized,

> I was not prepared . . . for the feeling of safety and abundance and freedom that I find here, wherever I turn. I was not prepared for the endless friendliness, which surrounded me from the moment I crossed the border. . . . And this joy and happiness and friendliness, this utter absence of any embarrassment over a "race question" is all the more keenly felt by me because of the day spent in Berlin on the way here . . .

Robeson, who stressed particular amazement that children in the Soviet Union had not been taught to fear black men, further elucidated that "I felt like a human being for the first time since I grew up. Here I am not a Negro but a human being. . . . Here, for the first time in my life, I walk in full human dignity."[5] Robeson in fact felt so empowered by his experiences of equality and freedom that he enrolled his young son, Paul Jr., in a Soviet school while in the country in 1936.

Homer Smith, a member of the *Black and White* cast to which Hughes also belonged, described his experiences in the Soviet Union in similar terms. He stressed that he left the United States to "be free, to walk in dignity . . . to breath total freedom in great exhilarating gulps, to avoid all the hurts that were increasingly becoming the lot of men (and women) of color in the United States."[6] Smith, like Hughes, emphasized riding in sleeping compartments on trains and expressed amazement that he was at times assigned to the same compartment as a white female passenger. Smith's experiences—like those of Robinson, Hughes, and others—were adulterated by an awareness of Soviet leaders' propagandistic motives in denouncing U.S. racism. Three months after the *Black and White* cast arrived in Moscow, Comintern officials canceled the film out of fear of potentially jeopardizing the establishment of diplomatic relations with the United States, which at the time finally seemed imminent. Four cast members denounced Soviet officials for acquiescing to the same American racial prejudice that they claimed to oppose. Yet the majority of the group, including Hughes and Smith, publicly defended the Soviet Union. While of course extremely disappointed in the Soviet leaders' decision, they had nonetheless been afforded an equality that they were historically and routinely denied in their homeland—a situation that they emphasized in their public statements. Moreover, they saw nothing positive to be gained from aligning themselves with the same U.S. leaders who sanctioned their inequality.

Many of the cast members extended their stays in the Soviet Union either by touring other regions of the country like Langston Hughes, or by accepting jobs as Smith did. Smith explained his decision by emphasizing that as a black man his chances of working for a major U.S. newspaper were extremely slim, even though he had a degree in journalism from the University of Minnesota. In the USSR, Smith supplemented his income as a post office consultant and inspector for the Commissariat of Posts and Telegraphs by serving as a Moscow correspondent for the *Chicago Defender* and *Afro-American* under the pen name Chatwood Hall. Thus, like Robinson's, Smith's decision to remain in the Soviet Union was intimately connected to the frustrations at occupational advancement that he knew he would encounter in the United States as a result of his skin color.

After the Stalingrad attack and subsequent trial had propelled him to the status of worker-hero, Robinson continued working at the Stalingrad Tractor Factory until he was transferred in mid-1932 to the First State Ball Bearing Plant in Moscow. Robinson excelled in his new surroundings. He served as an instructor to Russian apprentices in the skill of toolmaking, helped remedy the plant's inefficiencies especially in the gauge department, and was responsible for numerous inventions including several delicate instruments and mechanical devices. As a result of his invaluable contributions, which helped reduce the factory's production costs, Robinson received labor awards, monetary rewards, and additional vacation days. Then, in December 1934, much to his great surprise, his coworkers at the ball bearing plant returned him to celebrity status by electing him deputy to the Moscow city soviet. Not only was Robinson's election covered in the Soviet press, but his name and photograph also appeared yet again across the Atlantic in newspapers like the *Chicago Defender* and *Afro-American*, and in popular mainstream magazines such as *Time*. Just as he had not welcomed the attention that accompanied the Stalingrad trial, Robinson was even more dismayed with his election to the largest city legislature in the USSR. He particularly feared how U.S. authorities would respond, and was aware of how his status as a city deputy furthered Soviet propaganda. As long as this black worker continued to live in and could be shown prospering in the Soviet Union, the country's identity as a society without racism remained relatively secure.

Since Soviet officials' interest in representing the USSR as the homeland of all oppressed peoples served as the underlying reason for his election, Robinson was not the first foreigner or even black man of Caribbean descent who became a member of this body. George Padmore, the famous black radical who was born in Trinidad and migrated to the United States to pursue an education in 1924 (the year after Robinson), had also become a deputy on the Moscow city soviet in 1930. In contrast to Robinson, however, at the time of his election Padmore was a dedicated Communist who was in the capital as a political actor participating in congresses and meetings. Hence he was not concerned about U.S. authorities' response to his election. Interestingly, as a deputy of the Moscow soviet, Padmore had served on a commission to investigate the assault on Robinson in Stalingrad. The fact that Soviet authorities did not consider adequate an apology from Robinson's white American attackers had an extremely strong impact on him. Even after he had renounced Communism in the mid-1930s, Padmore continued until his death in 1959 to cite the trial of Robinson's assailants as evidence that the USSR was the only country that had effectively eradicated racial discrimination.

Just as Robinson had suspected, following his election to the Moscow city soviet the U.S. State Department ordered him to return to the United States immediately. He protested the validity of the order but to no avail. Forced to consider his options, Robinson envisioned returning to the United States in 1935. His prospects were grim. He would not simply be reentering a world in which his skin color would again disqualify him from receiving consideration for any skilled positions in his profession. This situation would be made even worse by the severe economic depression and the stigma that accompanied having worked in the Soviet Union. U.S. employers were extremely reluctant to hire any Americans who had worked in the USSR because they perceived them as troublemakers who would have a negative influence on other workers. But this was particularly the case in regard to black laborers who, it was widely feared, would return to the United States extremely pompous and demand equality with white men. The depositions that white American engineers, architects, and laborers made to U.S. State Department officials when they returned to the country after working in the USSR indicate that they played a significant role in fueling this perception. Many stressed that the "the reception and kindly treatment which American Negroes have had in Russia," where they are "well looked after," had caused them to adopt an "extremely offensive" attitude toward all white Americans.[7]

Considering this situation, if Robinson returned to the United States, then he would most likely be barely able to provide for himself, let alone support his elderly mother, to whom he continued to send a substantial amount of money each month. Faced with this stark reality, the skilled black worker decided to accept his hero-worker status: He reported to the Moscow city soviet to receive his assignment as a new deputy and renewed his work contract, which was about to expire. Robinson initially believed that he had made the right decision by remaining in the Soviet Union, because shortly thereafter, he received word from the Evening Institute of Mechanical Engineering that he had been accepted into a four-year program. Since he was a young boy growing up in Cuba, Robinson had aspired to attend Tuskegee Institute in Alabama and become a mechanical engineer. By enrolling at the Institute of Mechanical Engineering, he would therefore be able to realize his lifelong dream. From Robinson's perspective, fulfilling his professional goals, which was impossible for most black men in America at this time—and the primary reason for his decision to leave the country in 1930—was more important than obeying the same U.S. officials who through occupational racism prevented him and many other black men from realizing manhood.

Yet after he had defied American authorities' order to leave the country, Robinson was forced to exchange his U.S. citizenship for Soviet citizenship.

This did not necessarily inhibit him professionally. Robinson received his mechanical engineering degree in 1944, and was recognized with over twenty medals and awards for the contributions that he made to production at the First State Ball Bearing Plant. It did however seriously circumscribe his mobility. By assuming Soviet citizenship, Robinson did not realize that he would be surrendering his ability to migrate freely, something that heretofore had been a defining feature of his life. As a Soviet citizen of foreign birth, Robinson became the subject of authorities' constant suspicion and surveillance, and his requests for permission to leave the Soviet Union, which he began submitting at the end of World War II, were routinely denied. According to Robinson, Soviet officials could not have their celebrity black worker and symbol of the Soviet Union's racial enlightenment leave the country and thereby jeopardize its image as a society without racism. It was not until 1974 that he received a passport and visa to travel to Uganda, where he served as an instructor at the Uganda Technical College for four years. From there, at the age of seventy-two, Robinson managed to receive permission from the American government to return to the United States in 1978, where he lived as a permanent resident until his American citizenship was restored in 1986. Although ecstatic to be back on U.S. soil, Robinson was profoundly disheartened and disappointed that in the forty-eight years since his departure the political, economic, and social conditions of U.S. blacks had not dramatically improved. Rather, he found that in places like Harlem conditions had deteriorated. Consequently, Robinson was immediately reminded of some of the critical factors that had originally encouraged him to make that fateful, courageous decision to migrate to the Soviet Union in the late spring 1930.

To be sure, while curiosity about what the Soviet Union could offer black people in the 1930s was not the primary motivation to journey there for workers like Robert Robinson and Communists such as Harry Haywood, it nonetheless played a role. That is to say, to some degree, Robinson and all black migrants to the Soviet Union were "pushed" from the United States by the intensification of American racism after the First World War, and "pulled" to the USSR by the promise and hope of freedom from it. After a lifetime of migration that had taken him from Jamaica to Cuba, the United States, the Soviet Union, and Africa, Robinson had become intimately acquainted with the diverse forms, problems, and limitations of "freedom" as it applied to black men. During a brief period in the early 1930s, he, like many other persons of African descent, was able to experience another kind of freedom in the Soviet Union—one that was by no means perfect or unproblematic—but which allowed Robinson to ascend to heights that were then denied him in the United States.

Suggested Readings

Baldwin, Kate A. *Beyond the Color Line and the Iron Curtain: Reading Encounters between Black and Red, 1922–1963*. Durham, NC: Duke University Press, 2002.

Blakely, Allison. *Russia and the Negro: Blacks in Russian History and Thought*. Washington, DC: Howard University Press, 1986.

Garb, Paul. *They Came to Stay: North Americans in the U.S.S.R.* Moscow: Progress Publishers, 1987.

Haywood, Harry. *Black Bolshevik: Autobiography of an Afro-American Communist*. Chicago: Liberator Press, 1978.

Hooker, James R. *Black Revolutionary: George Padmore's Path from Communism to Pan-Africanism*. New York: Frederick A. Praeger, 1967.

Hughes, Langston. *I Wonder As I Wander: An Autobiographical Journey*. New York: Hill and Wang, 1956.

James, Winston. *Holding Aloft the Banner of Ethiopia: Caribbean Radicalism in Early Twentieth-Century America*. London: Verso, 1998.

Khanga, Yelena. *Soul to Soul: A Black Russian American Family 1865–1992*. New York: W. W. Norton, 1992.

Matusevich, Maxim. *Africa in Russia, Russia in Africa: Three Centuries of Encounters*. Trenton, NJ: Africa World Press, 2007.

Robeson, Paul. *Paul Robeson Speaks: Writings, Speeches, Interviews, 1918–1974*, edited by Philip S. Foner. New York: Brunner/Mazel, 1978.

Robeson, Paul, Jr. *The Undiscovered Paul Robeson: An Artist's Journey, 1898–1939*. New York: John Wiley & Sons, 2001.

Smith, Homer. *Black Man in Red Russia*. Chicago: Johnson Publishing Company, 1964.

Trotter, Joe William, Jr., ed. *The Great Migration in Historical Perspective*. Bloomington: Indiana University Press, 1991.

~

CHAPTER ELEVEN

Vicente Ferreira Pastinha (1889–1981)

The "Angolan" Tradition of Capoeira

Maya Talmon-Chvaicer

The transformation of capoeira is a symbol of the mutations of cultural expressions in the African diaspora. A martial art used by gangs in the streets of Brazilian cities in the nineteenth century, capoeira is today a gamelike performing art identified with Africanness worldwide, much like hip-hop and rap, that empowers youth from lower-class backgrounds and affords them a rich identity. Historian Maya Talmon-Chvaicer recounts the history of this transformation, through the biography of one capoeira master, Pastinha, a black Brazilian who learned the philosophy and the movements of self-defense from one of Bahia's last African slaves, Benedito Angola. During Pastinha's life, and thanks to his own efforts, capoeira, which had been considered a threat and was repressed by the police, was recognized as a cultural tradition of the people of African descent, and as that, became part of Brazilian identity and heritage. Capoeira is now practiced by young people worldwide.

Not much is known about Vicente Ferreira Pastinha's family and early life. He was born on April 5, 1889, in Salvador, Bahia, to José Pastinha, a Spaniard who worked as a peddler, and Raimunda dos Santos, a black woman. As a child he suffered a lot from the aggression of an older child named Honorato, who beat him up often. One day, a black man saw his distress and offered to teach him capoeira so that he could deal with his aggressor face-to-face. At the age of ten he took his first lessons with Angola-born Benedito. After a few months he was ready for his first important performance. The unsuspecting Honorato, who continued annoying him, was defeated in a few seconds, never to bother him again. At the age of twelve, in 1902, Pastinha entered the naval school (Escola de Aprendizes-Marinheiros), where he taught capoeira informally to his classmates for the next eight years until he left the navy. Pastinha admitted that

> as a result of things I did as a young and poor boy, the police were often after me. . . . When they tried to catch me I remembered my master—Benedito, and defended myself. They knew I played capoeira and wanted to humiliate me in front of the people. Therefore sometimes with no intention to take advantage of the situation I hurt the police but only to defend my honor and body.

It is generally agreed that the first capoeiristas in Brazil were slaves of West Central African origin. In the 1840s and 1850s, creole (Brazilian-born) slaves and freedmen joined the ranks of capoeira. The authorities saw them as dangerous drifters who committed criminal acts and threatened public order. They were perceived as dangerous and violent offenders when they trained for purposes of recreation, and even more so when their gatherings ended in wild rioting. Consistent efforts were made to obliterate capoeira by a variety of methods. Writs were signed stating that capoeiristas must be arrested and severely punished. Urgent letters were addressed to police inspectors and army officers, demanding that they tighten up patrols and vigilance in trouble spots. Anybody suspected of violating these orders was arrested. Capoeiristas had to sign a promise to obey the law, maintain public peace, and behave properly. Breaking this commitment would lead to arrest and punishment by being recruited into the army. White people's sense of superiority induced them to seclude themselves and show no interest in the culture of African slaves and their descendants, who cultivated their traditions, adapted from those of their homelands. Consequently, official descriptions, as well as reports by tourists and the press, of the blacks' performances and of capoeira were merely synoptic, superficial, and incomplete. In the late nineteenth and early twentieth centuries Brazil was undergoing crucial social and political changes. Slavery was abolished in 1888, and a year later the monarchy was replaced by a republican regime. The concept of *branqueamento* (whitening) prevailed, based on the quasi-scientific racial theories that were taking root in Europe and the United States, utilizing biological "evidence" to affirm the superiority of the white race. The "experts" claimed that, for the sake of eugenics (race improvement), it was imperative to take certain measures to minimize the influence of the blacks and to improve the white genes. These measures included encouraging massive immigration from Europe, prohibiting immigration of blacks and Asians, and forbidding intermarriage. In the last decade of the nineteenth century, European immigrants flooded into Rio, and unemployment, poverty, and disease plagued the city. The government now lacked the means to control the masses, as was not the case in the time of slavery, when owners were held accountable for their slaves' deeds and conduct. The freedmen and the unemployed free men, the lowest and poorest stratum of society, were perceived as posing a threat to the rest of the citizens. Authorities tried to instigate a work ethic as a major value, a reflection of a stable, civilized, and progressive society opposed to hooliganism, idleness, and vagrancy. In this context the new regime, struggling against social and economic instability, began to wage a relentless war on capoeira. The policy of suppression eventually got expressed in the penal code signed on October 11, 1890, when capoeira was outlawed. It was defined as "training and exercise of physical agility and skill practiced in the streets and public squares . . . disorderly walking, running, with or without weapons or tools that may cause physical injury, provocation, disorder or riots, aggressive behavior towards a person that may arouse fear or cause harm."

The picture of capoeira as a martial art and a violent way to solve problems presented by the authorities was partial and biased. There was an obvious contradiction of interests between the authorities and the lower classes, who not only were trying to preserve their African traditions, but also found further ways to express their protest and criticism of the authorities. Despite the government's attempts to present capoeiristas as a threat to the public peace and as enemies of society, the masses admired their skillful and thorough mastery of the game displayed in the squares on festive days and religious processions, thereby making fun of the authorities and turning them into an object of scorn and derision as is evinced in a well-known capoeira song:

Não estudei para ser um padre	I didn't learn to be a priest
Nem também para ser doutor	Nor how to be a doctor
Estudei a capoeira	I learned capoeira
Para bater no inspector	To beat up the inspector

According to Pastinha, in 1910 he opened his own capoeira school in Campo da Pólvora, which he ran for twelve years. The newspaper A *Tarde* published in 1969 an interview with Pastinha, who told the story of those old days:

As a young man, when the youth frequently visited the famous Campo da Pólvora, Vicente Pastinha often "fechou o tempo," threw several policemen to the ground with one blow. He was always persecuted, but never arrested by the police. One day he decided to show up in front of the secretary of public security. Dr. Álvaro Cova, after finding out the truth about some legends related to him, granted him permission to work as a doorman of a music hall.[1]

Campo da Pólvora was not an institutionalized school, and Pastinha had to supplement his income by working as carpenter, newspaper vendor, gambling house bouncer, shoeshine, gold miner, and so on.

Pastinha claimed that capoeira undoubtedly came to Brazil with the African slaves. Enslaved persons were usually forbidden to use weapons and some resorted to this form of martial dance as a means of self-defense. He explained,

> In the days of the great plantations, the owners took a dim view of the capability for mayhem which the natives possessed. Practitioners of capoeira suffered great persecution at the hands of the owner-dominated police. In order to avoid this persecution, the capoeiristas began to camouflage their "sport" by turning it into a weird dance, consisting of pantomime, music, and dances. Capoeira ceased to be a matter of violence and death, and became an amusement.[2]

But some capoeiristas put this art to a violent and aggressive use. Pastinha explained, "This has tarnished the history of capoeira. Is the gun responsible for the crimes it practiced? and the knife? How about the canons? and the bombs?" He justified the authorities' policy: "Capoeira was severely repressed by the police that . . . tried to prevent individuals who abused it from benefiting from aggressive and disorderly conduct since capoeira attracted the lowest strata of society."[3]

Pastinha didn't practice capoeira for nearly the next twenty years. During these years a significant turnabout was evident in the attitude toward capoeira on the part of the intellectuals and the authorities as well as on the part of the lower classes, who were mainly black.

Severe economic problems resulting in poverty and unemployment heightened by the Great Depression's impact on the Brazilian economy, military discontent, and the rise of a new and active elite that advocated change led to a bloodless coup d'état on October 24, 1930. Three social groups were striving to bring about the desired change—the young officers who were eager to climb the social ladder, engineers who used their technical expertise to establish close connections with the military, and industrialists. Others with similar aspirations were the liberal professionals—lawyers and doctors who, despite their conservative upbringing, subscribed to and supported the new reforms imported from Europe. Rejecting the obsolete views of the decadent landed oligarchy, they struck root in the cities. They believed in treating a person according to his or her achievements rather than social class, and supported and encouraged new economic initiatives and attempts to emulate Europe. The military, traditionally active in Brazilian politics, installed Getúlio Vargas as provisional president followed by an entirely different policy toward the capoeira. Under the Estado Novo (the New State) in 1937–1945, Vargas abolished opposition political parties, imposed rigid censorship, established a centralized police force, and filled prisons with political dissidents, while evoking a sense of nationalism that transcended class and bound the masses to the state. Getúlio Vargas's policy advocated the image of a unified Brazil in which whites, blacks, mulattos, *mestiços*, and others could live in harmony, without racial strife. Social scientists inspired by Gilberto Freyre began stressing the positive contributions of the African and Indian cultures to Brazilian society. Their perceived backwardness, seen until then as the result of their origin, was now regarded differently, and explained in terms of cultural differences, lack of education, and poor hygiene. There began an intensive preoccupation with the creation of a national identity, with emphasis on homogeneity as embodied in the new mixed type—the *mestiço*. At the same time, influenced by Nazi theories of race prevailing in Europe, physical education in Brazil was increasing in importance. Capoeira was adopted as Brazil's national sport. Capoeira, like other cultural manifestations such as samba, Candomblé, and carnival had metamorphosed from an activity associated exclusively with blacks into a respectable and significantly Brazilian entity. The authorities' purpose was to usher the blacks into Brazilian society, to legitimize their culture and nationalize it, thereby decreasing their antagonism toward the privileged classes. This process included Candomblé and samba, which received the authorities' approval on condition that they were practiced at certified and known *terreiros de Candomblé* (places of worship of the orishas) or *escolas de samba* (samba schools). But the lower classes also benefited from this policy. The acceptance of their values, traditions, and customs made them feel like acknowledged partners in the creation of a Brazilian national identity. Despite the supervision forced upon them, they could now hold their dances, celebrations, and ceremonies in the open without having to hide from the authorities anymore. Capoeira was also an important tool for inculcating the new values. The most significant change in the concept of capoeira was introduced by capoeira teacher Manoel dos Reis Machado, known as Mestre Bimba, who founded in the 1930s the first Capoeira Regional school. The new capoeira, which by its very name presumed to reflect a local, regional creation, and the product of authentic Brazil, incorporated movements from other Brazilian martial arts like the *batuque* (leg fighting game), and Asian martial arts, like judo, karate, jujitsu, and so on. Manoel dos Reis Machado was born in the neighborhood of Brotas in

Salvador in 1900, the youngest of twenty-five children. He learned capoeira from an Angolan ex-slave named Bentinho. Bimba practiced and gained his experience in capoeira on the docks with black sailors, porters, wagon drivers, storage keepers, and other such laborers. Bimba realized that the attitude to capoeira had to change. Until then it had been identified with the lower classes. He decided to bring capoeira from the street into a school building, and added a further important dimension by turning it into a combat sport. This was why he called his school Centro de Cultura Física e Capoeira Regional (Center of Physical Culture and Regional Capoeira). He also incorporated into capoeira movements from other martial arts hoping that this feature would make it more attractive to people from higher socioeconomic strata of society and would grant it social acceptance. His policy succeeded, as it served government needs as well. On July 9, 1937, his capoeira course received an official seal of approval from the Ministry of Education. This was, in fact, the most significant change in status for capoeira, which was transformed from an activity banned by law to a sport that could be taught in schools. Moreover, the center of capoeira moved from Rio de Janeiro to Bahia. The transfer was a complex process affected by two contradictory trends that happened to coincide, namely, the disrepute of capoeira in Rio, and the declaration that Bahia was the city that reflected authentic African culture in Brazil. Declaring capoeira a healthy sport made it easier for the authorities, and for Getúlio Vargas as their leader, to welcome famous and charismatic capoeiristas from Bahia and ignore those from Rio. Getúlio Vargas himself met with Mestre Bimba, shook his hand, and granted his art the title of "the only authentic national Brazilian sport."

A group very vigorously opposed to the changed status of capoeira, headed by Pastinha, announced the establishment of Capoeira Angola. On February 23, 1941, Pastinha's life took a different turn at Jingibirra fim de Liberdade. Amorsinho, a famous capoeirista from the older generation, owner of the place, asked him to teach capoeira. Based on Amorsinho's reputation, he opened a capoeira school and named it Centro Esportivo de Capoeira Angola (Capoeira Angola Sports Center). Nobody knows when the term *Capoeira Angola* was first used. In the records of the early twentieth century in Rio de Janeiro and Bahia it was called *capoeira* only, and Bimba added the title Regional to the name of his school. Pastinha must have wanted to distinguish his version of capoeira from Bimba's, and wrote in his book *Esportivo de Capoeira Angola* (*Sportsman of Capoeira Angola*):

> I, Mestre Pastinha, hereby declare to all the capoeiras, students, friends and admirers, that I own a Capoeira Angola academy, one of the most well-known in

Salvador, capital of Bahia. It provides first of all physical training in Capoeira Angola and it also provides practice against the misguided philosophy. To sum up, this is what we designate the Capoeira Angola fight.[4]

Although Capoeira Regional was not specified as "the misguided philosophy," everybody in the field knew what he referred to. Despite the numerous objectors to Bimba's methods, and the staunch devotees of the "pure traditional" Capoeira Angola, Pastinha did not succeed in attracting enough students and eventually had to close his academy. He claimed that "when Senhor Amôrsinho died, the center became unprofitable because it was abandoned by all the capoeira masters."[5] In February 1944, he made another attempt to open a school with former students and friends, but failed again for lack of interest. In 1949, he finally managed to establish the center for the studies of Capoeira Angola, which thrived and was officially recognized in 1952. An elected board of directors and various professional and distinguished officers helped him to attract many people from higher social circles that contributed to his school financially as well as politically. The directorate could choose one honorary president and a judge to whom all capoeiristas' grievances were addressed. Pastinha assigned prestigious roles to gifted and diligent capoeiristas, such as an orchestra master, training master, and master's assistant. The center's members met at least once a month, organized public performances, and invited government officials. In these events, Pastinha succeeded in attracting the attention of many tourists as well as of intellectuals such as writer Jorge Amado and painter Carybé. He was soon crowned the cultural representative of the city of Salvador. In April 1966, he was appointed member of the Brazilian delegation to the first international festival of black cultures (FESTAC) held in Senegal.

Pastinha used to declare on every occasion that capoeira originated in Angola. This is evident in the name chosen for his center and a famous song popular among the Angoleiros (those who practice Capoeira Angola): "Sou Angoleiro que vem d'Angola" (I am an Angoleiro who comes from Angola). Folklorist Camara Cascudo cited in 1967 the Luanda-born poet, painter, and ethnographer Albano de Neves e Souza, who contended that

the Mucope in southern Angola have the zebra dance—the "n'golo"—performed in the course of the "Efundula"—the girls' rite of passage, when they stop being "muficuemas"—young girls, and become young women, ready to marry and bear children. The boy who wins in the "n'golo" can choose his wife among the new eligible brides without having to pay a dowry. The "n'golo" is capoeira. The slaves who came from the tribes that went there [to Brazil] through the trading port of Benguela, took with them the tradition of the

leg fighting. With time, what was first a tribal tradition became a defensive
and offensive weapon that helped one survive in a hostile environment. . . .
Another reason that has convinced me that capoeira originated in Angola
is that hoodlums in Brazil play an instrument called berimbau which we call
"m'bolumbumba" or "hungu," depending on the place, and is typically played
[in Africa] by herdsmen.[6]

This explanation became the founding myth of Capoeira Angola. It has
two major goals: first, to designate capoeira as an activity created by free
Africans and perpetuated by their descendants, who are proud of their roots,
and second, to connect capoeira to the ongoing and unceasing social and cultural struggle of the blacks in Brazil's unequal and hierarchical society. The
Angoleiros, who came at that time from the lower socioeconomic strata of
society, raised the banner of the struggle for justice and social equality. This
is evident especially in the popular Angoleiros' songs that deal with slavery,
extol heroes connected to the struggle for independence and social equality,
and stress the contribution of capoeira to Brazil. A case in point is a song
written about Pastinha:[7]

A capoeira rasga o véu dos algozes	Capoeira tore the veil of the hangmen
Na convicção da fé contra escravidão	With conviction of faith against slavery
Doce voz dos teus filhos e heróis	Sweet voice of your sons and heroes
A capoeira ama abolição.	Capoeira loves the abolition of slavery.

Pastinha dedicated his life to setting out the qualities of capoeira that
should grant it respect and honor. He composed a rule of conduct that reflected this attitude: "The fundamental principle of our center is propriety
of conduct. Social education, human solidarity, and above all the practice of
good. Never use the powerful weapon of capoeira unless it is for legitimate
defense or for the good of the motherland. This is the only way to honor my
vision and work for the benefit of our primitive fight—Capoeira Angola."[8]

According to him, "a capoeirista has to keep in mind that capoeira is not
solely an individual preparation for attack or defense against an aggressor, but
should develop, through physical and mental exercises, a real state of psycho-
physical balance. This will make him an authentic sportsman, a person who
controls himself before he can defeat his adversary."[9]

Pastinha perceived capoeira as a "play" in the African sense of the word—
it is part and parcel of a philosophy of life, a way to understand life, to prepare
for it. Capoeira contains all the necessary ingredients one needs to live well
physically and spiritually. It prepares one's body, muscles, and limbs to move
flexibly, steadily, and harmoniously. Music was another important part of ca-

poeira, as he explained: "The musical or rhythm band is not essential in the practice of capoeira, but it is obvious that the 'Capoeira Angola game,' with the rhythm of the typical band accompanying the songs and improvisations of the singers, infuses grace, gentleness, magic and mystery that sparkle with the capoeiras' spirit."[10]

One may deduce from these words, published in 1964, that Pastinha distinguished between Capoeira Angola as a game and capoeira as a contest. While the latter did not need musical accompaniment, in the former the music was an indispensable and vital element imbuing the game with mysticism, elegance, and style. According to Pastinha, "the berimbau [one-string musical arc with resonance box made of calabash] is the primitive teacher. It teaches through sound. It charges our body with vibrations [energy] and 'ginga' [basic movement in capoeira]. The percussion band with the berimbau is not a modern-day set-up, no, it is elementary."[11] Pastinha expresses the African worldview in which the instruments' sounds and rhythms are a means of communication infused with supernatural forces that grant strength and energy and convey messages. Pastinha claimed, "Capoeira is not mine. It is from the Africans. Something from the Africans remained for me. I have inherited something. I am the inheritor of the art of the Africans. But capoeira is Brazilian, it is a national heritage."[12] Pastinha was and felt Brazilian. He also subscribed to the emerging nationalism that characterized the whole period of 1930–1985. His most significant achievement was in formalizing the rules for a Capoeira Angola game that included the "traditional" movements, the trilogy of capoeira songs used in each game (ladainha, chula, and corrido), and institutionalizing the musical instruments used in the roda (circle).

Mestre Bimba, on the other hand, decided to eliminate African elements that didn't fit his vision of capoeira as a martial art. He explained, "In Capoeira Angola the kicks are prescribed or regulated by the berimbau and the pandeiro [tambourine]. But in real capoeira we defend ourselves and attack the enemy. Do I have to wait for the berimbau to tell me how to react when I am attacked? No berimbau and no pandeiro!"[13]

This is a very important observation, because it sheds light on the fundamental differences that had evolved in the roles of capoeira. It was now defined as a martial art that prepared the capoeirista to defend himself against enemy attacks and threats, and as a wholesome social activity, a game and a pastime, a sport for the development of physical skills and for practicing the capability to cope with the vicissitudes of life.

The authorities supported these changes and backed up both styles: Capoeira Angola as a part of Brazilian folklore and Capoeira Regional as a sport. During the 1970s, during the military dictatorship, Capoeira Regional flourished together with other sports, especially soccer. This was a result of the authorities' policy, which used sports as a political tool to redirect the concern of the masses from their daily problems. Capoeira Regional increasingly became the Brazilian national martial art. On the other hand, Capoeira Angola almost became extinct as the authorities persecuted its supporters. Pastinha, who fought for the survival of his center, appealed to the governor of Bahia to award his academy the authorities' recognition as part of Bahian folklore, which could grant him a small fund. "I came to the palace to pay my respects to Dr. Luiz Vianna Filho," he said. "I'm very happy that he is the governor. I came here to ask for assistance. I don't have unreasonable demands . . . only ask for assistance to restore the school."[14]

He tried in vain to get support, but it never arrived. Disappointed and despairing, he complained, "And all this, in Brazil! Brazil that has enough to give, sell, throw away and deny its sons. But everything depends on decrees. Edicts are issued and become ineffectual, ineffectual as the cry for independence."[15]

Embittered and ignored, Pastinha accused the ungrateful authorities' policy that both denied the value of his lifework and prevented his education. "All I have is first grade education. All the rest, I picked up myself. Life taught me to see. We see things that scholars, professors, or politicians don't. I wanted to learn more, but can one who must earn his daily bread, sit and read a dictionary?"[16] With no assistance from the government, Pastinha faced serious economic problems, which worsened with the loss of his eyesight. "I can't see anything, anything at all. Darkness, darkness, always darkness. . . . I live in poverty but I am not begging for charity yet. . . . Jorge Amado doesn't want me to beg for bread, simply because he doesn't want me to become a beggar. But—open your arms and raise them: I live in poverty."[17]

The building where Pastinha had his school was closed in 1971 for renovation, and a restaurant was opened instead. In 1979, when Pastinha was ninety, after incessant pleas, Mario Mendonça de Oliveira, director of the Heritage Foundation, signed a contract with Pastinha allowing him to open a capoeira school on Gregório de Matos Street. Pastinha's devoted and famous students João Pequeno, João Grande, and Angelo taught the practical lessons while he was sitting on a chair and guiding them verbally. The contract included a paragraph obliging Pastinha to teach a number of students free of charge. Students who could afford to pay preferred other schools. A few months later Pastinha had a stroke and was hospitalized, which led to the demise of the school. He died in 1981 at the age of ninety-two, destitute, penniless, and generally forgotten by all but a very few students.

Shortly before Pastinha's death and especially after it, Capoeira Angola saw a renaissance. This was the result of a number of events: First, there were many references in the press to his frail health and the privation he suffered, which may have led to his miserable death; then the open debate as to the condition of capoeira in general and Capoeira Angola in particular became an item of the public agenda. The renaissance was also the result of a special political conjunction of interests. Middle-class blacks now began to speak out against the latent racism in Brazil that barred their way to all key positions. They contended that national identity was merely another form of discrimination. In 1978 black social and political organizations such as the Movimento Negro Unificado (United Black Movement) were established. These movements supported and helped the black community, finding jobs, building shelters for homeless children, instituting education for children and adults; advocated black employee rights as well as the rights of prostitutes, battered women, and street children; and fought for better health care. Another factor for the renaissance of Capoeira Angola was the accelerated development of tourism in Salvador. This aroused great interest and wishes to encourage capoeira as part of the Bahian folklore. Capoeira was presented in front of tourists and guests who bought tickets to watch the performances. These performances, which were advertised as representing Brazilian culture and folklore, were usually performed in halls, sometimes in town squares, in front of middle- and upper-class audiences, for profit or publicity. Pastinha, in an interview a short time before his death, reminisced that during his time "tourists could walk freely visiting everywhere, which is not the case now, when group tours are organized with fixed itineraries depending on the interests of the travel agencies." This was one of the reasons for the decline of many academies including his own.[18] Pastinha stated that "the secret of capoeira dies with me and with many other *mestres*. Today there is lots of acrobatics and little capoeira."[19] A great number of capoeiristas resented the commercialization of the sport and advocated the need to bring capoeira back to its African roots and restore its pristine splendor. The newspaper *Tribuna da Bahia* wrote on September 15, 1981, "Mestre Pastinha became famous and legendary because he taught and disseminated the most authentic way of the capoeira warfare, the one brought from Angola."[20]

In the 1980s, in the wake of the weakening of the military regime until its collapse in 1985, and as a result of similar processes taking place in the United States, radical social changes significantly affected the reevaluation and revived interest in traditions, customs, and values of the African cultures. The rising popularity of soul music in the United States inspired a large number of black Brazilians from the city suburbs to celebrate punk dances and to form carnival groups of blacks, like the Ile Aiye. Different strictly black groups performed in the course of the processions skits on subjects related to the history of Brazil and its blacks. Themes like slave revolts and opposition to slavery included capoeira shows as a means to glorify the blacks. Slogans such as "Black is beautiful" and "black power," imported directly from the United States, were proudly welcomed by many blacks in Brazil. A new style of clothes, hairdos, music, and dance diffused throughout the public at large and was followed by a renewed interest in Africa and its traditions. The carnival festivities, capoeira shows, samba dances, and Candomblé meets became tourist attractions that, apart from being remunerative for the organizers and participants, resulted in greater self-esteem and awareness of the significance of these cultural expressions. Brazilians of African descent saw a massive return to the "sources" and attempts to connect once again with the traditions of the "motherland." Due to the popularity of the subject, a large-scale convention was organized in 1980 on the subject of capoeira; it was called the First Regional Seminary of Capoeira and the Festival of Capoeira Rhythms. It was held in Salvador for five days and included debates, lectures, and demonstrations that attracted a large audience of tourists, capoeira and physical education teachers, officials, and journalists. One of the challenging arguments was that Capoeira Angola had disappeared altogether. Some veteran capoeiristas were incensed at this claim and decided to open a new center of Capoeira Angola in which they would be able to meet and create open capoeira circles. The consequent opening in 1982 of academies by Pastinha's devoted student João Pequeno, named Centro Esportivo de Capoeira Angola and another one called Grupo de Capoeira Angola Pelourinho, reinvigorated the field and gave it a boost. These processes rekindled the embers of interest in this almost defunct style, and new students enrolled in these schools. The Angoleiros stressed more than ever the African elements. They emphasized the style of movement they recognized and sanctioned—the bent knees and the direct and constant contact with the ground.

The differences between Capoeira Angola and Capoeira Regional can be analyzed along the lines of the differences between African and Catholic Portuguese worldviews. When the capoeiristas themselves try to distinguish between the styles of Capoeira Angola and Capoeira Regional, they describe them respectively as *jogo baixo* (low game) and *jogo alto* (high game). The reason is that while in Capoeira Angola the players are bent and frequently touch the ground and the movements are relatively slow, in Capoeira Regional the movements are fast, vertical, and upward, involving a lot of acrobatics and kicks. Some of Capoeira Regional members believe that the differences are due to the age of the founder of Capoeira Angola, Mestre Pastinha, who was fifty-two when he opened his capoeira school in 1941. Owing to his advanced age, he would have adapted capoeira to his own physical limitations. This explanation is an example of the lack of comprehension and ignorance of the essence of Capoeira Angola. African religions are geocentric (with the earth as their center). They are based on the benevolence of the forces of nature or on polytheistic properties whose characteristics represent various aspects of the nature of man. The gods connect with man when the believers personify them in ceremonial dances, hence the dance and the dancers are expressions of the human soul and the gods' spirit. This also explains the constant need to reach toward the ground and feel it with the bent legs. In Christianity, the soul and the spirit are separate from the body. Christian philosophy is based on the paternalistic and monotheistic belief that God is not in man but high above him, in a superior sphere, in an eternal heaven. Hence the distinction between the physical and the spiritual aspects of man, and the reason the latter controls the former. This worldview is expressed in the dance style embodied in the aspiration to elevate the dancer to exalted spiritual heights. The entrance of capoeiristas with a European aesthetic outlook was expressed in the attempt to straighten the bent body, the addition of turning somersaults and cartwheels with straight legs and knees, and the reduction of the downward bending and ground touching. Nowadays veteran *mestres* cry out against young men who lack the knowledge and understanding of the African Brazilian cultures and see capoeira as only a sport and a martial art accompanied by music that creates the right ambience. They express scathing criticism especially against new *Regionais* who lack the understanding, affinity, and respect for music in general and the berimbau in particular. They say that many capoeiristas regard the music as mere accompaniment and act in the circle as they wish with no regard for the berimbau's instructions. This ever-increasing tendency distinguishes even more clearly between the styles, a new phenomenon led by some relatively new teachers. Since for them capoeira is a martial art and a sport, they focus on its technical and acrobatic aspects. The wish to present capoeira as a sport and a martial art that surpasses the foreign martial arts has forced out mystical elements and rituals perceived by many capoeiristas as witchcraft or superstitions. Today, however, more than ever before, there are capoeiristas who try to bridge the gap between Capoeira Angola and Regional, even though these styles represent diametrically opposed philosophies of life. These people adopt what they like from the two styles, and create countless hybrids, depending mostly on the masters' predilections.

Pastinha's cry that the secret of capoeira died with him was only partially true. The goals, essence, characteristics, and language of capoeira have become diversified. The variations on the theme of capoeira incorporate numerous traditions, which are influenced, among other things, by different perceptions of esthetics, as well as by African, African Brazilian and Catholic/Christian convictions, rituals, symbols, and religious beliefs.

But Capoeira Angola has not perished, nor has its secret. New capoeira *mestres* continue, in their way, to teach this wonderful art using Pastinha's perceptions and worldview. A relatively new song written by one of the most famous contemporary teachers, Mestre Moraes, sums up the essence and function of Capoeira Angola today:

Capoeira é uma arte	Capoeira is an art
Que o negro inventou	Invented by the black man
Foi na briga de duas Zebras	In the fight between two zebras
Que o N'golo se criou	The N'golo was created
Chegando aqui no Brasil	Arriving in Brazil
Capoeira se chamou	It was called capoeira
Ginga e dança que era arte	Ginga and dance that were art
Em arma se transformou	Became weapons
Para libertar o negro da senzala	To liberate the black man from the
do senhor	master's slaves' quarter
Hoje aprendo essa cultura para me	Today I learn this culture for my
conscientizar	conscience
Agradeço ao pai Ogun	I am grateful to father Ogun [God of war]
A força dos Orixás	To the power of Orishas
Camaradinha	Comrade

Nowadays Capoeira Angola is thriving in Salvador Bahia thanks to a number of academies run by top teachers like Mestre João Pequeno, Mestre Curió, Mestre Moraes, Mestre Valmir, and others. Capoeira Angola has spread throughout the globe, especially in the United States, where Mestre João Grande, Mestre Acordeon, Mestre Cobra Mansa, and others teach it. It is also popular in Europe: in Germany, France, Switzerland, Sweden, Denmark, Portugal, and England.

Mestre Pastinha's legacy is alive and sung by all the capoeiristas:

Jogo de dentro	Inside game
Jogo de fora	Outside game
Jogo bonito	It is a beautiful game
Esse jogo de Angola	This game of Angola

Suggested Readings in English

Assunção, Matthias Röhrig. *Capoeira: The History of an Afro-Brazilian Martial Art.* London: Routledge, Taylor & Francis Group, 2005.

Browning, Barbara. "Headspin: Capoeira's Ironic Inversion." In *Everynight Life: Culture and Dance in Latino/a America,* edited by Celeste Fraser and Jose Esteban Munoz. Durham, NC: Duke University Press, 1997.

Butler, Kim. *Freedoms Given, Freedoms Won.* Piscataway, NJ: Rutgers University Press, 1998.

D'Aquino, Iria. *Capoeira: Strategies for Status, Power and Identity.* PhD diss., University of Illinois, Urbana-Champaign, 1983.

Downey, Gregory John, *Incorporating Capoeira: Phenomenology of a Movement Discipline,* PhD diss., Department of Anthropology, University of Chicago, 1998.

Holloway, Thomas. "'A Healthy Terror': Police Repression of Capoeiras in Nineteenth-Century Rio de Janeiro." *Hispanic American Historical Review* 69, no. 4 (November 1989): 637–676.

Lowell, Lewis. *Ring of Liberation: Deceptive Discourse in Brazilian Capoeira.* Chicago: University of Chicago Press, 1992.

Talmon-Chvaicer, Maya. *The Hidden History of Capoeira: A Collision of Cultures in the Brazilian Battle Dance.* Austin: University of Texas Press, 2008.

———. "The Criminalization of Capoeira in Nineteenth-Century Brazil." *Hispanic American Historical Review* 82, no. 3 (2002): 525–548

CHAPTER TWELVE

~

Malcolm X (1925–1965)

A Pan-African Revolutionary

Alan Bloom

The twentieth century saw the emergence of a number of critical and charismatic po-
litical leaders of African descent throughout the Atlantic World. They often shared
the diagnosis of the problems afflicting their folk, yet differed in their approaches to
tackling them. Pan-Africanism was one of the strongest ideological currents of the
century, an ideal to unite Africans and their descendants in the diaspora as one
people in the struggle against colonial dominance, economic exploitation, and racial
discrimination. Pan-Africanism motivated political actions, such as the foundation
of the Organization of African Unity, and also fueled the struggle for civil rights,
giving an international tone to African American demands. Malcolm X was one of
the most influential black leaders of the century, and historian Alan Bloom brings
us a nuanced analysis of his trajectory, putting him in the context of the civil rights
campaign, and arguing that Malcolm's goals rested beyond desegregation and fran-
chise: He struggled for human rights for all people of African descent.

Comparisons between Martin Luther King and Malcolm X often juxtapose
the optimistic King with his dream for an integrated America to the pes-
simistic Malcolm X with his critique of what he called the American nightmare. But students and scholars alike would be remiss to take this comparison
too far, for Malcolm X also had a dream—a dream, like Martin Luther King's,
that was based on the ultimate objective of achieving freedom and equality
for people of color. Malcolm X, however, chose to pursue a different path

than King and the other mainstream civil rights leaders. Malcolm X believed that the integrationist, reform policies of the civil rights movement were not the answer, because they always could be co-opted by powerful people who opposed change. Instead, he favored a more radical approach that aimed to internationalize the problem of racial oppression by creating a united front of exploited people from around the globe. Malcolm X wanted not integration, but black liberation; he wanted not civil rights on a national level, but human rights on an international one. To that end, in the last year of his life Malcolm X founded the Organization of Afro-American Unity (OAAU), which he hoped would be the catalyst for a Pan-African revolution. That prospect for revolutionary change, ultimately, was Malcolm X's dream.

But to understand the Malcolm X who became a Pan-African revolutionary in 1964–1965, it is necessary to go back and examine his earlier years. Malcolm X led a life of drastic changes. Born in 1925 in Omaha, Nebraska, Malcolm Little was to become an enigmatic figure who over the course of his lifetime would take on many different names and identities. According to one scholar, it is best to divide his life into four periods: "Malcolm Little: the Exploited; Detroit Red: the Exploiter; Malcolm X: the Self-Emancipator; and El-Hajj Malik El-Shabazz: the Social Liberator."[1]

Exploitation best defines Malcolm Little's earliest years, as it was racism that ultimately caused his family's demise and left him scarred as a young boy. Malcolm came from an activist family in which both his parents championed the back-to-Africa movement of Marcus Garvey and his Universal Negro Improvement Association (UNIA). After the family moved to Lansing, Michigan, the young Malcolm occasionally attended UNIA meetings, where he witnessed his father, Earl, inspire fear—and anger—in the white community because he refused to accept the so-called proper place that white society demanded of him. In 1928, white supremacists burned down the family home, and just a few years later, in 1931, they reportedly murdered Earl. After his father's death, the Little family quickly disintegrated; the state institutionalized his mother, separated the children, and placed the half-orphan Malcolm in a detention home. As a young, bright pupil, Malcolm had his world crushed further when a teacher told him that he should not seek to be a lawyer, but, as a good Negro, should be sure to keep his expectations low.

During the next phase of his life, Malcolm Little transformed into "Detroit Red," the streetwise, urban hustler who believed that the game was either exploit or be exploited. He chose the former. Moving among Boston, Detroit, and New York City, Red held some menial jobs, but mostly embraced the "hustler ideology" and participated in all sorts of scams, including drug trafficking, prostitution, bootlegging, playing the numbers, and burglary.[2] In 1946, this parasitic life ended when he was imprisoned for breaking and entering, larceny, and possession of firearms.

Behind bars at Charlestown prison in Massachusetts, Malcolm experienced religious and educational awakenings that triggered his self-emancipation phase. During his first few years of incarceration, however, Malcolm was not ready for such a change; in fact a vicious disposition earned him the nickname "Satan" from his fellow inmates. In time, though, at the behest of a few of his siblings, Malcolm joined with a group of prisoners who had become members of the Nation of Islam (NOI), an organization that was to transform Malcolm's life yet again. The NOI provided him with discipline, moral rectitude, and a religious foundation. Moreover, through the teachings of Elijah Muhammad, the leader of the NOI, Malcolm developed a philosophy that could explain the racist world that surrounded him. Under Elijah Muhammad's tutelage, Malcolm heard that the white man was "a devil" and "the enemy" and that the only path to fulfillment was through separation from whites. Malcolm's burgeoning intellectual curiosity developed in earnest when he became a voracious reader consuming books by W. E. B. DuBois and Carter Woodson. These volumes provided him with "intellectual vitamins" and introduced him to forgotten episodes of African American history that had been whitewashed by the official keepers of America's history.

Upon leaving prison in 1952, Malcolm Little claimed a new identity for himself by replacing the Little surname with an X. In the process, he rejected the legacy of slavery that previously had determined his very name and took on an X that represented his lost African surname—and symbolically the surname every African American had lost because of slavery. With his newfound freedom Malcolm soon turned his energy toward building the NOI, a job he mastered so completely over the next decade that he became Elijah Muhammad's national spokesperson. Under Malcolm's charismatic leadership, the NOI grew dramatically, building more than two hundred new temples across the United States and having its membership increase from a few hundred to perhaps fifty thousand.[3] Throughout the 1950s, then, while Martin Luther King and the modern civil rights movement adopted the tactics of mass demonstrations and nonviolent resistance to fight for African American rights and tear down a society based on segregation, Malcolm turned his back on white society and channeled his efforts into the NOI. While King became the voice of the civil rights movement and integration, Malcolm voiced his appeal for black separatism.

Despite Malcom's successes within the NOI, on March 8, 1964, the relationship between Malcolm X and Elijah Muhammad became untenable, and Malcolm was forced to break from the organization. What caused them to split apart? Elijah Muhammad and the Nation of Islam claimed that the split stemmed from Malcolm's controversial statement that President John F. Kennedy's assassination was a case of "the chickens coming home to roost." Clearly, though, Malcolm X had worn out his welcome in the NOI before this incident. His extensive power and public visibility caused many of his fellow ministers to seethe jealously. Moreover, Malcolm's campaign to expose Elijah Muhammad's extramarital affairs and illegitimate children further inflamed the situation. Finally, an increasingly politically active Malcolm X found himself out of step with the NOI. While proud that Muhammad's organization had championed economic self-determination for African American communities over the years, he also was chagrined that the NOI took an apolitical stance when it came to the larger battle that African Americans were waging against oppression. Less than a week after the separation Malcolm X announced the formation of his own new religious organization, the Muslim Mosque, Incorporated (MMI). This institution was to be the religious base of Malcolm's movement, and he hoped that it would provide "the spiritual force necessary to rid our people of the vices that destroy the moral fiber of our community." It also would work "to eliminate the political oppression, the economic exploitation, and the social degradation suffered daily by twenty-two million Afro-Americans."

After leaving the NOI, Malcolm radically changed his identity once again; this time he would alter his religious and political orientations, take on the name El-Hajj Malik El-Shabazz, and in the process become a social liberator. The trigger for this transformation occurred in the spring of 1964 with his journey to the Middle East and Africa. In his "Letter from Mecca" Malcolm explained how his pilgrimage to the holiest of Muslim sites brought him to an entirely new awareness about Islam and race relations. As he joined together in the same ritual experiences as his fellow pilgrims, Malcolm encountered "a spirit of unity and brotherhood" of all races that he believed never would have been possible in the United States. Through these experiences Malcolm developed a more nuanced understanding of race, which allowed that brotherhood could transcend racial differences. Moreover, he concluded that Islam was the one true religion capable of overcoming such racial animosities.

While the trip to Mecca transformed Malcolm's views on race and religion, his ventures in Africa had no less a dramatic influence on his political philosophy. Freed from the apolitical agenda of the NOI, Malcolm became an activist bent on social liberation; in short he became a Pan-African revolutionary. Malcolm had long had a fascination with Africa, and while stationed in Harlem he had been able to develop it further. He not only studied, but also applauded the Pan-African movements of Marcus Garvey and W. E. B. DuBois, which called for the liberation of Africa from colonial control, as well as attempted to unite the peoples of Africa with those of the African diaspora. In the late 1950s Malcolm forged relationships with African leaders from Ghana, Kenya, and Egypt, while cultivating similar bonds with leaders from Asia, the Middle East, the Caribbean, and the United Nations. In 1959 he even traveled to Africa. In 1964, after going to Mecca, Malcolm continued to build on these earlier experiences by embarking on a political and diplomatic mission to Africa inspired by Julian Mayfield, an African American expatriate who lived in Ghana, "the very fountainhead of Pan-Africanism." Indeed, Ghana's expatriate community formed a Malcolm X Committee, which planned a jam-packed calendar for its charismatic visitor. As the first African American leader of his generation to go to Africa and discuss the common plight of America's disenfranchised black population and Africa's postcolonial peoples, Malcolm was greeted with much fanfare. Wherever Malcolm traveled he was treated as a diplomat, and by the end of his visit he had gained private audiences with prominent leaders from Egypt, Ghana, Nigeria, Tanzania, Kenya, Uganda, and Algeria. Moreover, Malcolm developed a pride in Africa because of its great natural resources, its potential to be a breadbasket to the world, and its strategic location between East and West.

These travels in Africa transformed Malcolm from a black nationalist into a Pan-Africanist. As a black nationalist, Malcolm believed that African Americans should have control of their own separate communities. But Malcolm had an epiphany. He began to reject the term *black nationalism*; he began to think more broadly. No longer, he believed, should African Americans emphasize their own parochial problems; instead, they must think internationally and reach out to people of African descent from around the globe. Indeed, Malcolm maintained that "the single worst mistake of the American black organizations, and their leaders, is that they have failed to establish direct brotherhood lines of communication between the independent nations of Africa and the American black people." But that mistake could and should be rectified, he argued; it was time for African Americans to join the world's Pan-African movement. Upon returning to the United States, Malcolm asked Americans to ponder "what can happen, what would certainly happen, if all of these African-heritage peoples ever *realize* their blood bonds, if they ever realize they all have a common goal—if they ever *unite*?" Indeed, Malcolm hoped that Pan-Africanism could accomplish for people of the African diaspora what Zionism had done for the Jews who were scattered during their own diaspora. Malcolm observed that Jews often had a strong relationship with Israel even though they never traveled there. Likewise, Malcolm suggested that while African Americans "might remain in America physically . . . we must 'return' to Africa philosophically and culturally and develop a working unity in the framework of Pan-Africanism."

Malcolm was convinced that conducting an effective Pan-African campaign against oppression demanded a series of paradigm shifts. Foremost, Malcolm became an internationalist. According to Malcolm, African Americans could no longer be narrowly or nationally focused in their efforts, and rather than continue to battle on "the American stage," they would have to set up camp on "the world stage." He suggested that activists abandon their overreliance on American support for their cause, and instead, reach out to nonwhite peoples around the globe. After all, there was an abundance of natural allies in Africa, Asia, and Latin America, since many countries in these regions were seeking their independence from Western powers. Additionally, Malcolm maintained that African Americans had to change their focus from *civil rights*, which were domestic concerns, to *human rights*, which were international ones. The battle over civil rights, as Malcolm accurately pointed out, was seen by other countries as inherently an American problem that demanded American solutions. In contrast, human rights were inherently a world problem. The key, then, as Malcolm saw it, was to turn the movement for civil rights into a movement for human rights. In this light, it became helpful to point out that the abuses heaped upon African Americans in the United States were akin to those experienced in the Congo and South Vietnam. Finally, Malcolm argued that African Americans would be wise to seek justice not before the federal government of the United States, but before the leaders of the United Nations. Whereas African Americans had little to no leverage in Washington, D.C., Malcolm recognized that the members of the United Nations offered the potential for a sympathetic hearing. In particular, Malcolm relished the image of how embarrassing it would be to the United States if, as the so-called leader of the free world, it was charged with violations of the UN charter of human rights, as South Africa had been. As a reporter for the *New York Times* noted in January 1965, there was great wisdom in Malcolm's tactics, since placing racial problems in an international context at the time of the Cold War "would give the African states more leverage in dealing with the United States and would in turn give American Negroes more leverage in American society."

Malcolm believed that for his idealistic notions of Pan-Africanism to be successful, it was essential to have unity among the oppressed people of color across the globe. Malcolm noted that Africans and African Americans must see their problems as inseparable. In Malcolm's estimation, race relations in the United States and postcolonial politics in Africa were linked: "You can't understand what is going on in Mississippi if you don't understand what is going on in the Congo. . . . They're both the same. The same interests are at stake." To facilitate such an understanding, Malcolm pleaded with people of color across the globe to submerge their small differences so that they could join together and address their oppressors. As Malcolm explained it, "we have a common enemy. . . . We have a common oppressor, a common exploiter, and a common discriminator. But once we all realize that we have a common enemy, then we unite—on the basis of what we have in common." The unity shared by the United States and Africa, Malcolm explained, could not be an end in itself; rather, this notion of unity also had to extend to the rest of the third world. As an example of such potential, Malcolm often pointed to the Bandung Conference of 1955, which included twenty-nine states from Africa and Asia. The conference called for Afro-Asian economic and cultural development and resistance to Western forces of imperialism and colonialism. In the Bandung Conference, then, Malcolm saw a model for his evolving notion of internationalism.

There was an additional reason that Malcolm embraced internationalism. For Malcolm, who as a hustler had run numbers, the civil rights movement in the United States simply never added up. Malcolm never saw the efficacy of concentrating so much energy on civil rights in America, because as a minority in the United States African Americans always would be at a disadvantage. Without the power of numbers, he explained, African Americans always would have to approach their government "as beggars, with our hat in our hands." Consequently, Malcolm wanted to improve his odds, and from his travels abroad he found a way to do so. By forging alliances in the United States, Malcolm calculated that African Americans always would be limited in power by their sheer lack of numbers, but if they reached out to African, Arab, Asian, and Latin American allies, the situation would shift decidedly. Although African Americans were a minority in the United States, as part of the world's nonwhite population they were on the side of the majority. Or, as Malcolm put it, once the downtrodden saw their shared experiences, then "the oppressed people of this earth make up a majority, not a minority—then we approach our problem as a majority that can *demand*, not as a minority that has to beg."

Thus in the last year of his life, Malcolm evolved into a Pan-African revolutionary. He did not seek integration, but liberation; moreover, he rejected reform through nonviolence in favor of revolution by any means necessary. Malcolm believed that political change came through violence and was fond of saying that leaders of the American Revolution like George Washington and Patrick Henry did not preach nonviolence. After all, Malcolm concluded, "There is no such thing as a nonviolent revolution. . . . Revolution is bloody, revolution is hostile, revolution knows no compromise, revolution overturns and destroys everything that gets in its way." To eschew revolution, then, was to eschew the most important tactic in the quest for human rights. It was to ignore the recent lessons from the Mau Mau Rebellion in Kenya and the guerrilla resistance in Algeria, two cases where oppressed people had embraced revolutionary ideology and the tactics of military insurgency in order to undermine European colonial power. Malcolm was loathe to do so, however, as he considered the Mau Mau the "greatest African patriots and freedom fighters." Indeed, he thought that the Mau Mau were great revolutionary role models and that black Americans could learn much from following their path. As Malcolm put it, "In Mississippi we need a Mau Mau. In Alabama we need a Mau Mau. Right here in Harlem, in New York City, we need a Mau Mau." Ultimately, Malcolm touted the Mau Mau's military exploits against the British and the Algerians' guerilla resistance against the French, because he believed that these efforts were essential to the cause of freedom. Clearly, he was proud of the achievements of these African independence movements against Western forces. Likewise, he also was impressed by the resistance movement in Vietnam. Violence in Malcolm's eyes was a prerequisite for change, and it was inspiring to have several models to point to when calling for a worldwide revolution of the oppressed against their oppressors.

On June 28, 1964, soon after Malcolm's return from his trip to the Middle East and Africa, Malcolm X and a number of his compatriots founded the Organization of Afro-American Unity (OAAU) based on these revolutionary principles. The organization was Malcolm's greatest effort in his campaign to internationalize the black liberation movement. The founders of the OAAU, realizing that the religious platform of the MMI attracted only Muslims, created a secular organization that would have a broader appeal. Moreover, they modeled their organization "after the letter and spirit" of the Organization of African Unity (OAU), which was established in Ethiopia in May 1963. The OAU embraced a Pan-African philosophy in its campaign to foster unity, end colonialism, furnish security, and advance economic development throughout Africa. Over the final eight months of Malcolm's life, the OAAU remained very much a work in progress that would evolve significantly. While Malcolm and the other founders had begun to lean toward a Pan-African internationalism, the organization's original agenda did not fully measure up to those aspirations. Indeed, the OAAU's "Statement of Basic Aims and Objectives" reflects an agenda that was steeped more in the localized tradition of black nationalism than a full-fledged Pan-African internationalist outlook.

The OAAU's Statement had six central tenets. Foremost, the OAAU preached unity. It called for "the unification of all people of African descent" in the Western Hemisphere, including cooperation among the various civil rights organizations. To encourage solidarity the OAAU also recommended that African Americans submerge all their differences by "establishing a non-religious and non-sectarian . . . program for human rights." Second, the OAAU asserted that African Americans had the right to self-defense. This right came from the Constitution of the United States, and the necessity for such self-preservation stemmed from a government that was "either unable or unwilling to protect the lives and property of our people." Consequently, the OAAU argued that African Americans had the right "to protect themselves by whatever means necessary," and it was "the duty of every Afro-American and every Afro-American community throughout this country to protect its people against mass murderers, bombers, lynchers, floggers, brutalizers and exploiters." Third, the OAAU stressed the need for an educational program that would help African Americans "rediscover their identity and thereby increase self respect." Reflecting the narrow geographical backgrounds of the organization's members, the OAAU called on New York City's board of education to turn over poorly run schools to the African American community. In time, the OAAU hoped to spread this program of self-improvement to other African American communities across the country.

Fourth, the OAAU vowed to cultivate political and economic power. It sought to organize a voter-registration drive, create political clubs, run candidates for office, and support politicians sympathetic to African Americans. Also, it planned to start a housing self-improvement program that would include rent strikes. Fifth, the OAAU wanted to help African American communities take the lead in solving problems such as police brutality, organized crime, drug addiction, juvenile delinquency, and illegitimacy. The final tenet, though, best embraced the spirit of Pan-Africanism that Malcolm had experienced in his travels. The OAAU wanted to launch a cultural revolution that would serve to "unbrainwash an entire people," who had been denied access to their past, and then bring them "closer to [their] African brothers and sisters." The cornerstone of this revolution, however, still reflecting the parochialism of the OAAU, would be a cultural center in Harlem.

Despite the narrowness of the OAAU's original agenda Malcolm continued to expand his vision for a Pan-African movement. In July 1964,

Malcolm embarked on another extended trip to Africa. Indeed, in the last year of his life, Malcolm spent nearly half his time abroad. During this final trip to Africa he visited eleven nations on the continent, where he had the opportunity to speak to each of these nations' head of state and to address most of their legislatures. But his most important business was to attend the OAU's second summit. As chairman of the OAAU, Malcolm served as an observer who represented the United States' twenty million African Americans. On July 17, he delivered an eight-page memorandum that asked the independent African states to bring up before the United Nations the issue of human rights violations against African Americans. Appealing to a shared history of Western slavery, racism, and colonialism, Malcolm stressed his belief that African problems were African American problems and vice versa. In that light, Malcolm hoped that the OAU would lend the weight of its international support to the African American cause by recommending "an immediate investigation" of the United States by the United Nations Commission on Human Rights. Ultimately, however, the independent African nations were not ready to go before the United Nations with a resolution. Quite simply, as Malcolm recognized, they already had enough problems, including the fact that they were too dependent on the United States and the West for their economic livelihoods to be so bold. Instead, in a more measured response, the OAU, while acknowledging the United States' Civil Rights Act of 1964, also declared that it was "deeply disturbed" by the continued practice of discrimination against African Americans. Though Malcolm's efforts at the summit did not develop exactly as he had hoped, it is clear that he was forging stronger relationships between Africa and the peoples of the African diaspora. Moreover, Malcolm's activities at the OAU conference constituted a major threat to the United States in two ways. First, there can be no gainsaying that Malcolm had begun developing his own foreign policy independent of the official one sanctioned by the federal government in Washington, D.C. Second, Malcolm's quest for censure of America before the United Nations held out the possibility of great embarrassment for the United States. Indeed, it is for this reason that the Central Intelligence Agency (CIA) and the United States Information Agency (USIA) increasingly saw Malcolm X and the OAAU as threats to American foreign policy.

Upon Malcolm's return to the United States, the OAAU had an opportunity to hone its philosophy and its policies. First, though, Malcolm had to rebuild an organization that had begun to splinter in his absence. By mid-February 1965 the OAAU was back on its feet, and Malcolm's brain trust had put together a Basic Unity Program. Like the previous statement from

June 1964, this later program called for a cultural revolution that would allow the Africans of the diaspora to unite with their brethren in Africa not physically, but culturally, psychologically, and economically. In the process African Americans would rediscover their history and their "true African culture." The OAAU asserted that African American communities had the right to self-determination. The OAAU also pledged to submerge the "artificial differences" that previously had plagued black groups by forging "a grand alliance" of people from Africa and the African diaspora. In terms of membership, the OAAU still limited itself to people of African origin, but in an effort to reach out to more people, the OAAU leaders did allow for the creation of branches of their organization regardless of ideology or geography. The only stipulation was that the new branches had to be dedicated to the OAAU's one goal: "freedom from oppression."

While the new program, in many ways, grew out of the earlier OAAU's plans, this later effort clearly had a much stronger Pan-African voice. The OAAU emphasized the need to "internationalize the problems of Afro-Americans" and lamented the fact that their people "have been too slow in recognizing the link in the fate of Africans with the fate of Afro-Americans." In particular, the OAAU drew up five strategic points that centered on Pan-African goals. First, the OAAU believed that it was essential to restore communication between Africans in the Western Hemisphere and those that remained in the homeland. These lines of communication, the OAAU's organizers argued, had been severed by their enslavers, but it was time to use media and education to reconnect those lines. Second, African Americans must reorient themselves. Instead of limiting their "thinking to the shores of America," they must understand that their "struggle is part of a larger world struggle of oppressed peoples against all forms of oppression." In particular, the OAAU hoped to facilitate this reorientation through reading and travel to Africa and the Caribbean. Third, the OAAU aimed for African American communities to gain complete control of their own education. In particular, the OAAU leaders wanted to "liberate" their children "from the vicious lies and distortions" perpetuated by the public school system. Through educational workshops, liberation schools, and control of textbooks, the OAAU wanted to provide for the next generation an education that would reflect an awareness and pride in their African culture. Fourth, to free black peoples across the globe from "economic slavery," the OAAU aspired to create a labor pool of talented technicians that could be employed in the Western Hemisphere, as well as "the newly independent nations of Africa." This project was based on the principle of "mutual cooperation and mutual benefit" among all people of African descent. The fifth element of the new program had nothing to do with Pan-Africanism, but it did reflect the revolutionary nature of the OAAU. Because African Americans had had to endure a history of racial violence and concomitant governmental neglect in the United States, the OAAU affirmed its "right and obligation" to practice self-defense "*by any means necessary.*" Although the call for self-defense was not couched in Pan-African terms, it is important to note that the OAAU, in keeping with its internationalist outlook, considered the racial violence against blacks in the United States to be not just a violation of the Constitution of the United States, but a violation of the United Nations Charter of Human Rights.

Unfortunately, Malcolm never had a chance to present the Basic Unity Program. On February 21, 1965, he was assassinated at the Audubon Ballroom in New York, and in essence, the OAAU died that day as well. Malcolm often described himself as the "angriest black man in America," but clearly he was more than that. In the last year of his life he made a concerted effort to reach out to oppressed people across the globe. Malcolm realized that fighting a revolution as a minority in the United States was not a promising proposition. In contrast, forging a Pan-African coalition or reaching out to nonwhites in Asia and Latin America held out greater possibilities. To that end, Malcolm, who increasingly saw the world divided less by race and more by the legacy of colonial oppression, wanted to link the domestic fight for civil rights with the global struggle against the vestiges of European colonialism to form a broader international campaign for human rights. Moreover, Malcolm's tactic of trying to embarrass the United States—the self-proclaimed moral leader of the free world—was inspired statesmanship. Of course, there were flaws with this vision. The OAAU suffered from a small membership; large divisions concerning nationality, race, and tactics; and an overdependence on Malcolm's charisma. Some of his critics contended that Malcolm's brand of Pan-Africanism suffered from too broad a focus, because it included peoples who simply did not share Malcolm's view that their problems were inseparable. Others, such as civil rights worker Archie Epps, dismissed "Malcolm X's hands-across-the-water strategy with Africa" as a misguided view of humanity that "seem[ed] to be based on the same irrelevant dream" that Marcus Garvey held. Also, while the OAAU might have been able to embarrass the United States in front of the United Nations, it was highly unlikely that the United Nations ever would act forcefully against a superpower such as the United States. Finally, Malcolm never clarified exactly how a violent revolution would work in conjunction with the OAAU's effort to reach out to mainline civil rights organizations that espoused nonviolence. Nevertheless, Malcolm's incipient international campaign for human rights definitely posed a challenge to the political power of the Western world and pricked its collective conscience. It also boosted black pride and enlivened a fading Pan-African tradition. Indeed, Malcolm, like Martin Luther King, had a dream: Malcolm was a Pan-African revolutionary.

Suggested Readings

Alkalimat, Abdul. "Malcolm X: A Research Site." Chicago: Twenty-First Century Books. www.brothermalcolm.net/ (access date June 27, 2009).

Asante, Molefi Kete. *Malcolm X as Cultural Hero and Other Afrocentric Essays*. Trenton, NJ: Africa World Press, 1993.

Breitman, George. *The Last Year of Malcolm X: The Evolution of a Revolutionary*. New York: Schocken Books, 1968.

———, ed. *Malcolm X Speaks: Selected Speeches and Statements*. New York: Grove Press, Inc., 1965.

Clark, Steve, ed. *February 1965: The Final Speeches*. New York: Pathfinder Press, 1992.

Clarke, John Henrik, ed. *Malcolm X: The Man and His Times*. New York: Collier Books, 1969.

Collins, Rodnell P. *Seventh Child: A Family Memoir of Malcolm X*. New York: Birch Lane Press, 1998.

Cone, James H. *Martin and Malcolm and America: A Dream or a Nightmare?* Maryknoll, NY: Orbis Books, 1991.

Dyson, Eric. *Making Malcolm: The Myth and Meaning of Malcolm X*. New York: Oxford University Press, 1995.

Epps, Archie, ed. *Malcolm X: Speeches at Harvard*. New York: Paragon House, 1991.

Gallen, David, ed. *Malcolm X: As They Knew Him*. New York: Carroll & Graf Publishers, Inc., 1992.

Goldman, Peter. *The Death and Life of Malcolm X*. Champaign: University of Illinois Press, 1979.

Jenkins, Robert L., and Mfanya Donald Tryman, eds. *The Malcolm X Encyclopedia*. Westport, CT: Greenwood Press, 2002.

Malcolm X, with Alex Haley. *The Autobiography of Malcolm X*. New York: Grove Press, 1964.

Perry, Bruce. *Malcolm: The Life of a Man Who Changed Black America*. New York: Station Hill Press, Inc., 1991.

———, ed. *Malcolm X: The Last Speeches*. New York: Pathfinder Press, 1989.

Sales, William W., Jr. *From Civil Rights to Black Liberation: Malcolm X and the Organization of Afro-American Unity*. Boston: South End Press, 1994.

T'Shaka, Oba. *The Political Legacy of Malcolm X*. Chicago: Third World Press, 1983.

~

CHAPTER THIRTEEN

Romare Bearden (1911–1988)

Artist, Intellectual, Activist

Sally Price and Richard Price

Art has been one of the most important avenues of expression for peoples of the African diaspora throughout modern times. Often used as resistance against oppression, the singing, dancing, drumming, performing, writing, or painting were sometimes repressed yet could never be silenced. In the twentieth century, while racism and segregation kept the lives of blacks and whites apart, the cultural expression of African descendants in the Americas became part of mainstream Western culture. Anthropologists Sally Price and Richard Price bring us a thoughtful analysis of the intersection of art and race relations, through the trajectory of Romare Bearden. Bearden was a versatile American artist best known for his colorful collages who was highly critical of the fact that African American artists were classified in a separate section of American art. Art should know no racial boundary, according to Bearden, whose work established dialogue with New York jazz musicians and Caribbean literary figures, and made a decisive contribution to the use of color in contemporary art.

A documentary film on Romare Bearden might well open with a scene from a little over a decade into the twentieth century, projecting it in sepia tones, with an old upright piano playing ragtime in the background. There, Fred Romare Howard Bearden is born into a comfortable four-generation African American family in Charlotte, North Carolina. His great-grandfather is a prominent member of the community, both parents are college educated, and his mother, Bessye, devotes special attention to the upbringing of her light-skinned "baaby."

Cut to Harlem three years later, where Bessye is an active participant in the worlds of politics, music, theater, and art, and hostess to a constant stream of visitors, from Fats Waller and Duke Ellington to Marcus Garvey and Eleanor Roosevelt. Then a year in Canada, where Romare's father works as a railroad steward; three years with his grandmother in Pittsburgh; childhood summers in North Carolina, creating a store of memories, impressions, images; and a teenage summer in Pittsburgh, working in the dust and din of a steel mill. College, studying mathematics and doing political cartoons for two student magazines, but eventually graduating with a degree in education. Serious involvement in baseball: varsity pitching for Boston University, then semipro ball with the Boston Tigers (once pitching against Satchel Paige), a summer with the Pittsburgh Crawfords of the Negro League, and a chance to play in the majors if only he were willing to pass for white (which he isn't).

By the mid-1930s, Bearden is pursuing his increasing commitment to drawing at the Art Students League. But he's also doing cartoons for the *Baltimore Afro-American*, writing essays on subjects such as the Negro artist and modern art, and getting involved with other artists. The Harlem Artists Guild leads into the Harlem Community Art Center, for which Bessye's friend Eleanor Roosevelt attends the opening in 1937, and the WPA Federal Art Project provides funds for Harlem's "306"—artists, writers, and musicians who meet informally in the studio of Bearden's childhood friend Charles Alston, downstairs from the Harlem Art Workshop on 141st St. Everyone's there—Richard Wright, Langston Hughes, Ralph Ellison, Katherine Dunham, the young Jacob Lawrence, and his future wife Gwendolyn Knight. . . . And around the corner is the Savoy Ballroom, where artists get in free to hear Duke Ellington, Cab Calloway, Earl Hines, Benny Goodman. In 1938 Bearden becomes a caseworker for the New York City Department of Welfare, a job that he'll continue to hold for the next three decades.

The 1940s. Bearden has taken a studio on 125th St. and has had his first solo show. Jamaican novelist and poet Claude McKay is his neighbor and friend. A three-year stint in the army during the war doesn't take him away from New York, and he continues to paint, showing The Passion of Christ as a one-artist exhibition at the Kootz Gallery, where he meets artist Carl Holty. Their correspondence (Bearden in New York, Holty teaching at the University of Georgia) develops into detailed reflections on art making that provide the substance for a coauthored book on structure and space in painting and a second book-length manuscript on color.

In 1950, the GI Bill gives Bearden nine months in Paris, where he is rarely behind the easel but daily in museums, jazz clubs, and cafés. There are walks in the Jardin du Luxembourg and evenings on the banks of the Seine, student fares for opera and movies, French cigarettes, a trip to Italy, a visit with Picasso, friendships with Constantin Brancusi and Jean Hélion, cheap wine and rich conversation with James Baldwin, Herbert Gentry, and Myron O'Higgens, and occasional socializing with Richard Wright, Wifredo Lam, Georges Braque, and Sidney Bechet. There's art talk with Wifredo Lam, Brancusi, and Braque, and at the cafés of Montparnasse, Matisse and Giacometti are regulars. Bearden, impressed when a frail, octogenarian Matisse walks by on the arm of a nurse and receives a standing ovation from the waiters, exclaims, "How you gonna beat this goddam Paris, man?! How y'gonna beat it?"

The early 1950s mark a low point in Bearden's artistic productivity. He picks up his job as a social worker, tries his hand at songwriting (creating one hit tune, "Seabreeze," recorded by Billy Eckstine and later Tito Puente), flirts briefly with abstract expressionism, spends several years copying photostatic reproductions of great works of art—copying, copying, doing nothing but copying—and finally has a nervous collapse that lands him in a hospital psychiatric ward. But by this time he's also met Nanette Rohan, daughter of immigrants from the island of Saint Martin, at a benefit for victims of a Caribbean hurricane, and she's become his wife. With her help, he pulls himself out of the emotionally and artistically stagnant period he's been through, and they move to a fifth-floor walk-up on the edge of New York's Chinatown that doubles as studio and living quarters. They do some traveling, and in 1960 they take their first trip to the Caribbean. The next year it's Europe, where Bearden is disappointed in Paris, finding that it's "sleeping artistically," and writing to Holty that "this doesn't seem to be the same place in many ways that I left 10 years ago. . . . In going around to the art galleries, I was appalled. . . . There ain't nobody trying anything new."

Bearden's apartment becomes the initial meeting place for fifteen artists concerned with the role of art in the context of the civil rights movement who take on the name Spiral to symbolize their goal of moving "outward embracing all directions, yet constantly upward." Bearden proposes a collective project using cutouts from magazines to create group collages, which the others greet unenthusiastically, but which constitutes a turning point in his own artistic career. His 1964 exhibit, Projections, four-by-eight-foot "montage paintings" made by enlarging typing-paper-size collages, catches the critics' attention, and Bearden's art begins to make its appearance on newsstands, and then on the covers of *Fortune* magazine, *Time*, and the *New York Times Magazine.*

Retiring from the Department of Welfare, Bearden continues to be concerned with the plight of black artists in the United States and, together with two others, convinces the Ford Foundation to underwrite the establishment of an exhibition space for young Afro-American artists. Rigorous reflection on art continues alongside this commitment to social concerns—his book on structure and space in painting is published in 1969, and in collaboration with writer Harry Henderson, he's beginning his important book on the history of African American art.

By 1970, the Caribbean has become a cruise-ship escape from the pressures of life in New York, and plans are made for a house in Saint Martin, to be built on land owned by Nanette's family. They begin spending several months each year on the island, where Bearden turns most of his new-felt energy to watercolor. Back in the United States, he's receiving increasing recognition—a Guggenheim Fellowship in 1970, a one-man retrospective at the Museum of Modern Art in 1971, election to the National Institute of Arts and Letters in 1972, an honorary degree at the Pratt Institute in 1973. The late 1970s bring more awards, more honorary degrees, commissions from the *New York Times* and the Alvin Ailey Dance Company, and a long profile in the *New Yorker*. Bearden produces a collage series on the travels of Odysseus that's set in the Caribbean, and continues his artistic output on a range of themes from New Orleans and jazz to *conjur* women and Southern gardens. The aqueous forms and luminous colors that capture the tropical sunsets and seascapes and market scenes of the Caribbean carry over into his New York studio, and by the 1980s, childhood memories of the U.S. South and images of Harlem jazz clubs have become saturated with the rich chromatics of the Caribbean.

The 1980s get off to a blockbuster start with a retrospective, Romare Bearden, 1970–1980, which shows in five major museums. Bearden collaborates on multimedia projects with poet Derek Walcott (providing both illustrations and overall design for their book) and with alto saxophonist Jackie McLean (in Sound Collages and Visual Improvisations). He creates a cityscape for a John Cassavetes film and does murals for Manhattan College, the City University of New York, and the Baltimore subway. He's portrayed on the cover of *Newsday Magazine* and *ARTnews*. There are more honorary degrees, a documentary film, a lifetime achievement award from New York's Mayor Koch, and the National Medal of Arts presented by Ronald Reagan.

In March 1988, a major obituary in the *New York Times* recognizes him as "the nation's foremost collagist."

In reviewing Bearden's reputation as the collagist chronicler of Harlem and the U.S. South, as the artistic ethnographer of the world of jazz, and as a modern-day narrator of Odyssean voyages, we inevitably confront the relative roles—and the delicate interaction—of form and content. How did his exceptionally insistent focus on structure, spatial relations, and the visual dynamics of a flat surface play into his gift for capturing the heartbeat of urban scenes, the complex fragrances of a Southern garden, the mellow tones and percussive heat of a jazz session, or the sultry air of the Louisiana bayous that have so indelibly marked his reputation as an American artist? His Caribbean artworks raise questions about the same tension. How did his concerns with the formal properties of a canvas work together with his ability to capture the exuberance of a carnival dancer, the otherworldliness of an Obeah in trance, the lush moisture of a tropical garden, or the magic of a flame-red Caribbean sunset?

In the two decades since his death, much has been written about Romare Bearden, and a major retrospective exhibit has brought a magnificent sampling of his art to museums across the United States. Most notably, Myron Schwartzman's *Romare Bearden: His Life and Art* and Ruth Fine's *The Art of Romare Bearden* provide comprehensive biographical information, extensive art historical assessments, and lavish illustrations of his art. In general, this literature adopts a North American perspective, focusing almost exclusively on Bearden in the United States with relatively brief allusions to the role of the Caribbean islands in his life and art. But Bearden was explicit that, for him, the Caribbean was vital: "Art will go where energy is," he said on more than one occasion. "I find a great deal of energy in the Caribbean. . . . It's like a volcano there; there's something underneath that still smolders." Throughout the final fifteen years of his life, when he was dividing his time between New York and the island of Saint Martin, all of Bearden's art was imbued with the colors and rhythms of the Caribbean. This essay, like our book *Romare Bearden: The Caribbean Dimension*, attempts to build the energy of that smoldering volcano into his biography and to explore its relationship to Bearden's role as a North American artist, intellectual, and social activist.

Beginning in the 1970s, aqueous tropical colors saturate paintings with Caribbean themes and seep into Romare Bearden's portrayals of Harlem and the U.S. South, imbuing them with a new luminosity. Diaphanous faces mark a state of deep trance, and the roosters of Mecklenburg County farmyards give way to fighting cocks on the French/Dutch island of Saint Martin.

Bearden's imbrication in the Caribbean was gradual. At the beginning, he looked at the region with an external, American gaze. It's true that he had

had some relation with the Caribbean while he was growing up. He'd played baseball in Negro leagues that included Puerto Ricans and Cubans, hung out with Jamaican writer Claude McKay, and lived through Garvey's rise and fall in a Harlem that included many Caribbean immigrants. He'd even met his future wife at a benefit for Caribbean hurricane victims. But in the 1960s, he viewed the Caribbean mainly as a cruise-ship destination, a vacation land, and an escape from the pressures of New York.

During their first few years in Saint Martin, the Beardens engaged in very little social activity, but eventually they began stepping out in the community, going to local cultural events, and getting to know others on the island. Their circle was decidedly eclectic. Josianne Fleming was a cultural organizer and wife of the mayor. Nanette's father's cousin "Moti" played the concertina, Brooksie the taxi driver was the proud father of several dozen island children, "Uncle Oswald" raised goats, Louis Richardson owned a magnificent estate, Jeanne "Ma" Chance ran a creole restaurant, Bobo Claxton played the saxophone, and Fabian Badejo was a Hausa from Nigeria who directed the Council of the Arts. As for the artists in their circle, Gloria and Marty Lynn had left a fast-lane life in New York to recapture the idealism of their student days in the 1960s, Ruby Bute dreamed of opening an art school, Roland Richardson made etchings of historic buildings, Cynric Griffith was from Saint Kitts, Lucia Trifan was from Romania, and Mosera was a Rasta from Saint Lucia. In interviews with us, each one spoke of Bearden with affection, and each one had stories, and usually a painting or two, to back up these memories. Lasana Sekou, for example, told us how, a few days after he returned to the island during his undergraduate years at Howard and gave a black power poetry reading, Bearden appeared at his door with a watercolor for him—a fluid work incorporating fragments of one of the poems he'd read that evening.

Color was the first obvious change in Bearden's work more generally, once he moved to the Caribbean, and the critics were quick to pick up on the difference. A representative review commented that "vibrant, opulent color [has become] a constant, which Bearden attributes to sojourns in the West Indies." Even in his jazz works, such as *At Connie's Inn*, iridescent greens strongly recall paintings in a Caribbean series he was calling Martinique/Rain Forest. And his North American paintings, with American birds and plants, locomotives, and houses in the rural South, were gradually complemented by scenes from the Caribbean, with lush rain forest vegetation, egrets, and other tropical animals.

During the 1970s, much of Bearden's Caribbean work was landscape inspired (beaches, mountains, sunsets, flowers, fishing boats), but the 1980s saw an increasing engagement with Caribbean social realities, from carnival dances to magic and trance, as if he were gradually coming to grips in his work with the human element in the island.

Let's look at Bearden's late Caribbean experience through the eyes of Derek Walcott, who chose one of Bearden's two *Sea Nymph* paintings for the dust jacket of a collection of his poems on Caribbean themes. Walcott, not only as a Nobel laureate in literature, but also as a serious amateur painter, had come to have tremendous respect for Bearden both as an artist and as an intellectual. In speaking with us at his home in Saint Lucia, he seconded something that many others had already told us—that Bearden's knowledge of literature was wide and deep and solid, ranging from detective novels to Greek classics and nineteenth-century British poetry. A serious fan of Walcott's poetry, he had not only designed and illustrated the book they did together, but was also the one to make the selections of poetry.

When Walcott, who had crafted the great Caribbean epic *Omeros*, spoke to us about Bearden, who had created an important series of collages portraying a Caribbean Odysseus, he located their common ground in a relationship to the coral sea of the Caribbean, a sea as worthy of epic poetry and truly great art as that other one on the shores of the Greek islands. But he also located their common ground in Obeah, that special Caribbean brand of belief and healing, trance and sacrifice, drama and ritual that Bearden eventually took on in what is arguably his greatest Caribbean-based work.

In Saint Martin, Bearden heard countless stories about the ways Obeah intervened in people's daily lives, helping them deal with illness, affairs of love, political scandals, and domestic frictions. In the 1980s, the island's population of ritual practitioners included many Haitian immigrants as well as a few people from the Dominican Republic. The practitioner would sit in front of a table, conduct divination, and go into trance—often with the aid of a tape cassette playing ceremonial music from back home. And once the problem was identified, a solution would be prescribed, most commonly a ritual bath composed of herbs, roots, and perfumes. Native Saint Martin practitioners also read tarot cards and gazed into magical mirrors. The recourse to Obeah was never considered entirely "respectable," but it was very commonly used to explain why particular relationships, commercial dealings, or political affairs were developing as they were.

One critic described Bearden's exploration of this smoky, shadowy, often-invisible spirit world, known in Saint Martin as Obeah, by writing,

Bearden's stains . . . run over the figures, enveloping them in hypnotic fumes. In "Obeah in a Trance," the watery murk that eats into the figure like acid tells us that her personality has been dissolved by her trance. . . . [Bearden has dared] to penetrate the interior of the lives he portrayed and, having pierced the skin of those day-to-day lives, connect his people and events to larger more universal themes.

Another critic noted that Bearden had abandoned "the calm, ordered world of retrospection [characteristic of his North American work] . . . for the magical, otherworldly realm of the imagination. . . . Figures and images . . . emerge from and sink back into a lurid, hallucinatory world, a dreamlike space." Much of the power of the Obeah series stemmed from its resonances, for Bearden, with ancient and universal themes. But there were also other echoes, for example from his longtime fascination with the *conjur* woman of Southern Negro rural communities who prepared love potions, provided herbal cures for illnesses, and was consulted about vexing personal and family problems.

Bearden's main man, Al Murray, placed both the *conjur* woman and the Obeah paintings within the overarching theme he had named the Prevalence of Ritual, intending this as a tag that would embrace Bearden's entire philosophy of art. Ritual and ceremony had, in fact, always been part of Bearden's life. As Murray writes,

He spent his early years in the bosom of the church, as the old folks in the pews used to say . . . [where he] absorbed the spirituals, the traditional hymns, gospel songs and amen-corner moans in context and conjunction with the prayers, sermons, shouts, testifying shuffles and struts that made up the services and the rituals that gave rise to them in the first place.

By 1987, death had become been an insistent, stalking presence for Bearden. The year before, as the cancer eating away at his bones made climbing the stairs to their fifth-floor apartment impossible, the Beardens had taken a second-floor place and for the first time had canceled their summer stay in Saint Martin. Al Murray told us that "he [said that he] had these devils and so forth—menacing things in the bushes, and he said 'there are thorns.' He was having trouble with his back, and he was talking about his mortality—serious stuff."

On his two final visits to Saint Martin in 1987, Bearden worked, as one critic put it, "as if he were trying to outpaint death," producing a series of several dozen carnival images—exuberant celebrations of life, but with the grinning figure of Death lurking in the shadows. He also revisited a number of favorite Caribbean themes. *Lady and the God of the River*, for example, is a playful image in which a profoundly Afro-American figure, a river god, conveys all the mystery and translucence of the earlier Obeah figures.

Back in New York, in the weeks before he died, Bearden had the collaboration of his studio assistant in producing two collages with watercolor—*Eden Noon* (first called *The Hundred Animal Piece*), centered on "a nude bathing in a pool or stream surrounded by a playful fantasy-landscape composed of egrets, a blue dove, a gigantic bullfrog, and various fish," and *Eden Midnight* (first called *Enchanted Places*), in which the bathing nude is under a starry sky, in a landscape filled with "mythological, perhaps prehistoric creatures—a gigantic butterfly, an alligator, and a dinosaur." But he worked by himself to create his very last painting, *At Low Tide*, where a nude, half immersed in the sea, is standing at the edge of what looks very much like Saint Martin's Orient Bay.

Standing back from Bearden's total oeuvre, let's now shift our attention from the prevalence of ritual (in Afro-America) to what we might situate more in the realm of the prevalence of race (in the rest of America). How is Bearden's art seen within the larger context of world art? And where does his identity as a black man—or, more to the point, as a black artist—feed into that placement? Al Murray, speaking to us in his home in Harlem, and Derek Walcott, talking with us in Saint Lucia, both responded to that question with some passion after we dropped on them the astonishing fact that the *Grove Dictionary of Art*—a massive reference work that boasts 45,050 articles, occupies thirty-four hefty volumes, carries a price tag of $8,800, and has been regularly updated with new entries since its original publication in 1996—has no entry on Romare Bearden. Murray cast his reaction in a sports metaphor. He said, "Take Michael Jordan. You can't say he's a *black* basketball player. He *is* basketball! This is what Ralph [Ellison] and I . . . thought Romie had to be, 'cause . . . he could play with the rest of those guys in Yankee Stadium. . . . We're talking about Tiger Woods here!"

It's important to point out that naked racism—that is, exclusion on the basis of racial categories—isn't enough to explain Bearden's absence in the *Grove Dictionary*—or, for that matter, his absence from quite a few other recently compiled and allegedly "comprehensive" histories of art, such as the *Oxford Dictionary of Art and Artists* (1996), the *Yale Dictionary of Art and Artists* (2000), and the *Oxford History of Western Art* (2000). Other African American artists *are* included—from Faith Ringgold to Jean-Michel Basquiat—and Jacob Lawrence has now been added to the *Grove Dictionary*. Lawrence and Horace Pippin had just had major exhibitions when we spoke with Walcott, who had no difficulty finding an explanation.

Let's consider any establishment or orthodoxy that says, "Yeah, but it's so special—it has to do with black people catching hell in the South, or still being happy in a certain kind of a way." So you have this absurdity of an empire pronouncing its benediction on the very fucking suffering it caused! So it says, "Oh yes, Jacob Lawrence is fantastic." Why is he fantastic? Because he shows all these niggers tryin' to get to heaven, you know, material heaven. And that's why *he's* fantastic. . . . So he's fine. "Horace Pippin is fantastic," because he's a humble nigger who really couldn't paint very well, but he had that charm that is really a quality of the primitive. . . . But Romare . . . was genuinely erudite.

This explanation is relevant to a misreading of Bearden's art that appears over and over again in the critical literature, which is that, more than anything else, it's an art of social commentary. An exhibition brochure, for example, described his art as a depiction of the culture of African Americans in the 1960s with resonance for "the indignities of segregation and the political turmoil of the times," and a major reference source defines it as "propaganda art" built on its power to confront social realities and build racial pride.

This description quickly withers on the vine when challenged by more informed insights on his artistic priorities. Al Murray, for example, has written,

When black functions as a symbolic reference to so-called black people of Africa and the United States, it is not the reference that is of paramount importance but the design: how the black shape works with other shapes and colors. Moreover, black may or may not say Afro but inevitably says silhouette, and almost always has the effect of a cut-out in a collage. . . . Bearden has made it clear that his actual use of African art is based on aesthetic, not political and certainly not racial, considerations.

And Ralph Ellison, who like Murray was on an inside track with Bearden, wrote that his art

is not only an evaluation of his own freedom and responsibility as an individual and artist, it is an affirmation of the irrelevance of the notion of race as a limiting force in the arts. . . . It was as though Bearden had decided that in order to possess his world *artistically* he had to confront it *not* through propaganda or sentimentality, but through the finest techniques and traditions of painting. He sought to recreate his Harlem in the light of his painter's vision, and thus he avoided the defeats suffered by many of the aspiring painters of that period who seemed to have felt that they had only to reproduce out of a mood of protest and despair the scenes and surfaces of Harlem, in order to win artistic mastery and accomplish social transfiguration.

Bearden himself was, over and over again, quite explicit. Of all the problems facing the Negro artist, he said, the one he found the most perplexing was the pressure to use his art as an instrument to mirror the social injustices inflicted upon his people. "It is not necessary," he wrote, "that the Negro artist mirror the misery of his people."

A writer for the *New Yorker* who conducted in-depth interviews with Bearden in 1977 picked up on his feelings about the interpretation of his art as social protest:

> Inevitably, perhaps, in the emotional climate of the sixties, critics read social content into these powerful and evocative paintings . . . [calling his work] "propagandist in the best sense." Bearden has made it plain that this was not part of his intention. . . . [He] was concerned with art, not propaganda. . . . "Naturally, I had strong feelings about the civil-rights movement, and about what was happening in the sixties [he said]. But you saw that on television every night . . . and something was needed, I thought, other than to keep repeating it in art. I thought there were other means that would convey it better than painting."

And just months before his death, Bearden said it again: "There is nothing wrong with protest. But as I said before there are other things that do it better than art. Other ways. . . . People can protest much better now through other forms than through art."

"Other ways," in Bearden's case, included writing. In their book on the history of African American artists, for example, Bearden and Henderson had much to say regarding the racially based prejudice that blocked recognition of African American artists. For example, "A concrete example of the accepted attitude towards the Negro artist recently occurred in California where an exhibition coupled the work of Negro artists with that of the blind. It is obvious that in this case there is definitely a dual standard of appraisal."

Or again, in a discussion of Henry Ossawa Tanner (who in 1996 became the first African American artist to be represented in the permanent collection of the White House) they point to his absence from histories of American art and remark, "According to some art histories, the first African-American has yet to pick up a brush." They underscore the persistent racial abuse that Tanner suffered from his classmates, who dragged his easel out into the middle of the street one night, tied him to it, and left him there. They describe how, when Tanner was awarded a medal for *The Bagpipe Lesson*, his painting was not displayed with those of the other three winners, but rather in a specially designated building called the Negro Building. And how, when he won a prestigious international award in Paris for another painting, a Baltimore newspaper illustrated their coverage of this honor with a photo of a black dockworker, figuring that "any black face would do" for the purpose.

Noting that "there is a great blind spot in American art history, one that is color-sensitive, not color-blind," Bearden and Henderson point to exhibition policies of state fairs in the 1930s and 1940s, where work by black artists was often displayed in a special section alongside needlework by the handicapped. And they single out two particularly destructive misreadings of the work of African Americans:

> A somewhat demeaning, however sympathetic, sociological perspective [and a view] derived from stereotyped expectations about "primitive" people, . . . both perspectives neglected aesthetic consideration, a pattern that has continued to this day. The more talented the artists were, the more they were subjected to pressure to paint in ways that the majority perceived as "primitive." That perception required . . . a degree of awkwardness or crudity, violent color, and sensuality. Catering to that idea became the easiest way for an African-American artist or writer to gain attention from . . . the gatekeepers of recognition and acceptance.

They also make note of Langston Hughes's refusal to bend to the demand of a patron who wanted him to "be primitive and know and feel the intuitions of the primitive." But unfortunately, said Hughes, "I did not feel the primitive surging within me, and so I could not live and write as though I did. I was only an American Negro—who had loved the surface of Africa and the rhythms of Africa—but I was not Africa. I was Chicago and Kansas City and Broadway and Harlem."

One can see remnants of this race-based demand in the phrasing that critics have used to characterize Bearden's own work. One dubbed his paintings "willfully primitive." Another cited what he called his "tribal need to salvage his childhood." A third asserted that Bearden's art was essentially about "the abiding African mores that seethe beneath the surface of black life in the United States" and that his appreciation of African masks was based on "their power to invoke fear, awe, magic, ritual, ceremony"—a classic example of stereotypes of "primitive" art if ever there was one.

So how, in the end, do we gloss Bearden? Is he an African American artist? an *American* artist? an artist, period? And why have critics been so uniform in downplaying the art he did in the Caribbean? As Henry Louis Gates Jr. has pointed out, Bearden and his closest friends (that is to say, Bearden, Ralph

Ellison, and Al Murray) never tired of insisting on the essential American-ness of their project. Gates writes,

> At the heart of [their] joint enterprise was perhaps the most breathtaking act of cultural chutzpah this land had witnessed since Columbus blithely claimed it all for Isabella. In its bluntest form, their assertion was that the truest Americans were black Americans. . . . For generations the word "American" had tacitly connoted "white." [But they] inverted the cultural assumptions and the verbal conventions: in [their] discourse, "American," roughly speaking, means "black."

At the same time, Walcott, viewing Bearden's art from his perspective in the Caribbean, argues that it was a supremely universalizing project. When Walcott spoke with us about what the Caribbean means to him artistically in terms of the particulars of the relationship between the local and the universal (what Al Murray in an interview with us referred to as "processing the idiomatic particulars of Afro-American experience into aesthetic statements of universal relevance and appeal") he could, with only slight adjustment, have been speaking for Bearden:

> In terms of *Omeros*, I felt totally natural, without making it an academic exercise or a justification or an elevation of Saint Lucians into Greeks, or some such nonsense—because of the harbors of the Caribbean, the work of the people in the Caribbean, the light in the Caribbean. That sense of elation you get in the morning, of a possibility that is always there, and of the width of the ocean—that, to me, is Caribbean first of all.

That "sense of elation you get in the morning . . . the width of the ocean" echoes powerfully with the "renewed energy" Bearden felt whenever he was in the Caribbean—an energy that spilled over into all of his work, whatever its subject, during the final decades of his life.

Sources

This essay draws on materials in *Romare Bearden: The Caribbean Dimension*, by Sally Price and Richard Price (Philadelphia: University of Pennsylvania Press, 2006—French version, La Roque d'Anthéron: Vents-d'ailleurs, 2006). References for all citations in this essay may be found in that book. For copyright reasons, it is not possible to reproduce here any of the more than one hundred images, many in color, that appear in the book. See the

National Gallery of Art's site The Art of Romare Bearden: www.nga.gov/feature/bearden/index.shtm.

Suggested Readings

Bearden, Romare, and Harry Henderson. A History of African-American Artists from 1792 to the Present. New York: Pantheon, 1993.

Fine, Ruth. The Art of Romare Bearden. New York: Harry N. Abrams, 2003.

Price, Sally, and Richard Price. Romare Bearden: The Caribbean Dimension. Philadelphia: University of Pennsylvania Press, 2006.

Schwartzman, Myron. Romare Bearden: His Life and Art. New York: Harry N. Abrams, 1990.

~

Notes

Introduction

1. The photo taken by French photographer Pierre Verger can be found at www
.pierreverger.org (under Photo Library>Americas>Brazil>Bahia>Salvador, page 83,
26847) along with many others.

2. David Eltis, "Free and Coerced Migrations: From the Old World to the New,"
in *Coerced and Free Migration: Global Perspectives*, ed. David Eltis, 36 (Stanford: Stanford University Press, 2002).

3. Bernard Bailyn, *Atlantic History: Concept and Contours* (Cambridge: Harvard
University Press, 2005).

4. John Thornton, *Africa and Africans in the Making of the Atlantic World, 1400–1800*, 2nd ed. (Cambridge: Cambridge University Press, 1998).

5. Marcus Rediker, Cassandra Pybus, and Emma Christopher, "Introduction," in
Many Middle Passages: Forced Migration and the Making of the Modern World, ed. Emma
Christopher, Cassandra Pybus, and Marcus Rediker, 1–19 (Berkeley and Los Angeles: University of California Press, 2007); Livio Sansone, "Introduction," in *Africa,
Brazil and the Construction of Trans-Atlantic Black Identities*, eds. Livio Sansone, Elisée
Soumonni, and Boubacar Barry, 1–16 (Trenton, NJ: Africa World Press, 2008); Tiffany Ruby Patterson and Robin D. G. Kelley, "Unfinished Migrations: Reflections
on the African Diaspora and the Making of the Modern World," *African Studies
Review* 43, no. 1 (April 2000): 1–45; Kristin Mann, "Shifting Paradigms in the Study
of the African Diaspora and of Atlantic History and Culture," *Slavery and Abolition*
22, no. 3 (April 2001): 3–21.

6. See Rebecca C. Scott, *Degrees of Freedom: Louisiana and Cuba after Slavery* (Cambridge, MA: Belknap Press, 2005).

7. Robert W. Slenes, "'Malungu, Ngoma's Coming!' Africa Hidden and Discovered in Brazil," in *Mostra do Redescobrimento: Negro de Corpo e Alma, Black in Body and Soul*, ed. Nelson Aguilar (São Paulo: Associação Brasil 500 Anos Artes Visuais, 2000).

8. See, among others, Stephanie E. Smallwood, *Saltwater Slavery: A Middle Passage from Africa to American Diaspora* (Cambridge, MA: Harvard University Press, 2007); Michael Gomez, *Exchanging Our Country Marks: The Transformation of African Identities in the Colonial and Antebellum South* (Chapel Hill: University of North Carolina Press, 1998); and Gwendolyn Midlo-Hall, *Slavery and African Ethnicities in the Americas: Restoring the Links* (Chapel Hill: University of North Carolina Press, 1997).

9. W. E. B. DuBois, *The Souls of Black Folk*, 1st ed., 1903 (New York: New American Library, 1969).

10. James T. Campbell, *Middle Passages: African-American Journeys to Africa, 1787–2005* (New York: Penguin, 2007); Paul Gilroy, *The Black Atlantic: Modernity and Double Consciousness* (Cambridge, MA: Harvard University Press, 1993); Brent Hayes Edwards, *The Practice of Diaspora: Literature, Translation, and the Rise of Black Internationalism* (Cambridge, MA: Harvard University Press, 2003).

11. See "Documenting the American South: North American Slave Narratives," docsouth.unc.edu/neh/; and "Born in Slavery: Slave Narratives from the Federal Writers' Project, 1936–1938," at memory.loc.gov/ammem/snhtml/snhome.html, accessed on June 29, 2009. See also Philip Curtin, ed., *Africa Remembered: Narratives by West Africans from the Era of the Slave Trade* (Madison: University of Wisconsin Press, 1968).

12. João José Reis, "The Revolution of the Ganhadores: Urban Labour, Ethnicity and the African Strike of 1857 in Bahia, Brazil," *Journal of Latin American Studies* 29, no. 1 (1997): 355–393. For similar African-Brazilian unions in Rio de Janeiro, see Maria Cecília Velasco e Cruz, "Puzzling Out Slave Origins in Rio de Janeiro's Port Unionism: The Strike of 1906 and the Sociedade de Resistência dos Trabalhadores em Trapiche e Café," *Hispanic American Historical Review* 82, no. 2 (2006): 205–245.

13. See www.filhosdegandhy.com.br/historico.html, accessed on February 28, 2009.

14. Anamaria Morales, "O afoxé Filhos de Gandhi pede paz," in *Escravidão e Invenção da Liberdade*, ed. João J. Reis (São Paulo: Brasiliense, 1988), 264–274.

15. Interview of Agnaldo Silva to Emerson Nunes on January 24, 2006, atibahia .globo.com/entrevistas/, accessed on February 28, 2009.

Chapter 1 Alonso de Illescas (1530s–1590s)

1. See Ruth Pike, *Aristocrats and Traders: Sevillian Society in the Sixteenth Century* (New York: Cornell Press, 1972), especially her chapters on slavery (and slave life) and merchants.

2. Quotations in the chapter are drawn from the works included in the notes.

3. See Pike, *Aristocrats and Traders.*

4. Documents referencing the activities of the Illescas family in the New World are contained in the Archivo de Protocolos de Sevilla.

5. See James Lockhart, *Spanish Peru 1532–1560: A Colonial Society* (Madison: University of Wisconsin Press, 1968), and Frederick Bowser, *The African Slave in Colonial Peru: 1524–1650* (Stanford, CA: Stanford University Press, 1974).

6. The main sources of information about the Esmeraldas community are José Rumazo, *Documentos para la Historia de la Audiencia de Quito*, 8 vols. (Madrid: Afrodisio Aguado, S. A., 1948); Miguel Cabello Balboa, "Verdadera descripción y relación larga de la Provincia y Tierra de las Esmeraldas . . ." in *Obras*, vol.1, ed. Jacinto Jijón y Caamaño, 7–76 (Quito: Editorial Ecuatoriana, 1945); in addition to documents from the Archivo General de Indias, Sección Quito.

7. See Cabello Balboa, "Verdadera descripción."

8. See Linda Newson, *Life and Death in Early Colonial Ecuador* (Norman and London: University of Oklahoma Press, 1995).

9. See Cabello Balboa, "Verdadera descripción."

10. The source documents relating to López de Zúñiga's expedition and Rodrigo de Ribadeneyra's are contained in the documents Escribania 922b at the Archivo General de Indias.

11. See Rumazo, *Documentos*, vol. 4.

Chapter 2 Gregoria López (1680s)

1. Quotations in the chapter are drawn from the works included in the Sources.

2. Mark A. Burkholder, "Honor and Honors in Colonial Spanish America," in *The Faces of Honor: Sex, Shame, and Violence in Colonial Latin America*, ed. Lyman L. Johnson and Sonya Lipsett-Rivera, 18 (Albuquerque: University of New Mexico Press, 1998).

Chapter 3 Philip Quaque (1741–1816)

Quotations in the chapter are drawn from the works included in the Suggested Readings.

Chapter 4 Harry Washington (1760s–1790s)

Quotations in the chapter are drawn from the works included in the Sources.

Chapter 5 Rufino José Maria (1820s–1850s)

1. João José Reis, *Slave Rebellion in Brazil: The Muslim Uprising of 1835 in Bahia* (Baltimore: Johns Hopkins University Press, 1993).

2. There are two accounts of Rufino's life that complement each other, both based on his interrogation by the police. One was reported by an anonymous correspondent in Recife of a Rio de Janeiro newspaper, the *Jornal do Commercio*, September 25, 1853, who witnessed the interrogation; the other is the transcript of Rufino's interrogation, or "Auto de perguntas feitas ao preto forro Rufino José Maria," in Arquivo Nacional, Rio de Janeiro, IJ1 326 (1853–54), Pernambuco, Offícios do Presidente da Província ao Ministro da Justiça, as well as other enclosed documents pertaining to his arrest.

3. Instituto Histórico e Geográfico Brasileiro, Lata 310, Doc. 47: Carta de Henrique Beaupaire-Rohan ao IHGB, Curitiba, abril 22, 1855.

4. Manolo Florentino, "Alforria e etnicidade no Rio de Janeiro oitocentista: Notas de pesquisa," *Topói* 5 (2002): 25–40.

5. Jaime Rodrigues, *De costa a costa: escravos, marinheiros e intermediários do tráfico negreiro de Angola ao Rio de Janeiro (1780–1860)* (São Paulo: Cia. das Letras, 2005), 186–187.

6. Public Record Office (PRO), Foreign Office (FO), 315/17 fls. 550–553, 573–575, PRO, FO 84/392, fl. 39v.

7. Sigismund Wilhelm Koelle, *Polyglotta Africana* (Graz, Austria: Akademische Druck – U. Verlagsanstalt, 1963 [1854]), iii.

8. See PRO, FO, 84/391, fls. 178v, 188v, 257–314.

9. Fergusson and Melville to Aberdeen, January 25, 1842, PRO, FO 84/391, fls. 170v–171.

10. PRO, 84 391, fls. 187, 201–202.

11. PRO, FO 84/391, fls. 201–201v.

12. PRO, FO 315/17 fl. 550ff; and FO 84/391, 195–198, 253, FO 84/392, fl. 24, 91–92 and passim. See also Leslie Bethell, "The Mixed Commissions for the Suppression of the Transatlantic Slave Trade in the Nineteenth Century," *Journal of African History* 7, no. 1 (1966): 79–93; Bethell, "Britain, Portugal and the Supression of the Brazilian Slave Trade: The Origins of Lord Palmerston's Act of 1839," *English Historical Review* 80 (1965): 761–784; and Bethell, *The Abolition of the Brazilian Slave Trade: Britain, Brazil and the Slave Trade Question* (Cambridge: Cambridge University Press, 1970), 194–5.

13. "Auto de perguntas feitas ao preto forro Rufino José Maria."

14. *Jornal do Commercio*, September 25, 1853.

15. Marcus J. M. de Carvalho, "Agostinho José Pereira: The Divine Teacher," in *The Human Tradition in Modern Brazil*, ed. Peter Beattie, 23–42 (Wilmington, DE: Scholarly Resources, 2004).

Chapter 7 Blaise Diagne (1872–1934)

1. *Métis* is a French term meaning "mixed race." It is more commonly used today rather than *mulatto* because of the derogatory connotations of sterility associated with the word *mule*. In the nineteenth century, people of mixed racial ancestry in Senegal

were probably referred to as "mulatto." I use mulatto, *métis*, or Afro-European to refer to this group.

2. G. Wesley Johnson, *The Emergence of Black Politics in Senegal: The Struggle for Power in the Four Communes 1900–1920* (Stanford, CA: Stanford University Press, 1971), 155.

Chapter 8 Phyllis Ann Edmeade (1920s)

1. Cars arrived in 1953. In 1966, there were 375 telephone subscribers. The first electric streetlight was installed in Plymouth in 1950. Service was extended from twelve to twenty-four hours in 1960, and by 1966, the entire island had access to electricity. There was no reliable water supply until 1972. Howard A. Fergus, *Montserrat in the Twentieth Century: Trials and Triumphs* (Manjack, Montserrat: UWI School of Continuing Studies, 2000), 69–74.

2. *Tillinghast v. Edmead*, Transcript of Record, 11.
3. *Tillinghast v. Edmead*, 11.
4. *Tillinghast v. Edmead*, 11.
5. *Tillinghast v. Edmead*, 28.
6. *Tillinghast v. Edmead*, 22.
7. *Ex parte Edmead*.

Chapter 9 C. L. R. James (1901–1989)

Quotations in the chapter are drawn from the Suggested Readings.

Chapter 10 Robert Robinson (1930s)

The collections of the United States National Archives, the Russian State Archive of Social and Political History (RGASPI), and the State Archive of the Russian Federation (GARF) were critical to the composition of this essay.

1. Yelena Khanga, *Soul to Soul: A Black Russian American Family 1865–1992* (New York: W. W. Norton, 1992), 22.
2. "Negro Lawyer, in Moscow, Sees Communism at the Way," *The Liberator*, October 17, 1931.
3. Langston Hughes, *I Wonder As I Wander: An Autobiographical Journey* (New York: Hill and Wang, 1956), 212.
4. Robert Robinson, *Black on Red: My 44 Years inside the Soviet Union* (Washington, DC: Acropolis Books Ltd., 1988), 72.
5. Vern Smith, "'I Am at Home,' Says Robeson at Reception in the Soviet Union," *Daily Worker*, January 15, 1935.

6. Homer Smith, *Black Man in Red Russia* (Chicago: Johnson Publishing Company, 1964), 1.

7. *Records of the Department of State Relating to Internal Affairs of the Soviet Union, 1930–1939*, 861.5017—Living Conditions/371, 519, 575.

Chapter 11 Vicente Ferreira Pastinha (1889–1981)

1. *A Tarde*, February 22, 1969, in Antonio Liberac Cardoso Pires, *Bimba, Pastinha e Besouro de Mangangá* (Goiânia, Brazil: Editora Grafset, 2002), 66.

2. Pastinha, *Black Belt Magazine*, March 1964.

3. Vicente Ferreira Pastinha, *Capoeira Angola* (Salvador: Escola Gráfica N.S. de Loreto, 1964), 31.

4. Vicente Ferreira Pastinha, *Esportivo de Capoeira Angola* (Salvador: n.p., 1963), 5–6.

5. Angelo Augusto Decânio, *A Herança de Pastinha: A Metafísica da Capoeira* (Salvador: Coleção São Salomão, 1997), 7.

6. Luís de Camara Cascudo, *Folclore do Brasil* (São Paulo: Fundo de Cultura, 1967), 183.

7. Pastinha, *Esportivo de Capoeira Angola*, 15.

8. "Estatuto do Centro Esportivo de Capoeira Angola," in Pires, *Bimba, Pastinha*, 82.

9. Pastinha, *Capoeira Angola*, 35.

10. Pastinha, *Capoeira Angola*, 39.

11. Gregory J. Downey, "Incorporating Capoeira: Phenomenology of a Movement Discipline," PhD diss., Department of Anthropology, University of Chicago, 1998, 141.

12. *O Globo*, Rio de Janeiro, November 14, 1981.

13. Frederico José de Abreu, *Bimba é Bamba: A Capoeira no Ringue* (Bahia: P&A Gráfica e Editora, 1999), 68.

14. *Jornal do Brasil*, Rio de Janeiro, June 30, 1967.

15. *Revista Realidade*, Rio de Janeiro, Editora Abril, 1967, 80.

16. *Revista Realidade*, 80.

17. I. C. Salvador, July 2, 1967, 3, in Pires, *Bimba, Pastinha*, 85–86.

18. *A Tarde*, June 5, 1980.

19. Letícia Vidor de Souza Reis, "Negros e brancos no jogo de capoeira: a reinvenção da tradição," Dissertação de Mestrado em Ciências Sociais. Universidade de São Paulo, 1993, 103.

20. Fátima Góes, "Mestre Pastinha pede ajuda," *Tribuna da Bahia*, Salvador, September 15, 1981.

Chapter 12 Malcolm X (1925–1965)

1. William J. Sales Jr., *From Civil Rights to Black Liberation: Malcolm X and the Organization of Afro-American Unity* (Boston: South End Press, 1994), 28.

2. All quotations by Malcolm X or about Malcolm X and the Organization of Afro-American Unity are drawn from the texts included in the Suggested Readings.

3. For these numbers, see Sales, *From Civil Rights to Black Liberation*, 36, 68.

Suggested Readings by Topic

General and Theoretical

Andrews, George Reid. *Afro-Latin America, 1800–2000*. Oxford: Oxford University Press, 2004.

Blakely, Allison. *Blacks in the Dutch World: The Evolution of Racial Imagery in a Modern Society*. Bloomington: Indiana University Press, 1993.

———. *Russia and the Negro: Blacks in Russian History and Thought*. Washington, DC: Howard University Press, 1986.

Conniff, Michael, and Thomas J. Davis. *Africans in the Americas: A History of the Black Diaspora*. New York: St. Martin's Press, 1994.

Davis, Darien J. *Slavery and Beyond: The African Impact on Latin America and the Caribbean*. Wilmington, DE: Scholarly Resources Books, 1994.

Edwards, Brent Hayes. *The Practice of Diaspora: Literature, Translation, and the Rise of Black Internationalism*. Cambridge, MA: Harvard University Press, 2003.

Fabre, Geneviève, and Klaus Benesch, eds. *African Diasporas in the Old and New Worlds: Consciousness and Imagination*. Amsterdam: Rodopi, 2004.

Fredrickson, George M. *White Supremacy: A Comparative Study in American and South African History*. New York: Oxford University Press, 1981.

Gilroy, Paul. *The Black Atlantic: Modernity and Double Consciousness*. Cambridge, MA: Harvard University Press, 1993.

Gomez, Michael A. *Reversing Sail: A History of the African Diaspora*. Cambridge: Cambridge University Press, 2005.

———, ed. *Diasporic Africa: A Reader*. New York: NYU Press, 2006.

Harris, J. E. *Global Dimensions of the African Diaspora*. Washington, DC: Howard University Press, 1993.

Hine, Darlene Clark, and Jacqueline McLeod, eds. *Crossing Boundaries: Comparative History of Black People in Diaspora*. Bloomington: Indiana University Press, 1999.

James, Winston, and Clive Harris, eds. *Inside Babylon: The Caribbean Diaspora in Britain*. London: Verso, 1993.

Jayasuriya, Shihan De S., and Richard Pankhurst, eds. *The African Diaspora in the Indian Ocean*. Trenton, NJ: Africa World Press, 2003.

Lemelle, Sidney, and Robert D. G. Kelley, eds. *Imagining Home: Class, Culture and Nationalism in the African Diaspora*. London and New York: Verso, 1994.

Lovejoy, Paul, ed. *Identity in the Shadow of Slavery*. London and New York: Continuum International Publishing Group, 2000.

Lovejoy, Paul E., and David Trotman, eds. *Trans-Atlantic Dimensions of Ethnicity in the African Diaspora*. London and New York: Continuum, 2004.

Ogundiran, Akinwumi, and Toyin Falola, eds. *Archaeology of Atlantic Africa and the African Diaspora*. Bloomington: Indiana University Press, 2007.

Palmer, Colin A. "Defining and Studying the Modern African Diaspora." *The Journal of Negro History* 85, no. 1/2. (Winter–Spring, 2000): 27–32.

Peabody, Sue. *"There Are No Slaves in France": The Political Culture of Race and Slavery in the Ancien Regime*. New York: Oxford University Press. 1996.

Powell, Eve Troutt, and John O. Hunwick, eds. *The African Diaspora in the Mediterranean Lands of Islam*. Princeton, NJ: Marcus Wiener Publishers, 2002.

Segal, Ronald. *Islam's Black Slaves: The Other Black Diaspora*. New York: Farrar, Straus, & Giroux, 2002.

Terborg-Penn, Rosalyn, and Andrea Benton Rushing, eds. *Women in Africa and the African Diaspora: A Reader*, 2nd ed. Washington, DC: Howard University Press, 1997.

Thornton, John. *Africa and Africans in the Making of the Atlantic World 1400–1680*, 2nd ed. Cambridge: Cambridge University Press, 1998.

Yerxa, Donald A., ed. *Recent Themes in the History of Africa and the Atlantic World: Historians in Conversation*. Columbia: University of South Carolina Press, 2008.

Walvin, James. *Making the Black Atlantic: Britain and the African Diaspora*. London: Cassell, 2000.

Slave Trade

Bailey, Anne. *African Voices of the Atlantic Slave Trade: Beyond the Silence and the Shame*. Boston: Beacon Press, 2006.

Barry, Boubacar. *Senegambia and the Atlantic Slave Trade*. Cambridge: Cambridge University Press, 1998.

Curtin, Philip D. *The Atlantic Slave Trade: A Census*. Madison: University of Wisconsin Press, 1969.

Diouf, Sylviane A., ed. *Fighting the Slave Trade: West African Strategies*. Athens: Ohio University Press, 2004.

DuBois, W. E. B. *The Suppression of the African Slave Trade to the United States of America 1638–1870*. Baton Rouge: Louisiana State University Press, 1969. 1st ed. 1896.

Inikori, Joseph, and Stanley Engerman, eds. *The Atlantic Slave Trade: Effects on Economies, Societies and Peoples in Africa, the Americas and Europe*. Durham, NC: Duke University Press, 1992.

Klein, Herbert. *The Atlantic Slave Trade*. Cambridge: Cambridge University Press, 1999.

Law, Robin. *Ouidah: Social History of a West African Slaving Port, 1727–1892*. Athens: Ohio University Press, 2000.

Linebaugh, Peter, and Marcus Rediker. *The Many-Headed Hydra: The Hidden History of the Revolutionary Atlantic*. Boston: Beacon Press, 2000.

Miller, Joseph C. *Way of Death: Merchant Capitalism and the Angolan Slave Trade 1730–1830*. Madison: University of Wisconsin Press, 1988.

Northrup, David. *Africa's Discovery of Europe: 1450–1850*. New York and Oxford: Oxford University Press, 2002.

———, ed. *The Atlantic Slave Trade*. Boston: Houghton Mifflin, 2002.

Postma, Johannes. *The Dutch in the Atlantic Slave Trade, 1600–1815*. Cambridge: Cambridge University Press, 1990.

Smallwood, Stephanie. *Saltwater Slavery: A Middle Passage from Africa to American Diaspora*. Cambridge, MA: Harvard University Press, 2007.

Slavery and American Societies

Barickman, B. J. *A Bahian Counterpoint: Sugar, Tobacco, Cassava, and Slavery in the Recôncavo, 1780–1860*. Stanford, CA: Stanford University Press, 1998.

Berlin, Ira. *Generations of Captivity: A History of African-American Slaves*. Cambridge, MA: Harvard University Press, 2003.

———. *Many Thousands Gone: The First Two Centuries of Slavery in North America*. Cambridge, MA: Harvard University Press, 2000.

Bowser, Frederick P. *The African Slave in Colonial Peru, 1524–1650*. Stanford, CA: Stanford University Press, 1974.

Craton, Michael. *Searching for the Invisible Man: Slaves and Plantation Life in Jamaica*. Cambridge, MA: Harvard University Press, 1978.

———. *Testing the Chains: Resistance to Slavery in the British West Indies*. Ithaca, NY: Cornell University Press, 1982.

Diouf, Sylviane. *Servants of Allah: African Muslims Enslaved in the Americas*. New York: New York University Press, 1998.

Davis, David Brion. *Inhuman Bondage: The Rise and Fall of Slavery in the New World*. Oxford and New York: Oxford University Press, 2006.

Eltis, David. *The Rise of African Slavery in the Americas*. Cambridge: Cambridge University Press, 2000.

Gaspar, David Barry, and Darlene Clark Hine, eds. *More Than Chattel: Black Women in Slavery in the Americas*. Bloomington: Indiana University Press, 1996.

Helg, Aline. *Liberty and Equality in Caribbean Colombia, 1770–1835*. Chapel Hill: University of North Carolina Press, 2004.

Heywood, Linda M., and John Thornton. *Central Africans, Atlantic Creoles, and the Foundation of the Americas, 1585–1660*. Cambridge: Cambridge University Press, 2007.

Karasch, Mary C. *Slave Life in Rio de Janeiro, 1808–1850*. Princeton, NJ: Princeton University Press, 1987.

Landers, Jane G. *Black Society in Spanish Florida*. Champaign: University of Illinois Press, 1999.

Morgan, Philip. *Slave Counterpoint: Black Culture in the Eighteenth-Century Chesapeake and Lowcountry*. Chapel Hill and Williamsburg: University of North Carolina Press and the Omohundro Institute for Early American History and Culture, 1998.

Palmer, Colin A. *Slaves of the White God: Blacks in Mexico, 1570–1650*. Cambridge, MA: Harvard University Press, 1976.

Reis, João José. *Slave Rebellion in Brazil: The Muslim Uprising of 1835 in Bahia*. Baltimore: Johns Hopkins University Press, 1993.

Schwartz, Stuart B. *Sugar Plantations in the Formation of Brazilian Society: Bahia, 1550–1835*. Cambridge: Cambridge University Press, 1985.

———, ed. *Tropical Babylons: Sugar and the Making of the Atlantic World 1570–1670*. Chapel Hill: University of North Carolina Press, 2004.

Shepherd, Verene, and Hilary McD. Beckles, eds. *Caribbean Slavery in the Atlantic World: A Student Reader*. Kingston, Jamaica: Ian Randle, 2000.

Solow, Barbara, ed. *Slavery and the Rise of the Atlantic System*. Cambridge: Cambridge University Press, 1991.

Williams, Eric. *Capitalism and Slavery*. Chapel Hill: University of North Carolina Press, 1944.

Wood, Marcus. *Blind Memory: Visual Representations of Slavery in England and America, 1780–1865*. New York: Routledge, 2000.

Abolition and Emancipation

Adderley, Rosanne M. *"New Negroes from Africa": Slave Trade Abolition and Free African Settlement in the Nineteenth-Century Caribbean*. Bloomington: Indiana University Press, 2006.

Bethell, Leslie. *The Abolition of the Brazilian Slave Trade: Britain, Brazil and the Slave Trade Question, 1807–1869*. Cambridge: Cambridge University Press, 1970.

Brown, Christopher Leslie. *Moral Capital: Foundations of British Abolitionism*. Chapel Hill and Williamsburg: University of North Carolina and Omohundro Institute for Early American History and Culture, 2006.

Burin, Eric. *Slavery and the Peculiar Solution: A History of the American Colonization Society*. Gainesville: University Press of Florida, 2005.

Childs, Matt D. *The 1812 Aponte Rebellion in Cuba and the Struggle against Atlantic Slavery*. Chapel Hill: University of North Carolina Press, 2006.

Davis, David Brion. *The Problem of Slavery in the Age of Revolution, 1770–1823*. Ithaca, NY: Cornell University Press, 1975.

Diouf, Sylviane. *Dreams of Africa in Alabama: The Slave Ship Clotilda and the Story of the Last Africans Brought to America*. New York: Oxford University Press, 2007.

Dorsey, Joseph C. *Slave Traffic in the Age of Abolition: Puerto Rico, West Africa, and the Non-Hispanic Caribbean, 1815–1859*. Gainesville: University Press of Florida, 2003.

Dubois, Laurent. *A Colony of Citizens: Revolution & Slave Emancipation in the French Caribbean, 1787–1804*. Chapel Hill: University of North Carolina Press, 2006.

———. *Avengers of the New World: The Story of the Haitian Revolution*. Cambridge, MA: Harvard University Press, 2005.

Eltis, David. *Economic Growth and the Ending of the Transatlantic Slave Trade*. Oxford: Oxford University Press, 1987.

Ferrer, Ada. *Insurgent Cuba: Race, Nation, and Revolution, 1868–1898*. Chapel Hill: University of North Carolina Press, 1999.

Geggus, David P., ed. *The Impact of the Haitian Revolution in the Atlantic World*. Columbia: University of South Carolina Press, 2001.

James, C. L. R. *The Black Jacobins: Toussaint L'Ouverture and the San Domingo Revolution*. New York: Vintage Books, 1989.

Korieh, Chima J., and Femi J. Kolapo, eds. *The Aftermath of Slavery: Transitions and Transformations in Southeastern Nigeria*. Trenton, NJ: Africa World Press, 2007.

Murray, David. *Odious Commerce: Britain, Spain, and the Abolition of the Cuban Slave Trade*. Cambridge: Cambridge University Press, 1980.

Pybus, Cassandra. *Epic Journeys of Freedom: Runaway Slaves of the American Revolution and Their Global Quest for Liberty*. Boston, MA: Beacon Press, 2006.

Schama, Simon. *Rough Crossings: Britain, the Slaves and the American Revolution*. New York: Ecco, 2006.

Schmidt-Nowara, Christopher. *Empire and Antislavery: Spain, Cuba and Puerto Rico, 1833–1874*. Pittsburgh: University of Pittsburgh Press, 1999.

Scott, Rebecca. *Slave Emancipation in Cuba: The Transition to Free Labour, 1860–1899*. Princeton, NJ: Princeton University Press, 1985.

Scully, Pamela, and Diana Paton, eds. *Gender and Slave Emancipation in the Atlantic World*. Durham, NC: Duke University Press, 2005.

Walker, James W. St. G. *The Black Loyalists: The Search for a Promised Land in Nova Scotia and Sierra Leone*, 2nd ed. Toronto: University of Toronto Press, 1992.

Postemancipation in the Americas

Andrews, George Reid. *Blacks and Whites in São Paulo, Brazil, 1888–1988*. Madison: University of Wisconsin Press, 1991.

———. *The Afro-Argentines of Buenos Aires, 1800–1900*. Madison: University of Wisconsin Press, 1980.

Butler, Kim. *Freedoms Given, Freedoms Won: Afro-Brazilians in Post-Abolition São Paulo and Salvador*. Newark, NJ: Rutgers University Press, 1998.

Cooper, Frederick, Thomas C. Holt, and Rebecca J. Scott. *Beyond Slavery: Explorations of Race, Labor, and Citizenship in Postemancipation Societies*. Chapel Hill: University of North Carolina Press, 2000.

Foner, Eric. *Reconstruction: America's Unfinished Revolution, 1863–1877*. New York: HarperCollins, 1988.

Helg, Aline. *Our Rightful Share: The Afro-Cuban Struggle for Equality, 1886–1912*. Chapel Hill, University of North Carolina Press, 1995.

Hahn, Steven. *A Nation under Our Feet: Black Political Struggles in the Rural South from Slavery to the Great Migration*. Cambridge, MA: Belknap Press, 2003.

Holt, Thomas C. *The Problem of Freedom: Race, Labor, and Politics in Jamaica and Britain, 1832–1938*. Baltimore: Johns Hopkins University Press, 1992.

Litwack, Leon. *Been in the Storm So Long: The Aftermath of Slavery*. New York: Vintage Books, 1980.

Paton, Diana. *No Bond but the Law: Punishment, State, and Gender in Jamaican State Formation, 1780–1870*. Durham, NC: Duke University Press, 2004.

Scott, Rebecca J. *Degrees of Freedom: Louisiana and Cuba after Slavery*. Cambridge, MA: Harvard University Press, 2005.

Nineteenth- and Twentieth-Century Colonialism and Racism

Beattie, Peter M. *The Tribute of Blood: Army, Honor, Race, and Nation in Brazil 1864–1945*. Durham, NC: Duke University Press, 2001.

Ben-Ghiat, Ruth, and Mia Fuller, eds. *Italian Colonialism*. New York: Palgrave Macmillan, 2005.

Ben Jelloun, Tahar. *French Hospitality: Racism and North African Immigrants*. Trans. Barbara Bray. New York: Columbia University Press, 1997.

Clark, Nancy L., and William H. Worger. *South Africa: The Rise and Fall of Apartheid*. London: Longman, 2004.

Cooper, Frederick. *Decolonization and African Society: The Labor Question in French and British Africa*. Cambridge: Cambridge University Press, 1996.

———. *Colonialism in Question: Theory, Knowledge History*. Berkeley: University of California Press, 2005.

Cooper, Frederick, and Ann Laura Stoler, eds. *Tensions of Empire: Colonial Cultures in a Bourgeois World*. Berkeley: University of California Press, 1997.

Fanon, Frantz. *The Wretched of the Earth*. New York: Grove Press, 1968.

Gebrekidan, Fikru Negash. *Bond without Blood: A History of Ethiopian and Caribbean Relations, 1896–1991*. Trenton, NJ: Africa World Press, 2004.

Hochschild, Adam. *King Leopold's Ghost: A Story of Greed, Terror, and Heroism in Colonial Africa*. New York: Houghton Mifflin, 1998.

Klein, Martin A. *Slavery and Colonial Rule in French West Africa*. Cambridge and New York: Cambridge University Press, 1998.

Larebo, Haile M. *The Building of an Empire: Italian Land Policy and Practice in Ethiopia*. Trenton, NJ: Africa World Press, 1995.

Law, Robin, ed. *From Slave Trade to "Legitimate" Commerce: The Commercial Transition in Nineteenth-Century West Africa*. Cambridge: Cambridge University Press, 1995.

Miers, Suzanne. *Britain and the Ending of the Slave Trade*. New York: Longman, 1975.

Petré-Grénouilleau, Olivier, ed. *From Slave Trade to Empire: European Colonisation of Black Africa 1780s–1880s*. New York and London: Routledge, 2004.

Pratt, Mary Louise. *Imperial Eyes. Travel Writing and Transculturation*. London: Routledge 1992.

Ranger, Terence. "The Invention of Tradition in Colonial Africa." In *The Invention of Tradition*, edited by Eric Hobsbawm and T. Ranger, 211–263. Cambridge: Canto, Cambridge University Press, 1983.

———. "The Invention of Tradition Revisited: The Case of Colonial Africa." In *Development: A Cultural Studies Reader*, edited by Susanne Schech and Jane Haggis, 283–291. London: Blackwell, 2002.

Rodney, Walter. *How Europe Underdeveloped Africa*. Washington, DC: Howard University Press, 1981.

Young, Robert J. C. *Postcolonialism: An Historical Introduction*. Oxford: Blackwell, 2001.

Struggles for Civil Rights and Racial Equality

Ackah, William B. *Pan-Africanism: Exploring the Contradictions: Politics, Identity and Development in Africa and the African Diaspora*. Aldershot, UK: Ashgate, 1999.

Adi, Hakim. *Pan-African History: Political Figures from Africa and the Diaspora since 1787*. London and New York: Routledge, 2003.

Crawford, Vicki L., Jacqueline Anne Rouse, and Barbara Woods. *Women in the Civil Rights Movement: Trailblazers and Torchbearers, 1941–1965*. Bloomington: Indiana University Press, 1993.

Dittmer, John. *Local People: The Struggle for Civil Rights in Mississippi*. Champaign: University of Illinois Press, 1995.

DuBois, W. E. B. *The Souls of Black Folk*. New York: Bantam, 1989. 1st ed. 1903.

Franklin, John Hope, and Alfred Moss. *From Slavery to Freedom: A History of African Americans*. Boston: McGraw-Hill, 1994.

Joseph, Peniel E., ed. *Black Power Movement: Rethinking the Civil Rights–Black Power Era*. London and New York: Routledge, 2006.

Kelley, Robin D. G. *Hammer and Hoe: Alabama Communists during the Great Depression*. Chapel Hill: University of North Carolina Press, 1990.

Klarman, Michael J. *From Jim Crow to Civil Rights: The Supreme Court and the Struggle for Racial Equality*. New York: Oxford University Press, 2004.

————. *Unfinished Business: Racial Equality in American History*. New York: Oxford University Press, 2007.

Ling, Peter, and Sharon Monteith, eds. *Gender and the Civil Rights Movement*. Newark, NJ: Rutgers University Press, 2004.

Payne, Charles. *I've Got the Light of Freedom: The Organizing Tradition and the Mississippi Freedom Struggle*. Berkeley: University of California Press, 1997.

Ransby, Barbara. *Ella Baker and the Black Freedom Movement: A Radical Democratic Vision*. Chapel Hill: University of North Carolina Press, 1995.

Culture and Identity

Ball, Edward. *Slaves in the Family*. New York: Farrar, Straus, & Giroux, 1998.

Falola, Toyin, and Matt Childs, eds. *The Yoruba Diaspora in the Atlantic World*. Bloomington: Indiana University Press, 2005.

Gomez, Michael. *Exchanging Our Country Marks: The Transformation of African Identities in the Colonial and Antebellum South*. Chapel Hill: University of North Carolina Press, 1998.

Harding, Rachel. *A Refuge in Thunder: Candomblé and Alternative Spaces in Blackness*. Bloomington: Indiana University Press, 2000.

Heywood, Linda, ed. *Central Africans and the Cultural Transformations in the American Diaspora*. Cambridge: Cambridge University Press, 2002.

Holloway, Joseph E. *Africanisms in American Culture*, 2nd ed. Bloomington: Indiana University Press, 2005.

Johnson, Paul C. *Diaspora Conversions: Black Carib Religion and the Recovery of Africa*. Berkeley: University of California Press, 2007.

Mann, Kristin, ed. *Rethinking the African Diaspora: The Making of a Black Atlantic World in the Bight of Benin and Brazil*. London: Routledge, 2001.

Matory, J. Lorand. *Black Atlantic Religion: Tradition, Transnationalism, and Matriarchy in the Afro-Brazilian Candomblé*. Princeton, NJ: Princeton University Press, 2005.

Midlo-Hall, Gwendolyn. *Slavery and African Ethnicities in the Americas: Restoring the Links*. Chapel Hill: University of North Carolina Press, 2007.

————. *Africans in Colonial Louisiana: The Development of Afro-Creole Culture in the Eighteenth Century*. Bâton Rouge: Louisiana State University Press, 1995.

Mintz, Sidney, and Richard Price. *The Birth of African-American Culture: An Anthropological Perspective*. Boston: Beacon Press, 1992.

Murphy, Joseph M. *Working the Spirit: Ceremonies of the African Diaspora*. Boston: Beacon Press, 1994.

Naro, Nancy Priscilla, Roger Sansi-Roca, and David H. Treece, eds. *Cultures of the Lusophone Black Atlantic*. New York: Palgrave Macmillan, 2007.

Oboe, Annalisa, and Anna Scacchi, eds. *Recharting the Black Atlantic: Modern Cultures, Local Communities, Global Connections*. New York: Routledge, 2008.

Ohadike, Don C. *Sacred Drums of Liberation: Religious and Music of Resistance in Africa and the Diaspora*. Trenton, NJ: Africa World Press, 2007.

Okpewho, Isidore, Carole Boyce Davies, and Ali Mazrui, eds. *The African Diaspora: African Origins and New World Identities.* Bloomington: Indiana University Press, 1999.

Price, Richard. "The Miracle of Creolization: A Retrospective." *New West Indian Guide* 75 (2001): 35–64.

Saïd, Edward W. *Culture and Imperialism.* New York: Vintage, 1993.

Sansone, Livio. *Blackness without Ethnicity: Creating Race in Brazil.* New York: Palgrave Macmillan, 2003.

Sansone, Livio, Elisée Soumonni, and Boubacar Barry, eds. *Africa, Brazil and the Construction of Trans Atlantic Black Identity.* Trenton, NJ: Africa World Press, 2007.

Sweet, James C. *Recreating Africa: Culture, Kinship, and Religion in the African-Portuguese World, 1441–1770.* Chapel Hill: University of North Carolina Press, 2006.

Vianna, Hermano. *The Mystery of Samba: Popular Music and National Identity in Brazil.* Trans. John Chasteen. Chapel Hill: University of North Carolina Press, 1994.

Walker, Sheila, ed. *African Roots/American Cultures: Africa in the Creation of the Americas.* Lanham, MD: Rowman & Littlefield, 2001.

Journeys and Narratives of the Black Atlantic

Blight, David W. *A Slave No More: Two Men Who Escaped to Freedom Including Their Own Narratives of Emancipation.* Orlando, FL: Harcourt, 2007.

Brooks, Joanna, and John Saillant, eds. *"Face Zion Forward": First Writers of the Black Atlantic, 1785–1798.* Boston: Northeastern University Press, 2002.

Byrd, Alexander X. *Captives and Voyagers: Black Migrants across the Eighteenth-Century British Atlantic World.* Baton Rouge: Louisiana State University Press, 2008.

Campbell, James T. *Middle Passages: African American Journeys to Africa, 1787–2005.* New York: Penguin Press, 2006.

Carretta, Vincent. *Equiano, The African: Biography of a Self-Made Man.* Athens: University of Georgia Press, 2005.

Carretta, Vincent, and Philip Gould, eds. *Genius in Bondage: Literature of the Early Black Atlantic.* Lexington: University Press of Kentucky, 2001.

Curtin, Philip D., ed. *Africa Remembered: Narratives by West Africans from the Era of the Slave Trade.* Madison: University of Wisconsin Press, 1968.

Douglass, Frederick. *Life and Times of Frederick Douglass Written by Himself.* Hartford, CT: Park Publishing Co., 1884.

Eakin, Sue, ed. *Solomon Northup's Twelve Years a Slave and Plantation Life in the Antebellum South.* Lafayette: Center for Louisiana Studies, University of Louisiana at Lafayette, 2007.

Frost, Karolyn Smardz. *I've Got a Home in Glory Land: A Lost Tale of the Underground Railroad.* New York: Farrar, Straus, & Giroux, 2007.

Furtado, Júnia Ferreira. *Chica da Silva: A Brazilian Slave of the Eighteenth Century.* Cambridge and New York: Cambridge University Press, 2009.

Gates, Henry Louis, Jr., and William L. Andrews, eds. *Pioneers of the Black Atlantic: Five Slave Narratives from the Enlightenment, 1772–1815*. Washington, DC: Civitas, 1998.

Jeffrey, Julie Roy. *Abolitionists Remember: Antislavery Autobiographies and the Unfinished Work of Emancipation*. Chapel Hill: University of North Carolina Press, 2008.

Jesus, Carolina Maria de. *Child of the Dark: The Diary of Carolina Maria de Jesus*. Trans. David St. Clair; with a new afterword by Robert M. Levine. New York: New American Library, 2003.

Law, Robin, and Paul Lovejoy, eds. *The Biography of Mahommah Gardo Baquaqua: His Passage from Slavery to Freedom in Africa and America*. Princeton, NJ: Markus Wiener Publisher, 2007.

Lowly, Beverly. *Harriet Tubman: Imagining a Life*. New York: Doubleday, 2007.

Pettinger, Alasdair, ed. *Always Elsewhere: Travels of the Black Atlantic*. New York: Cassell, 1998.

Potkay, Adam, and Sandra Burr, eds. *Black Atlantic Writers of the Eighteenth Century: Living the New Exodus in England and the Americas*. Basingstoke, UK: Macmillan, 1995.

Rice, Alan J. *Radical Narratives of the Black Atlantic*. London: Continuum, 2003.

Sparks, Randy. *The Two Princes of Calabar: An Eighteenth-Century Atlantic Odyssey*. Cambridge, MA: Harvard University Press, 2004.

Sweeney, Fionnghuala. *Frederick Douglass and the Atlantic World*. Liverpool: Liverpool University Press, 2007.

Yellin, Jean Fagan. *Harriet Jacobs: A Life*. New York: Basic Civitas Books, 2004.

Walvin, James. *An African's Life: The Life and Times of Olaudah Equiano, 1745–1797*. London and New York: Cassell, 1998.

~

Selected Filmography
on the Black Atlantic

Adanggaman (director Roger Gnoan M'Bala, 2000), 90 minutes. Set in West Africa
   in the seventeenth century, a fictionalized account of enslavement and slave
   trade. King Adanggaman, who orders his soldiers to torch enemy villages, kill
   the elders, and capture the men to be sold to the slave trade, and Ossei, the main
   protagonist, whose family and love are killed, except for his mother, whom he
   has to find.
Adwa, An African Victory (director Haile Gerima, 1999), 97 minutes. Drama set
   during the 1896 Italian invasion of Ethiopia, focusing on the resistance waged
   by Ethiopians, whose victory in the battle of Adwa is seen as a landmark in the
   African resistance against colonialism.
Amazing Grace (director Michael Apted, 2006), 111 minutes. British abolitionist
   William Wilberforce spent decades lobbying his fellow members of Parliament to
   end their country's transatlantic slave trade, using the Christian hymn "Amazing
   Grace" to make an emotional, religious, and moral case. The Slave Trade Act
   finally passed in 1807, at great personal cost to Wilberforce.
Amistad (director Stephen Spielberg, 1997), 152 minutes. Based on the true story
   of a mutiny aboard the slave ship *Amistad* in 1839, led by a former African leader
   named Cinque. When the ship lands on United States territory, the rebels are
   seized as runaway slaves, and the case eventually makes its way to the Supreme
   Court, where former president John Quincy Adams argues on their behalf.
The Black Girl/La Noire de . . . (director Ousmane Sembene, 1966), 65 minutes.
   The first African feature film, this drama follows a young woman from Senegal as
   she moves to France to work for the same French family she served in Dakar. Her

dreams of consumption and mobility are shattered as her employers treat her as an exotic sample, and lowly maid, in the French Côte d'Azur.

Black Orpheus (director Marcel Camus, 1958), 107 minutes. Modern reinterpretation of the myth of Orpheus set in Brazil, during the Rio de Janeiro Carnival. Orpheus is a streetcar conductor who lives in the favela. Soundtrack is the now-classic bossa nova by Vinicius de Moraes and Tom Jobim.

The Black Press: Soldiers without Swords (director Stanley Nelson, 1999), 86 minutes. Documentary on black newspapers from the nineteenth century to the 1960s and the campaigns they defended, including rare footage and interviews with journalists and activists.

Burn! (U.S)/*The Mercenary* (Canada)/*Queimada* (director Gillo Pontecorvo, 1969), 112 minutes. Set in a fictional West Indian plantation island, the plot shows a British mercenary, Sir William Walker (played by Marlon Brando), brought in to instigate a slave revolt against the Portuguese rulers, claiming the superiority of free labor, in order to favor the British sugar trade, and years later brought back to deal with rebels who now threaten the British sugar interests.

The Color Purple (director Steven Spielberg, 1985), 154 minutes. Based on the Pulitzer Prize–winning novel by Alice Walker, the story follows the life of Celie Johnson, an African American woman in the early twentieth-century rural South, who endures abuse yet overcomes it.

Eyes on the Prize (director Henry Hampton, 1986), 360 minutes. This documentary series produced by Blackside, Inc., and aired on PBS gives a comprehensive account of the American civil rights movement in the 1950s and 1960s with rare archival footage and interviews with its leaders and participants. The sequel follows up on the fragmented agenda to the mid-1980s.

Guess Who's Coming to Dinner (director Stanley Kramer, 1967), 108 minutes. Sidney Poitier plays an African American doctor who is brought by a white young woman (Katharine Houghton) to meet her liberal upper-class parents. The script revolves around the prejudice toward interracial marriages, which were still illegal in seventeen Southern states until that year.

I Am Cuba, the Siberian Mammoth/*Soy Cuba, o Mamute Siberiano* (director Vicente Ferraz, 2005), 90 minutes. This fascinating documentary chronicles the making of the Soviet propaganda movie *I Am Cuba* in the early years after the Cuban Revolution, and its subsequent rejection by Cubans and Soviets alike. By trying to investigate the reason behind it, Ferraz brings back memories from Cuban and Soviet crew members and reveals the intrinsic incompatibility between the image the Soviets made of Cuba and that Cubans made of themselves.

Jazz (director Ken Burns, 2001). Made-for-TV ten-episode documentary series surveys the history of jazz, through the musicians that created it. From New Orleans to the East and West Coasts, from ensembles to free improvising, the history of this typically American art form is recounted having as a backdrop the history of twentieth-century America.

Jongos, Calangos e Folias: música negra, memória e poesia (directors Hebe Mattos and Martha Abreu, 2007), 48 minutes. Portuguese with English subtitles. Three cultural traditions of the African Brazilian communities of southeastern Brazil are explored in this documentary that bridges slavery to the present day through oral, musical, and religious practices of the descendants of the last slaves and explores their quest for land and full citizenship.

The Language You Cry In: Story of a Mende Song (directors Ángel Serrano and Alvaro Toepke, 1998), 52 minutes. Documentary showing the remarkable reconstitution of the cultural ties between the Gullah people of the coastal regions of the southeast United States and Sierra Leone, through an old burial song recorded among the Gullah people by anthropologist Lorenzo Turner in the 1930s, and then found among the Mende in Sierra Leone by anthropologist Joe Opala and ethnomusicologist Cynthia Schmidt in the 1980s.

Little Senegal (director Rachid Mouchareb, 2001), 98 minutes. Emotional journey through the contemporary African diaspora. Alloune, an old guide at the Gorée Island Slave Fort Museum, arrives in America to search for the descendants of his ancestors and meets people with different strategies of survival and adaptation in Little Senegal in Harlem, most of them insensible to his quest.

Lumumba (director Raoul Peck, 2000), 110 minutes. Fictionalized account of the last year in the life of Patrice Lumumba, who helped win independence from Belgium and became the first prime minister of the Democratic Republic of Congo in 1960, and who was executed through a conspiracy of U.S. intelligence, the Belgian government, and local traitors.

Malcolm X (director Spike Lee, 1992), 201 minutes. The life of activist and leader Malcolm X (played by Denzel Washington) is recounted by acclaimed filmmaker Spike Lee.

Manderlay (director Lars von Trier, 2005), 139 minutes. Second film in a trilogy about the American way of life, this one is set in a Southern plantation in the early 1930s, in which slavery still persisted decades after the Civil War and the Emancipation Proclamation. The central character, Grace (played by Bryce Dallas Howard), sets out to implement free labor relations and new egalitarian rules yet is surprised to discover the real workings of that community's daily life before her arrival.

Marcus Garvey: Look for Me in the Whirlwind (director Stanley Nelson, 2000). Made for the *American Experience* TV series. Film on the life and times of prominent Pan-Africanist leader Marcus Garvey, using rare archival footage from the early twentieth century, complementing it with interviews and reenactments.

'Non,' ou A Vã Glória de Mandar/ No, or the Vain Glory of Command (director Manoel de Oliveira, 1990), 110 minutes. Portuguese film that utilizes a narrator, a soldier marching through an African colony in 1972, to introduce episodes in Portuguese military history, ranging over several centuries, including Roman Lusitania, Vasco da Gama's discoveries, and colonial events in Africa and Brazil. Subtext comments on the fate of the contemporary dictatorship.

Ray (director Taylor Hackford, 2004), 178 minutes. Drama recounting the life and career of legendary pianist Ray Charles. Ray (played by Jamie Foxx) is depicted as someone who fought against adversity since childhood (having turned blind at age seven) but never bent to those who wanted to exploit his fame, and in his way, denounced the hypocrisy of racist America, where in some places blacks were denied entrance to his shows.

Return to Gorée/Retour à Gorée (director Pierre-Yves Borgeaud, 2007), 110 minutes. This documentary follows Senegalese musician Youssou N'Dour through the routes of the slave trade and the music of African slaves and their descendants in the Unites States and Europe and then back to Gorée Island, a symbol of the transatlantic slave trade, where he stages a concert to honor the victims, and also the legacy of the African diaspora.

Sankofa (director Haile Gerima, 1993), 125 minutes. An African American model is transported in time to live and suffer through the experience of Shola, a house servant in a plantation in the West Indies during slavery. Along with others, she runs away and joins a Maroon community. *Sankofa* is an Akan word that conveys a saying: One has to go back and learn from the past.

To Kill a Mockingbird (director Robert Mulligan, 1962), 129 minutes. Based on the Pulitzer Prize–winning novel by Harper Lee, this movie, set in the Depression-era U.S. South, is narrated from the viewpoint of Scout, the daughter of lawyer Atticus Finch (Gregory Peck), who defends a black man from an unfair accusation of raping a white woman. In this timely rendition of racism in the U.S. South, intolerance is seen from the children's eyes and weighed against Finch's example of firm righteousness.

Traces of the Trade: A Story from the Deep North (director Katrina Browne, codirector Alla Kovgan, 2008), 86 minutes. The documentary follows ten descendants from the DeWolf family, including the director herself, in a personal journey to the roots of their ancestors' fortune, built on slave trading, exploiting slave plantations, and processing slave-grown crops in Northern manufactures. The film exposes New England's deep connections with the slave economy, and also raises the question of reparations.

Unchained Memories (director Thomas Lennon II, 2002), 75 minutes. Documentary based on the first-person narratives of ex-slaves recorded in the 1930s and read by African American actors.

The Visitor (director Thomas McCarthy, 2007) 104 minutes. American academic is confronted with the human dimension of globalization when he is forced to interact with a man from Syria and a woman from Senegal who squatted in his apartment in New York City. His appreciation of their cultures and presence grows, and their interaction is abruptly cut short as a consequence of the treatment received by illegal immigrants in the United States.

The Voyage of La Amistad: Quest for Freedom (director H. D. Motyl, 1997), 70 minutes. Historically accurate documentary on the revolt aboard the Spanish ship *La Amistad* and the ensuing judicial fight between the Spanish merchants and the

U.S. government over the ship and its cargo. The film features court documents, transcripts, news stories, letters, and interviews with specialists.

When We Were Kings (director Leon Gast, 1996), 89 minutes. This Academy Award–winning documentary focuses on the famous "Rumble in the Jungle" heavyweight championship match between Muhammad Ali and George Foreman held in what was then called Zaïre (now called the DR Congo) on October 30, 1974. The film emphasizes the questionable ethics of locating the fight in Zaïre, as it was funded by the brutal dictatorship of Mobutu Sese Seko. It also contains footage of the "black Woodstock" soul music festival accompanying the fight. Deemed best documentary on Muhammad Ali.

Index

215

~

About the Editors and Contributors

Editors

Beatriz G. Mamigonian earned a PhD from the University of Waterloo, in Canada. She is a professor of history at the Universidade Federal de Santa Catarina in Brazil, having also been a visiting professor of history at Michigan State University. Her fields of study are comparative slavery and African diaspora, and her research interests focus on the impact of abolitionism on the Brazilian slave system throughout the nineteenth century and its human consequences. She has published a number of chapters in edited collections and journal articles in English and in Portuguese. She is completing a book manuscript on the fate of the Africans who were emancipated in the course of the suppression activities in Brazil.

Karen Racine received her PhD from Tulane University and is associate professor of Latin American history at the University of Guelph in Canada. She is the author of *Francisco de Miranda: A Transatlantic Life in the Age of Revolution* (2003), and coeditor of *Strange Pilgrimages: Travel, Exile and National Identity in Latin America 1800–2000* (2000). Her current research focuses on cultural connections between Britain and Latin America in the late eighteenth and early nineteenth centuries, and on patriotic civic culture in Spanish American independence. She is completing two book manuscripts, one on Latin American independence leaders in London, and the other on British poet laureate Robert Southey's work on the Luso-Hispanic world.

Contributors

Aaron P. Althouse received his PhD from Stanford University and is currently an assistant professor of history at the University of Tennessee, Chattanooga. He researches social relations and caste identity in the colonial Pátzcuaro, Mexico, region and is currently working on a book-length manuscript entitled *The Power of Language: Caste, Identity, and Society in Pátzcuaro, 1680–1750*.

Alan Bloom received his PhD in history from Duke University and is associate professor of history at Valparaiso University. He is writing a book entitled *"Where Else Can They Go?": Homelessness in Early Chicago, 1833–1871*, and has had essays appear in the *Journal of Urban History* and the *Journal of Illinois History*.

Marcus J. M. de Carvalho earned his PhD in history from the University of Illinois, Urbana-Champaign, and is professor of history at the Universidade Federal de Pernambuco in Brazil. He has published several papers on the social history of nineteenth-century Brazil and is the author of *Liberdade: Rotinas e Rupturas do Escravismo, Recife 1822–1850* (1998).

Flávio dos Santos Gomes is a professor of history at the Universidade Federal do Rio de Janeiro. He has written several books and articles on different aspects of the history of slavery and postemancipation Brazil, among them *Histórias de quilombolas: mocambos e comunidades de senzalas no Rio de Janeiro, século XIX* (2006), *A Hidra e os pântanos: mocambos, quilombos e comunidades de fugitivos no Brasil* (séculos XVII–XIX) (2005), and *Experiências atlânticas: ensaios e pesquisas sobre a escravidão e o pós-emancipação no Brasil*. He has also edited several books, more recently (with Olivia Cunha), *Quase-Cidadão. Antropologias e histórias da pós-emancipação no Brasil* (2007).

Hilary Jones earned her PhD in African history from Michigan State University. She held a postdoctoral fellowship at the Center for African and African American Studies at the University of Michigan and taught at Macalester College before joining the University of Maryland, College Park, as an assistant professor of history. Hilary Jones is the author of an *International Journal of African Historical Studies* article entitled "From mariage à la mode du pays to Weddings at Town Hall: Marriage, French Colonialism and Mixed Race Society in Nineteenth Century Sénégal." She is currently working on a book that deals with mixed-race identity and French citizenship in Senegal's nineteenth-century Atlantic port towns.

Charles Beatty Medina is an assistant professor of history at the University of Toledo. His research focuses on the African diaspora in Latin America with a concentration on Maroon societies and African resistance to colonial rule. His first book (in progress) examines the Maroons of Esmeraldas, and he is currently finishing the translation of one of the first full-length reports, written in 1578, on the Esmeraldas Maroon societies.

María de los Ángeles Meriño Fuentes completed her doctorate in history at Universidad de la Habana, and is a researcher at Instituto de Investigaciones Culturales Juan Marinello in Cuba. She published two books, including *El Alzamiento de los Independientes de Color. Una vuelta necesaria a mayo de 1912* (2006), and has coauthored, with Aisnara Perera Díaz, *Nombrar las Cosas: Aproximación a la Onomastica de la Familia Negra en Cuba* (2006), *Esclavitud, Família y Parroquia en Cuba. Otra Mirada desde la Microhistoria* (2006), *Un café para la micro historia. Estructura de posesión de esclavos y ciclo de vida en la llanura habanera, 1800–1886* (2007), and *Matrimonio y familia en el ingenio una utopía posible. La Habana,1825–1886* (2007), for which they obtained prizes in Cuba and in Mexico.

Aisnara Perera Díaz earned her doctorate in history from Universidad de la Habana and is a researcher at Instituto de Investigaciones Culturales Juan Marinello, in Cuba. She authored many books on Cuban history, among them *Africanía en las Charangas de Bejucal* (2005), and has coauthored, with Maria de los Ángeles Meriño Fuentes, *Nombrar las Cosas: Aproximación a la Onomastica de la Familia Negra en Cuba* (2006), *Esclavitud, Família y Parroquia en Cuba. Otra Mirada desde la Microhistoria* (2006), *Un café para la micro historia. Estructura de posesión de esclavos y ciclo de vida en la llanura habanera, 1800–1886* (2007), and *Matrimonio y familia en el ingenio una utopía posible. La Habana, 1825–1886* (2007), for which they obtained prizes in Cuba and in Mexico.

Richard Price received his PhD in anthropology from Harvard University. He has taught at Yale, Johns Hopkins (where he was founding chair of the Department of Anthropology), Stanford, and the Federal University of Bahia (Brazil) and now divides his time between the College of William and Mary in

Virginia, where he is Dittman Professor of American Studies, Anthropology, and History, and a home in Martinique, which serves as his base for research and writing. His many books include *First-Time*, *Alabi's World*, *The Convict and the Colonel*, and *Travels with Tooy*.

Sally Price received her PhD in anthropology from the Johns Hopkins University. She has taught at Minnesota, Stanford, Princeton, and the Federal University of Bahia (Brazil) and now divides her time between the College of William and Mary in Virginia, where she is Dittman Professor of American Studies and Anthropology, and a home in Martinique, which serves as her base for research and writing. Her books include *Co-Wives and Calabashes*, *Primitive Art in Civilized Places* (published in seven languages), and *Paris Primitive: Jacques Chirac's Museum on the Quai Branly*.

Cassandra Pybus received her PhD in history and holds an Australian Research Council Research Chair in history at the University of Sydney. She is the author of eleven books, most recently *Epic Journeys of Freedom: Runaway Slaves of the American Revolution and Their Global Quest for Liberty* (2006) and coeditor (with Marcus Rediker and Emma Christopher) of *Other Middle Passages: Forced Migration and the Making of the Modern World* (2007).

Ty M. Reese is an associate professor of history at the University of North Dakota. He is currently completing a monograph project, *Sortings and Slaves: Trade and Interaction at Cape Coast, 1750–1821*, and is working with Vincent Carreta on an edited edition of the writings of Philip Quaque. He has had articles appear in *Itinerario*, the *Journal of Religion in Africa*, and *Studies on Voltaire and the Eighteenth Century* and in two edited collections of essays.

João José Reis is a professor of history at the Universidade Federal da Bahia, in Brazil. Two of his books have been translated into English: *Slave Rebellion in Brazil: The 1835 Muslim Uprising in Bahia* and *Death Is a Festival: Funerary Rituals and Popular Rebellion in Nineteenth-Century Brazil*.

Lorna Biddle Rinear is a PhD candidate at Rutgers, the State University of New Jersey, having earned her BA from Wellesley College and her MA from Boston College. She is the coauthor and editor of *The Complete Idiot's Guide to Women's History* and has contributed to other reference resources. She currently teaches at Curry College and at Regis College.

Meredith L. Roman earned her PhD in the Comparative Black History Program at Michigan State University and is an assistant professor of history at the State University of New York, College at Brockport. She is the author of "Making Caucasians Black: Moscow since the Fall of Communism and the Racialization of Non-Russians," *Journal of Communist Studies and Transition Politics* (2002); and "Racism in a 'Raceless' Society: The Soviet Press and Representations of American Racial Violence at Stalingrad in 1930," *International Labor and Working-Class History* (2007).

Maya Talmon-Chvaicer received her PhD in history from the University of Haifa, Israel, where she taught at the Multidisciplinary Studies Department and acted as program director for the Center for the Study of the U.S. She is the author of *The Hidden History of Capoeira: A Collision of Cultures in the Brazilian Battle Dance* (2008) and the academic editor of *Capoeira: Ginga on the Razor's Point* (2005). She has had articles appear in the journals *Hispanic American Historical Review, Sport in Society, Historia,* and *Reflejos.*

Jerome Teelucksingh received his PhD in history and is a lecturer of history at the University of the West Indies. He is the author of *Caribbean-Flavoured Presbyterianism: Education as a Prescription for Socio-Political Development, 1868–2006* (2008). He has had articles appear in *Slavery and Abolition, Peace Review,* and *Humanitas.*